EBS 생수다
생생한 영어 수다

듣고 말하기

잉글리시헌트연구소

48 상황 완벽 대처하기

생생하게 살아 있는 영어 수다!

> 상대방이 말하는 영어를 **제대로** 듣고 싶어요.

> 들으면서 그 내용을 **바로 이해**하고 싶어요.

> 상황에 **적절한** 영어를 말하고 싶어요.

> 상대방과 함께 자연스럽게 **대화 주제를** 영어로 이어가고 싶어요.

> 내 생각을 영어로 **길게** 말하고 싶어요.

소리로 익혀 입에 새기는 영어
생수다

To the point!
핵심적인 음운 현상과 듣기 전략으로 듣고 말하는 실력이 쭉쭉 늘어나요.

Relevant!
48가지 여행과 업무 상황에서 쓰는 **적절한 표현을** 말할 수 있어요.

Authentic!
실제 생활에서 쓰이는 **실제적인 표현을** 말할 수 있어요.

Confident!
역할극, 원어민과 1:1 실전 연습을 통해 **자신 있게** 말할 수 있어요.

Active Learner!
대화형 말하기, 듣고 말하기 등 다양한 활동으로 **능동적 학습자**가 될 수 있어요.

- ☑ **POINT 1** **반복연습**으로 저절로 이해되는 영어!
- ☑ **POINT 2** 입에 바로 새기는 영어! **툭 치면 탁!** 영어가 술술 ~
- ☑ **POINT 3** 간단한 문장에서 **긴 문장까지 척척!**
- ☑ **POINT 4** 48가지 상황으로 익히는 **생생한 생활영어!**

이렇게 학습하세요!

하나, 교재로 학습하기

듣기 향상 팁 익히기
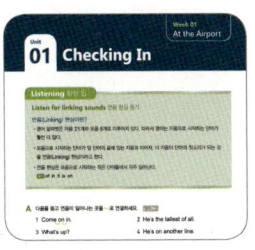
영어의 핵심 음운 현상과 듣기 향상 팁을 배워, 듣고 말하는데 효과적으로 적용할 수 있습니다.

48가지 상황 듣기
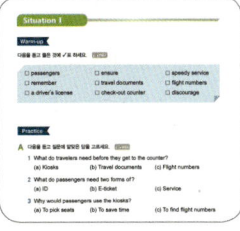
실제 업무나 여행에서 겪을 수 있는 48가지 상황을 듣고 단어와 내용을 파악합니다.

48가지 상황 이해하기

상황을 다시 한번 더 익혀 체득화 시킵니다. 툭! 치면 탁! 나올 때까지 연습!

48가지 상황 말하기
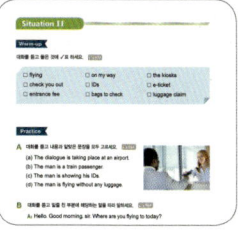
앞에서 배운 듣기 향상 팁과 상황별 내용을 응용하여 대화로 말해 봅니다.

두울, 온라인으로 학습하기

Lecture

생수다의 비법을 전하는 본 강의를 들어 보세요. 간단명료한 강의를 듣고, 보고, 따라하다 보면 듣기 실력과 회화 실력이 동시에 쑥쑥 올라갑니다!

Practice
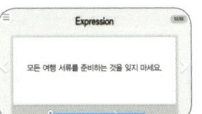
목표 문장 연습
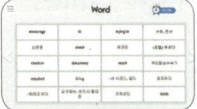
목표 단어 연습

듣고 문장배열

다양한 활동을 통해 목표 문장과 단어를 암기하고, 반복 학습하세요.
툭 치면 탁! 떨어지는 생생한 영어 수다를 경험할 수 있습니다.

Song

각 상황의 대화와 내용을 담은 뮤직비디오를 제공하여 48가지 상황을 노래로 재미있게 익힐 수 있습니다.

Recording
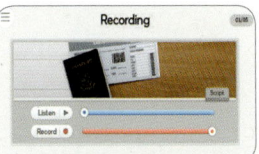
학습한 문장을 듣고 녹음하여 완벽히 습득했는지 확인하고 자신의 발음도 확인할 수 있습니다.

Conversation

원어민과의 가상대화를 통해 효과적으로 상황에 따른 역할극과 1:1 대화 연습을 할 수 있습니다.

www.ebslang.co.kr 에서 온라인/모바일 동시 학습이 가능합니다

WEEK 01 — At the Airport

Unit 01	Checking In	10
Unit 02	Security Checkpoint	14
Unit 03	Waiting to Board	18
Unit 04	Immigration Control	22
Vocabulary		26

WEEK 02 — On the Plane

Unit 01	Emergency Procedures on the Plane	30
Unit 02	Captain's Greetings	34
Unit 03	Duty Free Sales	38
Unit 04	Take-off and Landing Announcements	42
Vocabulary		46

WEEK 03 — At the Hotel

Unit 01	Reserving Rooms	50
Unit 02	Checking In	54
Unit 03	Complaining	58
Unit 04	Concierge Service	62
Vocabulary		66

WEEK 04 Transportation

Unit 01	Getting Directions to the Tour site	70
Unit 02	Buying Tickets	74
Unit 03	Finding the Right Stop	78
Unit 04	Missing a Train	82
Vocabulary		86

WEEK 05 At the Restaurant

Unit 01	Making a Reservation	90
Unit 02	Introducing a Restaurant	94
Unit 03	Advertising a New Product	98
Unit 04	Problems on Food	102
Vocabulary		106

WEEK 06 At the Mall

Unit 01	Mall Opening	110
Unit 02	Sales Announcement	114
Unit 03	Announcement About Parking	118
Unit 04	Mall Closing	122
Vocabulary		126

WEEK 07 On the Street

Unit 01	Getting Directions	130
Unit 02	Shopping for Souvenirs	134
Unit 03	Bargaining	138
Unit 04	Enjoying Street Food	142
Vocabulary		146

WEEK 08 At the Tourist Site

Unit 01	Purchasing Tickets	150
Unit 02	Booking a Tour	154
Unit 03	Rules at Tourist Sites	158
Unit 04	Touring a Site	162
Vocabulary		166

WEEK 09 On the Phone

Unit 01	Arranging a Meeting	170
Unit 02	Getting a Complaint Call	174
Unit 03	Transferring a Call	178
Unit 04	Changing a Project Schedule	182
Vocabulary		186

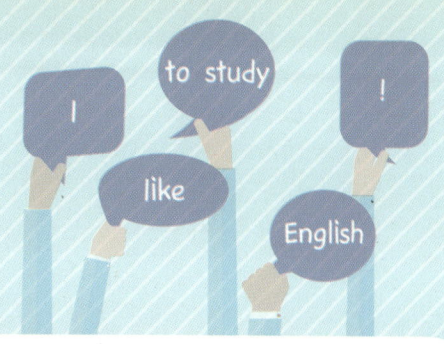

WEEK 10 At the office

Unit 01	Introducing the New Manager	190
Unit 02	Announcing a Training Session	194
Unit 03	Announcing a Conference	198
Unit 04	Overcoming Problems	202
Vocabulary		206

WEEK 11 Business Trips

Unit 01	Renting a Car	210
Unit 02	At a Meeting Place	214
Unit 03	Business Lunch	218
Unit 04	Accepting Invitations	222
Vocabulary		226

WEEK 12 Speech / Presentation

Unit 01	Opening and Closing a Presentation	230
Unit 02	Linking Ideas	234
Unit 03	Emphasizing Important Points	238
Unit 04	Describing Graphs / Charts	242
Vocabulary		246

정답 및 스크립트 250

EBS 생수다

생생한 영어 수다

Week 01 At the Airport

- **Unit 01** Checking In
- **Unit 02** Security Checkpoint
- **Unit 03** Waiting to Board
- **Unit 04** Immigration Control

Week 01
At the Airport

Unit 01 Checking In

Listening 향상 팁

Listen for linking sounds 연음 현상 듣기

연음(Linking) 현상이란?
- 영어 알파벳은 자음 21개와 모음 5개로 이루어져 있다. 따라서 영어는 자음으로 시작하는 단어가 훨씬 더 많다.
- 모음으로 시작하는 단어가 앞 단어의 끝에 있는 자음과 이어져, 이 자음이 단어의 첫소리가 되는 것을 연음(Linking) 현상이라고 한다.
- 연음 현상은 모음으로 시작하는 작은 단어들에서 자주 일어난다.
  예시 of in it is on

A 다음을 듣고 연음이 일어나는 곳을 ⌣로 연결하세요. 🎧 001

1 Come on in.
2 He's the tallest of all.
3 What's up?
4 He's on another line.
5 How much is it?
6 I'm not tired at all.

B 다음을 듣고 빈칸에 알맞은 단어를 쓰세요. 🎧 002

1 I'm tired _____ old shoes.
2 Is _____ _____ _____ building?
3 May I come _____?
4 Does _____ sound _____ right?

C 맞으면 T를, 틀리면 F를 고르세요.

1 연음이란 모음으로 시작하는 단어가 앞 단어에 붙어서 소리 나는 현상을 말한다.   T F
2 연음은 of, in, on 등과 같이 모음으로 시작하는 작은 단어에서 흔히 일어난다.   T F

Situation I

Warm-up

다음을 듣고 들은 것에 ✓표 하세요. 🎧 003

- ☐ passengers
- ☐ remember
- ☐ a driver's license
- ☐ ensure
- ☐ travel documents
- ☐ check-out counter
- ☐ speedy service
- ☐ flight numbers
- ☐ discourage

Practice

A 다음을 듣고 질문에 알맞은 답을 고르세요. 🎧 003

1 What do travelers need before they get to the counter?
   (a) Kiosks   (b) Travel documents   (c) Flight numbers

2 What do passengers need two forms of?
   (a) ID   (b) E-ticket   (c) Service

3 Why would passengers use the kiosks?
   (a) To pick seats (b) To save time   (c) To find flight numbers

B 다음을 듣고 질문에 알맞은 사진을 고르세요. 🎧 003

Q Where will passengers be right after this announcement?

(a)  (b) 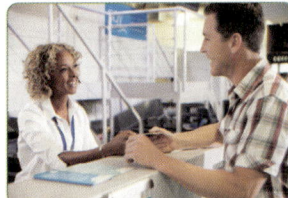 (c)

C 다음을 듣고 맞으면 T를, 틀리면 F를 고르세요. 🎧 003

1 Passengers should have their travel documents ready for quick service.   T F

2 Using the kiosks could be faster.   T F

Dictation

다음을 듣고 빈칸을 채우세요. 🎧 003

Attention, passengers. To ensure speedy service, please remember to ① _____ _____ your travel documents ② _____ before you reach the ③ _____ counter. Two ④ _____ _____ ID are required, or one form of ID plus ⑤ _____ _____. Self check-in kiosks are available for passengers with their travel documents and flight numbers ready. We ⑥ _____ _____ to use the kiosks for ⑦ _____ service.

* ▭ 부분은 연음(Linking)이 일어나는 부분입니다.

Situation II

Warm-up

대화를 듣고 들은 것에 ✓표 하세요. 🎧 004

- ☐ flying
- ☐ check you out
- ☐ entrance fee
- ☐ on my way
- ☐ IDs
- ☐ bags to check
- ☐ the kiosks
- ☐ e-ticket
- ☐ luggage claim

Practice

A 대화를 듣고 내용과 알맞은 문장을 모두 고르세요. 🎧 004

(a) The dialogue is taking place at an airport.
(b) The man is a train passenger.
(c) The man is showing his IDs.
(d) The man is flying without any luggage.

B 대화를 듣고 밑줄 친 부분에 해당하는 말을 따라 말하세요. 🎧 004

A: Hello. Good morning, sir. Where are you flying to today?

B: ① _____

A: Well, we can check you in here. Do you have your IDs or an e-ticket?

B: ② _____

A: No problem, sir. This will be fine. Any bags to check?

B: ③ _____

Week 01 At the Airport

Unit 02 Security Checkpoint

Listening 향상 팁

Listen for details 세부 사항 듣기

- 세부 사항 듣기는 성공적인 의사 소통을 하기 위해 꼭 필요한 듣기 능력이다.
  - 듣는 목적을 명확하게 파악한다.
  - 필요한 정보의 주요 부분을 나타내는 단어와 표현을 구별하여 듣고 이해한다.
    [예시] Please make sure that..., You should..., Please do not..., No...
  - 불필요하거나 연관이 없는 정보는 버린다.

A 다음을 듣고 질문에 알맞은 답을 고르세요. 🎧 005

1 What should passengers show to the security staff?
   (a) Boarding passes   (b) Laptops   (c) Change

2 Where should passengers put their keys?
   (a) On the conveyor belt   (b) In front of the staff   (c) In a plastic bin

B 다음을 듣고 빈칸에 알맞은 단어를 쓰세요. 🎧 006

1 The X-ray machine has a _____ that you can put your bags on.

2 Then, walk through the _____ .

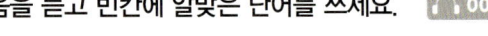

| conveyor belt | passport | metal detector | bin |

C 맞으면 T를, 틀리면 F를 고르세요.

1 성공적인 의사 소통을 하기 위해서는 모든 단어를 놓치지 말고 다 듣고 이해해야 한다. T F

2 세부사항을 들을 때 Please make sure..., You should..., Please don't... 다음에 오는 내용은 유의하여 듣는다. T F

Situation I

Warm-up

다음을 듣고 들은 것에 ✓표 하세요. 🎧 007

- ☐ liquids
- ☐ knives
- ☐ tablet PC
- ☐ 100ml or more
- ☐ carry-on bags
- ☐ basket
- ☐ exceptions
- ☐ scanning machine
- ☐ conveyor belt

Practice

A 다음을 듣고 질문에 알맞은 답을 고르세요. 🎧 007

1. Where do all liquids have to go?
   (a) To the security checkpoint
   (b) In a bag together
   (c) Inside of checked baggage

2. What do passengers NOT have to remove before scanning?
   (a) Coats   (b) Belts   (c) Socks

3. What should passengers take out of their bags?
   (a) Coats   (b) Bins   (c) Computers

B 다음을 듣고 질문에 알맞은 사진을 고르세요. 🎧 007

Q Which of the following can be allowed beyond the security checkpoint?

(a)
(b)
(c)

C 다음을 듣고 맞으면 T를, 틀리면 F를 고르세요. 🎧 007

1 Exceptions regarding liquids are sometimes made. T F

2 Tablets and laptops have to be scanned separately. T F

Dictation

다음을 듣고 빈칸을 채우세요. 🎧 007

All liquids must be ① _____ in one clear bag with ② _____ _____ of each liquid. ③ _____ _____ will be made. No ④ _____, _____, or other items that may be considered weapons will be allowed beyond the security checkpoint. ⑤ _____ your pockets and remove all ⑥ _____, _____, and belts before passing through the scanning machine. If you are carrying a laptop or tablet PC, please take it ⑦ _____ _____ your bag and place it in a bin on the conveyor belt.

* 부분은 세부 사항(Details)에 해당하는 부분입니다.

Situation II

Warm-up

대화를 듣고 들은 것에 모두 ✓표 하세요. 🎧 008

(a)

(b)

(c)

(d)

(e)

(f)

Practice

A 대화를 듣고 대화 내용과 맞도록 문장을 완성하세요. 🎧 008

1 The man is at the (immigration desk / security checkpoint).

2 The man has (something / nothing) on the banned item list.

3 The man wants to throw (a lighter / a knife) away.

B 대화를 듣고 밑줄 친 부분에 해당하는 말을 따라 말하세요. 🎧 008

A: Hello, sir. Please empty your pockets.

B: ① _____

A: Yes, sir. No exceptions I'm afraid.

B: ② _____

A: Do you have any items off the banned item list in your luggage such as lighters and knives?

B: ③ _____

Week 01
At the Airport

Unit 03 Waiting to Board

> **Listening 향상 팁**
>
> **Listen for key words** 핵심 단어 듣기
> - 모든 단어를 다 알아들어야만 상대방의 말을 이해하는 것은 아니다.
> - 모르는 단어가 많이 들려도 당황하지 말고 집중해서 계속 듣는다.
> - 주요 개념과 상황을 이해하면 핵심 단어를 찾기 쉽다.
>   **예시** 탑승구 변경(gate change), 출발시간 지연(departure delay)
> - 의문사가 있는 의문문은 첫 단어, 즉 의문사에 유의해서 듣는다.
>   **예시** When's your flight? 몇 시 비행기인가요? Where's the new gate? 새 탑승구는 어디인가요?

A 대화를 듣고 질문에 알맞은 답을 고르세요. 🎧 009

1 What is the new gate number?
 (a) C5   (b) C15   (c) C50

2 When will the flight begin boarding?
 (a) In 5 minutes   (b) In 15 minutes   (c) In 25 minutes

B 다음을 듣고 들은 것을 고르세요. 🎧 010

1 (a) 12   (b) 20   2 (a) 14   (b) 40

3 (a) 3:30   (b) 3:50   4 (a) 9:05   (b) 5:45

C 맞으면 T를, 틀리면 F를 고르세요..

1 모든 단어가 다 들릴 때까지 완벽하게 들을 수 있도록 반복해서 듣는다.

2 주요 개념이나 상황을 이해하면 핵심 단어를 찾기 쉽다.

Situation I

Warm-up

다음을 듣고 들은 것에 ✓표 하세요. 🎧 011

- ☐ flight 13
- ☐ the departure gate
- ☐ 50 minutes
- ☐ flight 30
- ☐ 18B
- ☐ 4:15
- ☐ New York
- ☐ boarding gate
- ☐ 4:50

Practice

A 다음을 듣고 질문에 알맞은 답을 고르세요. 🎧 011

1. Where is flight 30 laying over?
   (a) New York (b) Atlanta (c) Non-stop

2. How long is the boarding delay?
   (a) 15 minutes (b) 50 minutes (c) 13 minutes

3. What time can passengers board the plane?
   (a) In 50 minutes (b) At 4:15 (c) At 4:50

B 다음을 듣고 질문에 알맞은 그림을 고르세요. 🎧 011

Q What time was the flight 30 bound for New York supposed to board?

(a)  (b)  (c)

C 다음을 듣고 맞으면 T를, 틀리면 F를 고르세요. 🎧 011

1. The flight is bound for Atlanta. T F
2. The arrival gate has changed. T F

Dictation

다음을 듣고 빈칸을 채우세요. 🎧 011

Attention passengers on ①_____ _____ bound for New York with a stop in Atlanta. The departure gate has been changed to ②_____. The gate change has caused a boarding ③_____ of ④_____ minutes. Boarding will begin at ⑤_____. Again, please ⑥_____ that the boarding gate for flight 30 to New York has changed to 18B. Boarding will begin 15 minutes ⑦_____ at 4:50.

* _____ 부분은 핵심 단어(Key Words)에 해당하는 부분입니다.

Situation II

Warm-up

대화를 듣고 들은 것에 ✓표 하세요. 🎧 012

- ☐ flight 30
- ☐ changed
- ☐ 50 minutes
- ☐ New York
- ☐ boarding time
- ☐ Gate 18B
- ☐ 10B
- ☐ cancelled
- ☐ different terminal

Practice

A 대화를 듣고 질문에 알맞은 사진을 고르세요. 🎧 012

Q Where is the new gate?

(a)    (b)

B 대화를 듣고 밑줄 친 부분에 해당하는 말을 따라 말하세요. 🎧 012

A: Excuse me. is the gate for flight 30 bound for New York changed?

B: ① _____

A: Has the boarding time changed too then?

B: ② _____

A: Okay. good. Which way is Gate 18B?

B: ③ _____

Unit 04 Immigration Control

Week 01 At the Airport

Listening 향상 팁

Use your background knowledge 배경 지식을 이용하기

- 듣기는 주어진 내용을 수동적으로 단순 해독만 하는 것이 아니다.
- 듣기는 이전에 알고 있는 지식을 사용하여, 새로운 내용을 이해하고 그 의미를 만드는 적극적인 과정이다.
- 배경 지식(Background Knowledge)이 있으면 듣기 과정에서 예측과 예견을 할 수 있어 이해가 더 쉽게 된다.

A 출입국 관리소에서 들을 수 있는 아래 질문에 대한 대답을 듣고, 알맞은 대답을 고르세요. 🎧 013

1 How long are you going to stay here?   (a)   (b)
2 Where will you stay?   (a)   (b)
3 What is the purpose of your visit here?   (a)   (b)

B 공항에서 들을 수 있는 다음 질문을 듣고 알맞은 대답을 고르세요. 🎧 014

(a) Yes, here they are.
(b) My final destination is Boston.
(c) No, I'll keep it under the seat.
(d) Can I have an aisle seat, please?

1 _____   2 _____   3 _____

C 맞으면 T를, 틀리면 F를 고르세요.

1 듣기는 소극적인 의사 소통 과정이다.   T F
2 알고 있는 배경 지식을 활용하면, 더 잘 들리고 더 많이 이해할 수 있다.   T F

Situation I

Warm-up

다음을 듣고 들은 것에 모두 ✓표 하세요. 015

(a)  (b) (c)

Practice

A 다음을 듣고 질문에 알맞은 답을 고르세요. 015

1. What do immigration officers NOT need to see?
   - (a) Boarding pass
   - (b) Visa documents
   - (c) Seat assignment

2. Where should passengers line up?
   - (a) In front of the immigration officer
   - (b) Next to the immigration desk
   - (c) Behind the yellow line

3. How many people can be helped at the immigration desk?
   - (a) Only one
   - (b) One at a time
   - (c) At least two

B 다음을 듣고 질문에 알맞은 사진을 고르세요. 015

Q Which sign should passengers follow after the announcement?

(a)  (b)  (c)

C 다음을 듣고 맞으면 T를, 틀리면 F를 고르세요. 🎧 015

1 Passengers need to show their passports.　T　F

2 Onward travel documents are required for some. 　T　F

Dictation

다음을 듣고 빈칸을 채우세요. 🎧 015

Please be sure you have all your immigration documents ① _____ . Immigration officials will need to see your ② _____ , _____ _____ , and visa documentation. Those with return or forwarding flights need to show all of their onward travel documents to officers. Please wait ③ _____ _____ _____ line for the next ④ _____ officer. Only ⑤ _____ person at ⑥ _____ _____ is allowed to approach the ⑦ _____ desk.

* _____ 부분은 입국 심사 배경 지식(Background Knowledge)에 해당하는 부분입니다.

Situation II

Warm-up

대화를 듣고 대화와 관계 있는 사진을 고르세요. 🎧 016

(a)

(b)

(c)

Practice

A 대화를 듣고 내용과 알맞은 문장을 모두 고르세요. 🎧 016

(a) The man is going through immigration control.
(b) The man is showing his boarding pass and credit card.
(c) The man's couple will stay for two weeks.
(d) The man's wife was waiting next to him.

B 대화를 듣고 밑줄 친 부분에 해당하는 말을 따라 말하세요. 🎧 016

A: Next passenger. please step forward with all your immigration documents.

B: ① _____

A: Thank you. How long will you be traveling?

B: ② _____

A: Ma'am. Please wait behind the yellow line. Only one person at a time.

B: ③ _____

Week 01 At the Airport

Vocabulary

1	aisle seat	통로 좌석
2	arrival	도착
3	baggage claim	수하물 찾는곳
4	boarding pass	탑승권
5	carry-on	휴대용 가방
6	check-in counter	체크인 카운터
7	checked bag	위탁 가방
8	concourse	(공항 / 기차역의) 중앙 홀
9	connecting flight	연결 항공편
10	conveyor belt	컨베이어 벨트
11	customs	관세, 세관
12	delay	지연, 연착
13	departure	출발
14	direct flight	직항
15	duty free	면세, 면세품
16	duty free shop	면세점
17	economy class	보통석, 이코노미석
18	fragile	깨지기 쉬운
19	frequent flyer	(특정 항공사) 상용 우대 고객, 단골 고객
20	gate agent	탑승구 직원

Memo

#	English	Korean
21	gate number	탑승구 번호
22	immigration	출입국 관리소
23	layover	경유, 기착
24	lounge pass	라운지 입장권
25	luggage allowance	수하물 허용량
26	luggage cart	수하물 카트
27	missed connection	놓친 연결 항공편
28	overweight	중량 초과의
29	passport control	출입국 관리
30	priority boarding	(노약자나 우수 고객의) 우선 탑승
31	restricted items	제한 물품
32	seat preference	선호 좌석
33	security	안전, 보안; 보안 요원
34	self check-in	셀프 체크인[탑승 수속]
35	terminal	터미널
36	ticket	표, 티켓
37	transfer desk	경유 창구
38	upgrade	(좌석을) 업그레이드하다
39	weight limit	무게 한도[제한 중량]
40	window seat	창가 석

Memo

EBS 생수다
생생한 영어 수다

Week 02 On the Plane

- **Unit 01** Emergency Procedures on the Plane
- **Unit 02** Captain's Greetings
- **Unit 03** Duty Free Sales
- **Unit 04** Take-off and Landing Announcements

Week 02
On the Plane

Unit 01 Emergency Procedures on the Plane

Listening 향상 팁

Listen for meaningful chunks 의미 덩어리로 듣기

의미 덩어리(Meaningful Chunks)란?
- Meaningful Chunks는 '의미 덩어리'란 뜻으로 한꺼번에 하나의 단위처럼 사용할 수 있는 어구이다.
- 의미 덩어리에 따라 숨을 쉬기 때문에 문장 중간의 휴지(pause)는 의미 덩어리를 찾는데 도움이 된다.
- 보통 전치사 앞, 접속사 앞, 관계사 앞, to부정사 앞, 형용사구 앞, 부사구 앞, 명사구 앞에서 휴지(pause)를 두어 의미 덩어리의 구별을 돕는다.

A 의미 덩어리를 한 군데 골라 /로 표시한 후, 듣고 확인해 보세요. 🎧 018

1 There is a life vest under your seat.
2 I am sorry I can't. but I can give you a blanket.
3 She tried her best to succeed.
4 Unfortunately. it was delayed.

B 다음을 듣고 의미 덩어리의 개수를 쓰세요. 🎧 019

1 I left my cell phone in my room this morning. ____개
2 The plane for Chicago was delayed. ____개

C 맞으면 T를, 틀리면 F를 고르세요.

1 의미 덩어리가 중요한 이유는 의미 있는 단어들이 그룹지어 표현되기 때문이다.
2 휴지(pause)는 주로 접속사나 전치사 다음에서 일어난다.

Situation I

Warm-up

다음을 듣고 들은 것에 ✓표 하세요. 🎧 020

- ☐ safety picture
- ☐ cabin crew
- ☐ demonstration
- ☐ take a second
- ☐ indicating
- ☐ in the case of
- ☐ on the monitor
- ☐ under your seat
- ☐ at all times

Practice

A 다음을 듣고 질문에 알맞은 답을 고르세요. 🎧 020

1 Who is going to give the safety demonstration?
   (a) Cabin crew   (b) Captain   (c) Immigration officers

2 When should passengers assume the position on the screen?
   (a) During landing
   (b) In emergencies
   (c) During the safety demonstration

3 Where is the life vest?
   (a) By the exit   (b) Under the seat   (c) With the cabin crew

B 다음을 듣고 질문에 알맞은 사진을 고르세요. 🎧 020

Q Which picture is related to the announcement?

(a)  (b)  (c)

C 다음을 듣고 맞으면 T를, 틀리면 F를 고르세요. 🎧 020

1 The safety demonstration contains a video.   T F
2 There is a life vest in case of a water landing.   T F

Dictation

다음을 듣고 빈칸을 채우세요. 🎧 020

Please pay attention to the safety video and the cabin crew ① _____ we begin our safety demonstration. ② _____ _____ _____ to notice the cabin crew ③ _____ where the exits are. ④ _____ _____ _____ _____ an emergency landing, ⑤ _____ _____ the position shown on the screen. Should a water landing occur, there is a life vest ⑥ _____ _____ _____. Please follow the instructions of the cabin crew ⑦ _____ _____ _____.

* _____ 부분은 의미 덩어리(Meaningful Chunks)이거나 의미 덩어리가 시작하는 곳입니다.

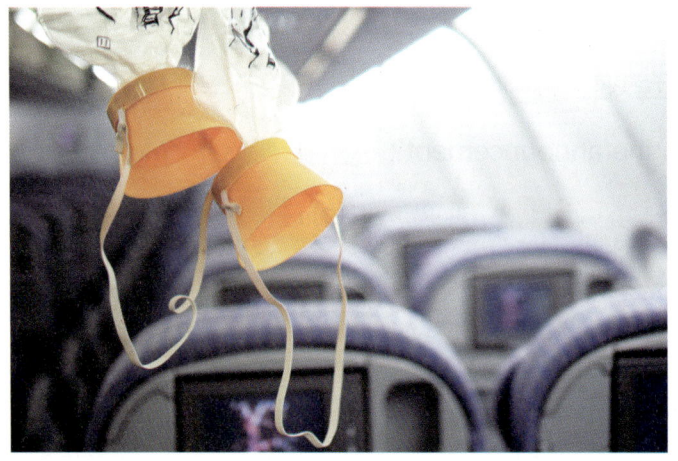

Situation II

Warm-up

대화를 듣고 대화와 관계 있는 사진을 모두 고르세요. 🎧 021

(a)  (b)  (c)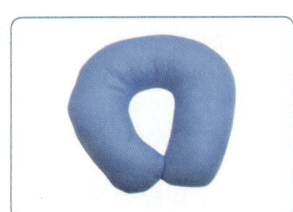

Practice

A 대화를 듣고 내용과 알맞은 문장을 모두 고르세요. 🎧 021

(a) The woman asked for snack.
(b) The woman felt very cold in her seat.
(c) The temperature was fixed.
(d) The man can adjust the air conditioning

B 대화를 듣고 밑줄 친 부분에 해당하는 말을 따라 말하세요. 🎧 021

A: Yes. ma'am. You rang for service?

B: ① _____

A: I'm sorry you are feeling cold. Unfortunately the air circulation system is what makes it feel cold.

B: ② _____

A: I'm sorry I can't, but I can offer you a blanket. Would you like one?

B: ③ _____

Week 02
On the Plane

Unit 02 Captain's Greetings

> **Listening 향상 팁**
>
> **Listen for specific words** 특정 단어 듣기
> - 특정 단어를 잘 들으면 내용을 유추하여 전반적인 내용을 이해할 수 있다.
> - 특정 단어를 듣는 연습은 기장의 인사말 방송과 같이 특수한 상황에서 듣는데 매우 효과적이다.
>
> 예시 We're **experiencing some turbulence**. 우리 비행기는 난기류를 만났습니다.
> All passengers, please **fasten your seat belts**. 승객 여러분 모두 안전벨트를 매주십시오.

A 다음을 듣고 빈칸에 알맞은 단어를 골라 쓰세요. 🎧 022

1 Serious turbulence is _____ soon.

2 Please remain _____ and do not use the _____.

3 Please _____ in your seats until the seat belt sign is _____.

| turned off | lavatory | expected | stay | seated |

B 다음을 듣고 해당 문장을 들을 수 있는 상황을 유추해 고르세요. 🎧 023

1 (a) 안전 교육 방송   (b) 착륙 안내 방송

2 (a) 기장 안내 방송   (b) 면세품 판매 안내 방송

3 (a) 극장 안내 방송   (b) 기내 방송

C 맞으면 T를, 틀리면 F를 고르세요.

1 특정 단어를 알면 기내 방송과 같은 상황에서 효과적이다.   T F

2 영어 듣기를 할 때는 특정 단어 위주로 내용을 모두 세세히 파악해야 한다.   T F

34 생생한 영어 수다

Situation I

Warm-up

대화를 듣고 대화와 관계 있는 사진을 고르세요. 🎧 024

(a)  (b)  (c)

Practice

A 다음을 듣고 질문에 알맞은 답을 고르세요. 🎧 024

1 Who is speaking?
   (a) The cabin crew   (b) The captain   (c) Ladies and gentlemen

2 How fast are they flying?
   (a) 30,000 ft/h   (b) 9,140 m/h   (c) 580 mph

3 How long will the flight be?
   (a) 9,140 meters   (b) 30,000 feet   (c) 4 hours

B 다음을 듣고 질문에 알맞은 그림을 고르세요. 🎧 024

Q Which is correctly indicating the temperature of the outside air?

(a) 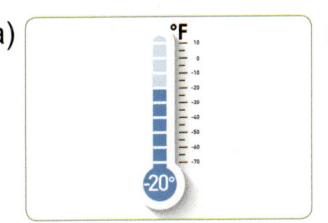 (b) 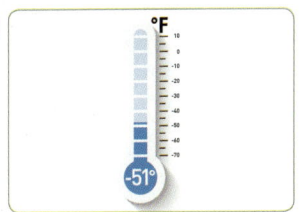 (c)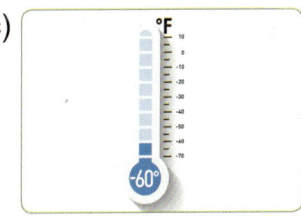

Week 02 • Unit 02   35

C 다음을 듣고 맞으면 T를, 틀리면 F를 고르세요. 🎧 024

1 The plane is traveling less than 1,000 km/h. [T] [F]

2 They are expecting a smooth flight. [T] [F]

Dictation

다음을 듣고 빈칸을 채우세요. 🎧 024

Good morning, ladies and gentlemen. This is your ①_____ speaking. We will be flying ②_____ _____ _____ of around 30,000 feet today with ③_____ _____ _____ of around 580 mph. That's 9,140 meters and about 930 km/h in ④_____. The outside ⑤_____ _____ is currently -60 °F, or -51 °C. We are looking at about a four-hour flight today. We are expecting some ⑥_____ during portions of the flight. As such, please be sure to keep your seat belt ⑦_____ when seated.

* 　　　 부분은 특정 단어(Specific Words)에 해당하는 부분입니다.

Situation II

Warm-up

대화를 듣고 들은 것에 ✓표 하세요. 🎧 025

- ☐ boarding pass
- ☐ passport
- ☐ seat 8K
- ☐ seat AJ
- ☐ aisle seat
- ☐ window seat
- ☐ galley
- ☐ first class cabin
- ☐ 4th row

Practice

A 대화를 듣고 대화 내용과 맞도록 문장을 완성하세요. 🎧 025

1. The dialogue is between a cabin crew and (a captain / a passenger).
2. The seat is located behind (a restroom / a galley).
3. The seat is (an aisle / a window) seat.

B 대화를 듣고 밑줄 친 부분에 해당하는 말을 따라 말하세요. 🎧 025

A: Welcome aboard, sir. May I see your boarding pass, please?

B: ① _____

A: You are in seat 8K, so please go through the galley and take a right.

B: ② _____

A: Yes, sir. You'll pass through the first class cabin, and then it will be the 4th row window seat.

B: ③ _____

Week 02 On the Plane

Unit 03 Duty Free Sales

Listening 향상 팁

Listen for Flap sounds 유음화 현상 듣기

- 유음화(Flap) 현상은 /t/, /d/가 모음이나 유성음 사이에서 짧은 /d/의 소리와 흡사하게 소리 나는 현상을 의미한다.
  예시 du**t**y bu**tt**er pre**tt**y
       /d/   /d/   /d/

- 단어와 단어가 연음이 될 때, 유음화 현상이 일어나는 경우가 종종 있다.
  예시 ou**t o**f righ**t a**way no**t a**t all

A 다음 단어를 듣고 유음화 현상이 일어나는 곳에 ○표 하세요. 🎧 026

1 water 2 metal 3 computer
4 better 5 item 6 Saturday
7 bottle 8 title 9 catalogue
10 idiot 11 matter 12 Seattle

B 다음을 듣고 빈칸에 알맞은 단어를 쓰세요. 🎧 027

1 I'll finish this _____ _____. 2 _____ _____ do you need?
3 I don't know _____ _____ do it. 4 This pizza is _____ _____ this world.

C 맞으면 T를, 틀리면 F를 고르세요.

1 유음화 현상은 /t/, /d/가 모음이나 유성음 사이에서 짧은 /d/처럼 변하는 음운 현상이다. [T] [F]
2 단어가 축약될 때 유음화 현상이 자주 발생한다. [T] [F]

Situation I

Warm-up

다음을 듣고 들은 것에 ✓표 하세요. 🎧 028

- ☐ announce
- ☐ look through
- ☐ a wide variety
- ☐ purchase
- ☐ review
- ☐ perfumes
- ☐ duty free items
- ☐ catalogue
- ☐ cigarettes

Practice

A 다음을 듣고 질문에 알맞은 답을 고르세요. 🎧 028

1. What is going to start soon?
   (a) Flight duty time   (b) Duty free sales   (c) An announcement

2. Where can passengers look for shopping items?
   (a) In the shopping center   (b) With the cabin crew   (c) In a catalogue

3. What can you NOT find in duty free?
   (a) Perfume   (b) Alcohol   (c) Snacks

B 다음을 듣고 질문에 알맞은 사진을 고르세요. 🎧 028

Q What can you find in the duty free catalogue?

(a)    (b)    (c)

C 다음을 듣고 맞으면 T를, 틀리면 F를 고르세요. 🎧 028

1 They have very few products to sell. T F
2 The cabin crew can answer questions about shopping. T F

Dictation

다음을 듣고 빈칸을 채우세요. 🎧 028

Attention, ladies and gentlemen. We are pleased to ① _____ that we will begin the sale of ② _____ free ③ _____ shortly. Please take a moment to look through the duty free ④ _____. You will find great savings on a wide ⑤ _____ of products including perfumes, liquor, jewelry, and other ⑥ _____ little accessories. If you have any questions, please ask any of the ⑦ _____ _____ members.

* 부분은 유음화(Flap Sounds) 현상에 해당하는 부분입니다.

Situation II

Warm-up

대화를 듣고 들은 것에 ✓표 하세요.

- ☐ sale
- ☐ duty free items
- ☐ good deals
- ☐ low prices
- ☐ cosmetics
- ☐ additional 10% off
- ☐ earrings
- ☐ necklace
- ☐ wife

Practice

A 대화를 듣고 질문에 알맞은 사진을 고르세요.

1 What is the man interested in?

(a)  (b)

2 Who does the man want it for?

(a)  (b)

B 대화를 듣고 밑줄 친 부분에 해당하는 말을 따라 말하세요.

A: Did you start the sale of duty free items yet?

B: ① _____

A: Are there any good deals right now?

B: ② _____

A: Oh. wow. I hope I can find a pretty necklace for my wife.

B: ③ _____

Week 02 On the Plane

Unit 04 Take-off and Landing Announcements

Listening 향상 팁

Listen for assimilation and glottal sounds 음운 동화 현상과 성문폐쇄음 듣기

음운 동화(Assimilation) 현상이란?
- 특정 자음끼리 만나서 소리가 나는 위치가 바뀌는 현상을 의미한다.

  예시 t + y → ch: Don't you like it?   d + y → j: Did you go there?
  s + y → sh: I miss you a lot.   z + y → zh: How's your work?

성문폐쇄음(Glottal Stop)이란?
- 성문폐쇄음은 목에 힘을 주어 목구멍의 성문(vocal cords)을 닫아서 공기를 완전히 움직이지 못하게 했다가 터뜨리는 소리이다.
- 가장 대표적인 성문폐쇄음은 /t/가 /n/ 앞에 올 때이다.

  예시 curtain   gotten

A 다음을 듣고 아래에서 해당하는 경우를 고르세요. 🎧 030

(a) t + y → ch   (b) d + y → j   (c) s + y → sh   (d) z + y → zh

1 How's your family? _____   2 What's your phone number? _____
3 Did you call her today? _____   4 Can't you understand? _____

B 성문폐쇄음이 있는 단어들을 듣고 따라 하세요. 🎧 031

1 mountain   2 fountain   3 captain
4 button   5 cotton   6 written

C 맞으면 T를, 틀리면 F를 고르세요.

1 음운 동화 현상에 따라 t가 y와 만나면 j로 소리 나는 위치가 바뀐다. T F

2 eaten, mountain을 발음할 때 성문폐쇄음 현상이 일어난다. T F

Situation I

Warm-up

다음을 듣고 내용과 알맞은 사진을 모두 고르세요. 032

(a)    (b)    (c)

Practice

A 다음을 듣고 질문에 알맞은 답을 고르세요. 032

1 What is the plane going to do?
   (a) To take off   (b) To land   (c) To leave New York

2 What should passengers do to get ready?
   (a) Get their bags   (b) Recline their seats   (c) Put on their seat belts

3 When can passengers take off their seat belts?
   (a) When the plane lands
   (b) When the crew says to
   (c) When the sign goes off

B 다음을 듣고 질문에 알맞은 사진을 고르세요. 032

Q Which picture is related to the announcement?

(a)    (b)    (c)

C 다음을 듣고 맞으면 T를, 틀리면 F를 고르세요.

1 The plane has landed. T F

2 Passengers need to stay seated after landing. T F

Dictation

다음을 듣고 빈칸을 채우세요.

Good afternoon, ladies and gentlemen. This is the ① _____ speaking. We are just approaching JFK International Airport and preparing for landing. Please be sure ② _____ _____ seats are in their upright positions and that your seat belts are securely ③ _____. Please also open all the window shades and return your tray tables to their original positions. After landing, ④ _____ _____ please ⑤ _____ seated with your seat belts fastened until the aircraft comes to a complete ⑥ _____ and the seat belt sign is ⑦ _____ _____ ? Thank you, and I hope you enjoyed your flight.

* _____ 부분은 음운 동화(Assimilation)나 성문폐쇄음(Glottal Stop)이 일어나는 부분입니다.

Situation II

Warm-up

대화를 듣고 들은 것에 ✓표 하세요. 🎧 033

- ☐ upright position
- ☐ landing
- ☐ approaching
- ☐ close
- ☐ shadow
- ☐ dinner table
- ☐ my bag
- ☐ overhead bin
- ☐ remain seated

Practice

A 대화를 듣고 대화 내용과 맞도록 문장을 완성하세요. 🎧 033

1. The man is (a cabin crew member / a passenger).
2. The airplane is about to (take off / land).
3. The woman has to open the (window shade / tray table).
4. The man will put (his / the woman's) bag in the overhead bin.

B 대화를 듣고 밑줄 친 부분에 해당하는 말을 따라 말하세요. 🎧 033

A: Excuse me, ma'am. I need to ask you to put your seat in an upright position.

B: ① _____

A: Yes, we are approaching JFK right now. Please also open the window shade and put your tray table up.

B: ② _____

A: Certainly. Please remember after we land to remain seated with your seat belt fastened.

B: ③ _____

Week 02 • Unit 04   45

Week 02 On the Plane

Vocabulary

#	English	Korean
1	amenity kit	위생용품 세트
2	arm rest	팔걸이
3	beverage cart	음료 카트
4	blanket	담요
5	cabin	객실
6	cabin crew	승무원
7	call button	호출 버튼
8	captain	기장
9	cockpit	조종석
10	ear plugs	귀마개
11	emergency exit	비상구
12	emergency light	비상등
13	eye mask	안대
14	flight crew	승무원
15	foot rest	발걸이
16	full flight	만석 비행기
17	galley	(기내) 주방
18	headset	헤드셋
19	in flight entertainment (IFE)	기내 오락시스템
20	in flight Wi-Fi	기내 와이파이

Memo

21	landing	착륙
22	leg room	다리 두는 공간(의자 사이 간격)
23	lie-flat bed	완전히 젖혀지는 침대[좌석]
24	meal preference	기내식 선호도
25	meal service	기내식 서비스
26	neck pillow	목 베개
27	overhead bin	(좌석 위) 짐칸
28	oxygen mask	산소 마스크
29	reading light	독서등
30	remote control	리모컨
31	seat	좌석
32	seat belt	안전벨트
33	seat pitch	좌석 사이 간격
34	smoke detector	연기 탐지기
35	take-off	이륙
36	tray table	쟁반 탁자
37	upright position	(좌석) 정위치
38	water landing	(비상) 수상 착륙[바다에 불시착]
39	window shade	창문 가리개
40	wing	비행기 날개

Memo

EBS 생수다
생생한 영어 수다

Week 03 At the Hotel

- **Unit 01** Reserving Rooms
- **Unit 02** Checking In
- **Unit 03** Complaining
- **Unit 04** Concierge Service

Week 03
At the Hotel

Unit 01 Reserving Rooms

Listening 향상 팁

Listen for frequently-used expressions 빈출 표현 듣기

호텔 예약 빈출 어휘 / 빈출 구문

빈출 어휘	빈출 구문
room rate / categories 객실 요금/유형 queen / twin room 퀸/트윈사이즈 침대방 available 이용 가능한 Internet access 인터넷 사용 expiration date 유효 기간 credit card information 신용카드 정보	start at $... ~달러부터 시작하다 Can I interest you in...? ~을 소개시켜 드릴까요? Is there availability on...? (몇 일)에 빈 방 있나요? finalize a reservation 예약을 확정 짓다

A 대화를 듣고 빈칸에 알맞은 단어를 쓰세요. 🎧 035

1 Q _____ _____ will you be staying?
   A I'll be staying for three _____.

2 Q What's the _____?
   A Your room is $250 _____ night.

B 방을 예약할 때 들을 수 있는 질문을 듣고 알맞은 대답을 고르세요. 🎧 036

(a) A double bed, please.
(b) Michael Lee
(c) It starts at $250 on weekends.
(d) By next July

1 _____   2 _____   3 _____

C 맞으면 T를, 틀리면 F를 고르세요.

1 '5월 5일에 빈 방 있나요?'는 'Is there availability on May 5th?'라고 한다.   T F

2 '그 방은 인터넷을 이용할 수 있다'는 'The room offers Internet access.'이다.   T F

Situation I

Warm-up

다음을 듣고 들은 것에 ✓표 하세요. 🎧 037

- ☐ lines
- ☐ busy
- ☐ as quickly as possible
- ☐ room rates
- ☐ for weekdays
- ☐ room categories
- ☐ extra charge
- ☐ continental breakfast
- ☐ hang up

Practice

A 다음을 듣고 질문에 알맞은 답을 고르세요. 🎧 037

1 Who answered the phone?
 (a) A receptionist (b) Nobody (c) A guest

2 How much would a room cost for Saturday night?
 (a) $115 (b) $125 (c) $165

3 What is offered for free to guests?
 (a) Breakfast (b) Rooms (c) Flights

B 다음을 듣고 질문에 알맞은 사진을 고르세요. 🎧 037

Q Which is NOT offered free of charge to guests?

(a) 　(b) 　(c)

C 다음을 듣고 맞으면 T를, 틀리면 F를 고르세요.

1 Rooms are the same price all week.   T F
2 Hotel guests can go to the airport for free.   T F

Dictation

다음을 듣고 빈칸을 채우세요.

Thank you for calling Sunny Day Inn. ① _____ _____ are currently busy, but we will answer your call as soon as possible. ② _____ _____ start at $125 for weekdays and $165 for weekends and ③ _____. All ④ _____ _____ include a ⑤ _____ continental breakfast. There is also a complimentary ⑥ _____ to the airport every hour. Please ⑦ _____ _____ _____ and we will be with you shortly.

* ____ 부분은 호텔 예약할 때 쓰이는 빈출 표현입니다.

Situation II

Warm-up

대화를 듣고 들은 것에 ✓표 하세요. 🎧 038

- ☐ missed
- ☐ what day
- ☐ weekend rates
- ☐ visit
- ☐ Saturday
- ☐ put the bags
- ☐ reservation
- ☐ 8th
- ☐ in the name of

Practice

A 대화를 듣고 맞으면 T를, 틀리면 F를 고르세요. 🎧 038

1. The woman wants to make a reservation for a concert.   T F
2. The woman makes a reservation for Saturday.   T F
3. The man will pay $165.   T F

B 대화를 듣고 밑줄 친 부분에 해당하는 말을 따라 말하세요. 🎧 038

A: Sorry we missed your call. How can I help you?

B: ① _____

A: What date do you want to make a reservation for?

B: ② _____

A: Weekend rates are $165.

B: ③ _____

Week 03
At the Hotel

Unit 02 Checking In

Listening 향상 팁

Listen for frequently-used expressions & idioms 빈출 표현과 관용어구 듣기

- 호텔 체크인 할 때 시간은 'at + 시각'으로 읽는다.
  [예시] It opens **at 6:00**. 6시에 문을 연다.

- 방 번호는 끝에서 두 자리는 방 번호이고, 그 앞은 층을 나타낸다.
  [예시] Room number 920 (**nine twenty**) 9층 20호   1503 (**fifteen**-o-three) 15층 3호

- 층은 서수로 나타낸다. [예시] The business center is on the **third** floor. 비즈니스 센터는 **3층**에 있다.

- 호텔 체크인 할 때 잘 쓰는 관용 어구
  [예시] around the clock 24시간 내내   at an additional [extra] charge 추가 비용 드는
  dial [press] 0 0번을 누르다   for a deposit 보증금으로

A 다음을 듣고 알맞은 방 번호를 쓰세요. 🎧 039

1 _____   2 _____   3 _____

B 다음을 듣고 알맞은 우리말 해석을 고르세요. 🎧 040

(a) 추가 비용을 내시면 룸서비스로 아침식사가 가능하십니다.
(b) 프런트데스크는 0번을 누르시면 됩니다.
(c) 룸서비스와 하우스키핑은 하루 종일 이용 가능합니다.

1 _____   2 _____   3 _____

C 맞으면 T를, 틀리면 F를 고르세요.

1 호텔 방 3117호는 'thirty-one, seventeen'이라고 읽는다.   T F

2 호텔의 층을 말할 때는 서수를 사용한다.   T F

Situation I

Warm-up

다음을 듣고 내용과 관계 있는 사진을 모두 고르세요.

(a) 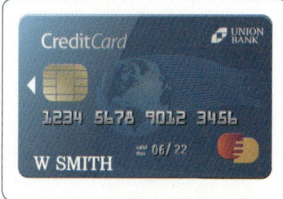   (b)    (c)

Practice

A 다음을 듣고 질문에 알맞은 답을 고르세요.

1 What does the speaker need?
   (a) A credit card   (b) Breakfast   (c) A reservation number

2 When is breakfast over?
   (a) At 6:30   (b) At 10:30   (c) 24 hours

3 How much does it cost to use the pool?
   (a) $10   (b) $30   (c) Nothing

B 다음을 듣고 질문에 알맞은 사진을 고르세요.

Q What is available to use around the clock?

(a)    (b)    (c)

C 다음을 듣고 맞으면 T를, 틀리면 F를 고르세요. 🎧 041

1 Housekeeping is always available.   T F

2 The pool is free to use.   T F

Dictation

다음을 듣고 빈칸을 채우세요. 🎧 041

I found your reservation, and I'll just need to see some ID and a credit card ① _____ ___ _____, please. I'll let you know that breakfast is in the ② _____ _____ from 6:30 to 10:30 a.m. ③ _____ _____ is 24 hours, and ④ _____ is also available ⑤ _____ _____ _____. The pool on the 5th floor is available to you ⑥ _____ _____ extra charge. Please note that ⑦ _____ is at noon on your final day.

* _____ 부분은 호텔 체크인 할 때 자주 쓰이는 표현이나 관용어구입니다.

Situation II

Warm-up

대화를 듣고 들은 것에 ✓표 하세요. 🎧 042

- ☐ checking in
- ☐ an ocean view
- ☐ holidays
- ☐ your driver's license
- ☐ eleventh hour
- ☐ a dime a dozen
- ☐ standard room
- ☐ rebooking fee
- ☐ my four cents' worth

Practice

A 대화를 듣고 내용과 알맞은 문장을 고르세요. 🎧 042

(a) The man wants a standard room with an ocean view.

(b) It is 11 o'clock now.

(c) The man can change rooms free of charge.

(d) The fee for the corner suite is two cents.

B 대화를 듣고 밑줄 친 부분에 해당하는 말을 따라 말하세요. 🎧 042

A: Hello, sir. Checking in? Can I see some ID, please?

B: ① _____

A: Let me see here. I have had an eleventh hour cancellation, so I can change your room for a small rebooking fee.

B: ② _____

A: If you want my two cents' worth, I'd suggest that you move to the corner suite.

B: ③ _____

Week 03 • Unit 02

Week 03
At the Hotel

Unit 03 Complaining

Listening 향상 팁

Listen for complaints 불평 듣기

불평하는 경우
- 불평하는 상황에서도 예의를 갖추고 상대방을 대하는 것은 중요하다.
- I feel, I think 등의 표현을 함께 사용하면 듣는 사람이 불편하지 않게 불평을 전달할 수 있다.
- 불평 내용 앞에 다음과 같은 표현을 자주 사용한다.
   예시 I'm afraid…, I'm sorry…, Excuse me…, Maybe you forgot to…

불평에 응대하는 경우
- 먼저 사과를 하고 즉각적인 조치를 약속한 후 신속히 처리한다.
   예시 I'm terribly sorry for this situation. Let me take care of it right away. I can assure you it won't happen again.

A 불평 상황과 관계 있는 아래 문장의 나머지 부분을 듣고 고르세요. 🎧 043

1 I'm terribly sorry for _____.   (a)   (b)   (c)

2 Let me take _____.   (a)   (b)   (c)

B 다음을 듣고 빈칸에 알맞은 단어를 쓰세요. 🎧 044

1 Maybe you _____ to send the room service.

2 I'm _____ that my watch doesn't go well.

C 맞으면 T를, 틀리면 F를 고르세요.

1 불평을 할 때 항상 강한 어조와 표현을 사용하는 것이 좋다.   T F

2 불평을 할 때 I'm afraid…나 Excuse me, but…으로 시작하면 공손하게 불만 사항을 전달할 수 있다.   T F

Situation I

Warm-up

대화를 듣고 들은 것에 ✓표 하세요. 🎧 045

- ☐ change
- ☐ booked
- ☐ a king bed
- ☐ immediately
- ☐ a mountain view
- ☐ double bed
- ☐ work
- ☐ family room
- ☐ available

Practice

A 대화를 듣고 질문에 알맞은 답을 고르세요. 🎧 045

1 Who is the woman?
   (a) A hotel guest   (b) A hotel employee   (c) A potential guest

2 What kind of view does the room have?
   (a) A city view   (b) An ocean view   (c) A family view

3 Why does the guest need more beds?
   (a) His family is there.   (b) He likes options.   (c) It's an ocean view room.

B 대화를 듣고 질문에 알맞은 사진을 고르세요. 🎧 045

Q Which room is the man calling from now?

(a)  (b)  (c)

C 다음을 듣고 맞으면 T를, 틀리면 F를 고르세요. 🎧 045

1 The guest booked a suite. T F

2 There are four guests total. T F

Dictation

대화를 듣고 빈칸을 채우세요. 🎧 045

A: Hello, sir. How may I help you?

B: I ①_____ _____ to change my room immediately! I just went to the room you gave me, and it's not going to ②_____ _____ us at all. I booked an ocean view ③_____ _____, but we have a ④_____ _____ with only one ⑤_____ _____. I am here with my wife and kids, so we need the ⑥_____ that has a king bed and two twin beds. Do you have another room ⑦_____ for us?

* _____ 부분은 불평을 공손하게 말하는 표현입니다.

Situation II

Warm-up

대화를 듣고 대화와 관계 있는 사진을 고르세요. 🎧 046

(a) 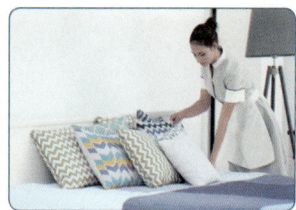 (b)  (c)

Practice

A 대화를 듣고 질문에 알맞은 사진을 고르세요. 🎧 046

1 Who will visit the woman soon?   2 What does the woman need?

(a)  (b)    (a)  (b)

B 대화를 듣고 밑줄 친 부분에 해당하는 말을 따라 말하세요. 🎧 046

A: Hello? Housekeeping. How may I help you?

B: ① _____

A: Oh, I'm terribly sorry for that, ma'am. You are in room 417, correct?

B: ② _____

A: Yes, ma'am. Right away. I will call the floor manager for the fourth floor right away and someone will come to your room immediately.

B: ③ _____

Week 03 • Unit 03   61

Week 03
At the Hotel

Unit 04 Concierge Service

Listening 향상 팁

Listen for specific information 특정 정보 듣기

- 컨시어지는 세탁, 호텔 시설에 관한 정보나 호텔 밖의 관광지, 레스토랑과 같은 장소를 안내하기도 하고, 공연표 예약, 여행에 필요한 교통편 안내 등의 포괄적 서비스를 제공한다.

  예시 Guest: Do you know if there're any more city tours?
  시내 관광이 더 있나요?

  Concierge: There's a half day tour that leaves in 30 minutes.
  30분 후에 출발하는 반나절 짜리 관광이 있습니다.

  Guest: Could you help us plan our route to this historic site?
  여기 역사 유적지로 가는 일정을 짜는 데 도와 주실래요?

  Concierge: No problem. Would you like to drive yourself, hire a driver, or rent one?
  그럼요. 직접 운전하실 건가요, 운전사를 고용하실 건가요, 아니면 차를 렌트하실 건가요?

A 다음 질문을 듣고, 질문에 알맞은 답변을 고르세요. 🎧 047

(a) Yes, I can suggest several newly opened shows that are very popular.
(b) Our shuttle service is free and leaves every hour on the hour.
(c) There are several nice restaurants within walking distance from here.
(d) If you just leave your suit in the laundry bag by your door, it'll be done for you.

1 _____   2 _____   3 _____   4 _____

B 맞으면 T를, 틀리면 F를 고르세요.

1 고객은 컨시어지에 드라이크리닝을 맡길 수 없다. T F
2 컨시어지는 고객에 관한 포괄적 서비스를 제공한다. T F

Situation I

Warm-up

다음을 듣고 들은 것에 ✓표 하세요. 🎧 048

- ☐ room keys
- ☐ something special
- ☐ your stay
- ☐ concierge desk
- ☐ sightseeing day
- ☐ truck rentals
- ☐ bus tickets
- ☐ theater
- ☐ escalator

Practice

A 다음을 듣고 질문에 알맞은 답을 고르세요. 🎧 048

1 Who is speaking?
   (a) The concierge   (b) Housekeeping   (c) Front desk staff

2 What can the concierge do for the guest?
   (a) Find a rental car   (b) Loan a car   (c) Call the elevator

3 Where is the concierge desk?
   (a) Near the bank   (b) Next to the elevators   (c) Upstairs

B 다음을 듣고 질문에 알맞은 사진을 고르세요. 🎧 048

Q What is the speaker mainly talking about?

(a)  (b)  (c)

C 다음을 듣고 맞으면 T를, 틀리면 F를 고르세요. 🎧 048

1 This information is given at check-in.　　　　　　　　　　T F

2 The concierge can help plan tourist activities.　　　　　　T F

Dictation

다음을 듣고 빈칸을 채우세요. 🎧 048

Here are your room keys, and ① _____ you need help with anything special during your stay, please visit the ② _____ _____. The concierge will be happy to help you with many different things such as planning a ③ _____ day, ④ _____ _____, train or bus tickets, or even ⑤ _____ for a tour or to the theater. The concierge desk is to the left of the ⑥ _____ _____, so please stop in ⑦ _____ _____.

* ____ 부분은 컨시어지 서비스에 관한 특정 정보 부분입니다.

Situation II

Warm-up

대화를 듣고 대화와 관계 있는 사진을 모두 고르세요. 🎧 049

(a)  (b)  (c)

Practice

A 대화를 듣고 대화 내용과 맞도록 문장을 완성하세요. 🎧 049

1 The woman is calling to the (room service / front desk).
2 The first four pages of the menu are available (in the evening / at any time).
3 The woman prefers (beef / vegetarian dishes) now.
4 The woman ordered (noodles and fruit / noodles and a soda).

B 대화를 듣고 밑줄 친 부분에 해당하는 말을 따라 말하세요. 🎧 049

A: Room Service, may I take your order please?

B: ① _____

A: The first four pages of the menu are, but the rest of the menu has the available times listed at the top of the page.

B: ② _____

A: Yes, we have lots of vegetarian dishes available such as the veggie burger, vegetable fried rice, sesame noodles and tofu, or the fruit platter.

B: ③ _____

Week 03 • Unit 04 65

Week 03 At the Hotel

Vocabulary

1	amenities	(호텔) 편의시설
2	bellhop	벨보이
3	buffet	뷔페
4	business center	(고객용) 비즈니스 센터
5	business hotel	(단기 숙박자용) 비즈니스 호텔
6	card key	카드 키
7	check-in	체크인[입실]
8	checkout	체크아웃[퇴실]
9	city view	시내 전망
10	concierge	컨시어지[안내]
11	continental breakfast	유럽식 아침 식사
12	convention	컨벤션, 대회의
13	deluxe room	디럭스룸
14	deposit	보증금; 맡기다
15	double occupancy	2인 1실 (사용)
16	duty manager	(프런트 / 하우스키핑의) 당직 매니저
17	early check-in	이른 체크인[입실]
18	fitness center	피트니스 센터
19	front desk	프런트 데스크
20	general manager	총지배인

Memo

#	English	Korean
21	housekeeping	하우스키핑, 집안 돌보기
22	in-room safe	실내 금고
23	late checkout	늦은 체크아웃[퇴실]
24	lobby	로비
25	minibar	미니바
26	no vacancy	공실[빈방] 없음
27	ocean view	바다 전망
28	package deal	패키지 행사
29	penthouse	펜트하우스 (꼭대기층을 통째로 쓰는 객실)
30	reception	리셉션[호텔 접수처]
31	room service	룸서비스
32	service bell	서비스 벨
33	shuttle bus	셔틀버스
34	spa	스파
35	superior room	슈페리어룸
36	swimming pool	수영장
37	upgrade	(방을) 업그레이드하다
38	upgraded room	업그레이드한 방
39	valet	발렛[주차대행] 서비스
40	welcome drink	환영 음료

Memo

EBS 생수다
생생한 영어 수다

Week 04 Transportation

- **Unit 01** Getting Directions to the Tour Site
- **Unit 02** Buying Tickets
- **Unit 03** Finding the Right Stop
- **Unit 04** Missing a Train

Week 04
Transportation

Unit 01 Getting Directions to the Tour Site

Listening 향상 팁

Listen for directions 길 안내 듣기

- 길을 안내할 때 도로 명칭이 항상 언급되므로 관련 어휘를 익히는 것이 좋다.

  [예시] Highway (Hwy.) 고속도로
  Avenue (Ave.) (도시에서 남북을 연결하는) 가
  Drive (Dr.) (주택가) 드라이브
  Boulevard (Blvd.) (가로수가 있는) 대로
  Street (St.) (차도와 인도가 모두 있는) 길
  Lane (Ln.) 레인(좁은 길)

- 길 안내에서 자주 사용되는 표현

  [예시] Turn left. 좌회전하세요.
  Keep going. 계속 가세요.
  Take the next right. 다음에 우회전하세요.
  Turn around. U턴 하세요.

A 다음을 듣고 알맞은 사진을 고르세요. 🎧 051

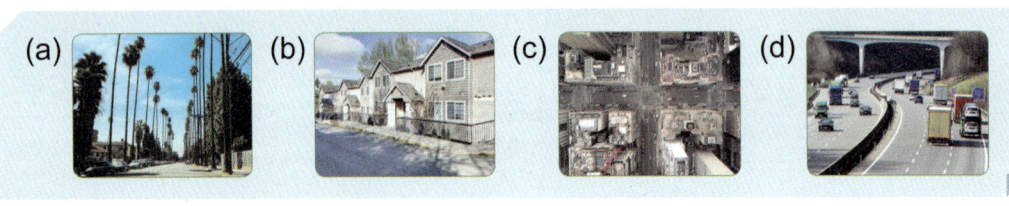

1. _____ 2. _____ 3. _____ 4. _____

B 다음을 듣고 빈칸에 알맞은 단어를 쓰세요. 🎧 052

1. From First _____, turn right.
2. Take the next left onto 7th _____.
3. Take the second left onto Green _____.
4. _____ going straight down three blocks.

C 맞으면 T를, 틀리면 F를 고르세요.

1. 'Highway'는 '고속도로'를 가리킨다. T F
2. 'Avenue'는 '주택가의 좁은 길'을 뜻한다. T F

Situation I

Warm-up

다음을 듣고 들은 것에 ✓표 하세요. 🎧 053

- ☐ walking tour
- ☐ information center
- ☐ turn left
- ☐ National Mall
- ☐ keep walking
- ☐ Madison Lane
- ☐ Exit 6
- ☐ in the same direction
- ☐ until you reach

Practice

A 다음을 듣고 질문에 알맞은 답을 고르세요. 🎧 053

1 Who is this information for?
   (a) Tourists   (b) Shoppers   (c) Commuters

2 Who can give good advice about planning a day?
   (a) Information center visitors
   (b) Information center workers
   (c) People in Smithsonian Castle

3 Where does the walking tour end?
   (a) In a mall   (b) At a monument   (c) At the information center

B 다음을 듣고 질문에 알맞은 사진을 고르세요. 🎧 053

Q What can you NOT see during the walking tour of the National Mall?

(a)  (b)  (c)

C 다음을 듣고 맞으면 T를, 틀리면 F를 고르세요. 🎧 053

1 The tour is given on a bus.   T F

2 The tour ends at Madison Dr. NW.   T F

Dictation

다음을 듣고 빈칸을 채우세요. 🎧 053

The ① _____ _____ of the National Mall is a great way to see the major sites of DC. Start early at Smithsonian Station. If you come out Exit 4 and ② _____ _____, you'll find the Smithsonian Castle and the information center. It's best to ask for staff advice when planning your day. ③ _____ _____ in the ④ _____ _____ until you reach 3rd St. SW, and then ⑤ _____ _____. After you ⑥ _____ Madison Dr. NW, you will turn left again and you can continue your tour down the National Mall until you reach the ⑦ _____ _____.

* _____ 부분은 길 안내를 할 때 자주 쓰는 빈출 표현입니다.

Situation II

Warm-up

대화를 듣고 대화에서 들은 방향을 고르세요. 🎧 054

(a)

(b)

(c)

Practice

A 대화를 듣고 내용과 알맞은 문장을 모두 고르세요. 🎧 054

(a) The woman is on Madison Dr. NW now.

(b) The woman wants to go to the Washington Monument.

(c) It takes 15 minutes to go to the White House from the place where the woman is.

(d) The White House is located on 15th St.

B 대화를 듣고 밑줄 친 부분에 해당하는 말을 따라 말하세요. 🎧 054

A: Excuse me. Do you know where Madison Dr. NW is?

B: ① _____

A: We are on a walking tour, and we are just trying to get back to the Washington Monument.

B: ② _____

A: Oh, that's cool. Is that far from the Washington Monument?

B: ③ _____

Week 04 • Unit 01 73

Week 04
Transportation

Unit 02 Buying Tickets

Listening 향상 팁

Listen for unstressed words 비강세 단어 듣기

비강세 단어(Unstressed Words) 듣기의 중요성
- 영어 문장은 내용어(Content Words)와 기능어(Function Words)로 이루어져 있다.
  - 내용어: 의미 표현이 주된 기능이며 강세가 있다.
    주로 명사, 동사, 형용사, 부사이다.
  - 기능어: 문장에서 문법적인 기능을 하며 강세가 없다.
    주로 전치사, 관사, 대명사이다.
- 강세가 없는 기능어를 못 들어도 의미 파악에는 지장이 없다.
- 기능어는 약하게 발음되지만, 연음, 유음화 등의 음운 현상을 일으켜 발음을 변형시키므로 제대로 듣는 것이 중요하다.

A 다음을 듣고 빈칸에 알맞은 단어를 쓰세요. 🎧 055

1 There are _____ _____ _____ tickets left for the 3:00 show.
2 Sorry, it is _____ _____ order.
3 It's _____ _____ expensive compared _____ _____ matinee.
4 It's been raining for two weeks. I'm _____ _____ it.
5 Reserve today _____ _____ evening of entertainment.
6 Book early _____ _____ discount _____ 10%.

B 맞으면 T를, 틀리면 F를 고르세요.

1 기능어는 전치사, 관사 등이 포함되고, 일반적으로 강세를 받지 않는다.

2 기능어는 약하게 발음되지만, 발음 변형을 시키는 경우가 많다.

Situation I

Warm-up

다음을 듣고 들은 것에 ✓표 하세요. 🎧 056

- ☐ a quick escape
- ☐ city center
- ☐ for more information
- ☐ country life
- ☐ all kinds of activities
- ☐ 15% off
- ☐ 50 minute train ride
- ☐ visit our homepage
- ☐ the first 15 visitors

Practice

A 다음을 듣고 질문에 알맞은 답을 고르세요. 🎧 056

1. What is the advertisement for?
   (a) A trip to the city (b) A visit to a farm (c) A cooking class

2. How long does it take to get there by bus?
   (a) 15 minutes (b) 35 minutes (c) 50 minutes

3. Who gets the daily 15% discount?
   (a) Everyday visitors (b) All the visitors (c) First come first served

B 다음을 듣고 질문에 알맞은 사진을 고르세요. 🎧 056

Q What is being advertised?

(a)  (b)  (c)

C 다음을 듣고 맞으면 T를, 틀리면 F를 고르세요. 🎧056

1 They offer meals at the ranch. [T] [F]
2 They have a website with more information. [T] [F]

Dictation

다음을 듣고 빈칸을 채우세요. 🎧056

Are you looking for a quick escape ① _____ _____ city? Come ② _____ visit us at the Lucky Farm for a day of fresh air, country life, and good home cooking! We are located a quick 35 minute train ③ _____ 50 minute bus ride from the city center, and offer all kinds ④ _____ activities for kids, adults, and groups. Visit our website or call us today for more information. We look forward ⑤ _____ welcoming you soon. Discounts of 15% ⑥ _____ entrance ⑦ _____ offered to the first 50 visitors every day!

* _____ 부분은 기능어인 비강세 단어(Unstressed Words)입니다.

Situation II

Warm-up

대화를 듣고 들은 것에 ✓표 하세요. 🎧 057

- ☐ front desk
- ☐ your train tickets
- ☐ to book
- ☐ the 9 a.m. train
- ☐ sold down
- ☐ other train
- ☐ the same city
- ☐ for three adults
- ☐ on that train

Practice

A 대화를 듣고 질문에 알맞은 그림을 고르세요. 🎧 057

Q What time will the train the man books leave tomorrow?

(a)    (b)    (c)

B 대화를 듣고 밑줄 친 부분에 해당하는 말을 따라 말하세요. 🎧 057

A: Hello? Is this Mr. Clarkson?

B: ① _____

A: Hello sir. This is the front desk, and I am calling about your train tickets for tomorrow. You had asked us to book tickets for you and your family on the 9 a.m. train tomorrow, but I'm afraid it is all sold out.

B: ② _____

A: Yes, sir. There is a train at 6 a.m. and one at 11 a.m. that both go to the same destination.

B: ③ _____

Week 04
Transportation

Unit 03 Finding the Right Stop

Listening 향상 팁

Listen for directions 길 안내 듣기

지하철 / 버스 이용 시 자주 사용하는 표현

예시 Excuse me, how can I get to the City Hall? 시청은 어떻게 가나요?
Take the red line at Central Station. 중앙역에서 빨간색을 타세요.
Transfer to the green line. 녹색선으로 갈아타세요.
Get off at City Hall Station. 시청역에서 내리세요.
Go out Exit 1. 1번 출구로 나가세요.

A 다음을 듣고 빈칸에 알맞은 단어를 쓰세요. 🎧 058

1 _____ the green line _____ Columbus Station.
2 _____ _____ at the K station, and _____ _____ the yellow line.
3 _____ three stops and get _____ at Main Street Station.
4 _____ _____ Exit 3.

B 다음을 듣고 알맞은 것을 골라 문장을 완성하세요. 🎧 059

1 (Get on / Take) the blue line from Fifth Avenue.
2 (Transfer to / Change to) the gray line at Martin Square.
3 (Get on / Get off) at 83rd Street.
4 Then, you can't (miss / reach) it.

C 맞으면 T를, 틀리면 F를 고르세요.

1 탈것을 탈 때는 get on, 내릴 때는 get off 표현을 주로 이용한다. T F
2 지하철 이용 시 빈출 표현은 take the... line, transfer to..., get off at... 등이 있다. T F

Situation I

Warm-up

대화를 듣고 들은 것에 ✓표 하세요. 🎧 060

- ☐ ask for
- ☐ in 4 more stops
- ☐ worried
- ☐ looking for
- ☐ almost there
- ☐ coming up shortly
- ☐ close
- ☐ perfect
- ☐ on the left

Practice

A 대화를 듣고 질문에 알맞은 답을 고르세요. 🎧 060

1 Where is the conversation taking place?
   (a) In an airport (b) On a ship (c) On a train

2 How much farther does the woman need to ride?
   (a) 2 stops (b) 3 stops (c) 5 stops

3 Where will the woman exit?
   (a) Exit 3 (b) On the left (c) On the right

B 대화를 듣고 질문에 알맞은 사진을 고르세요. 🎧 060

Q Where are the speakers now?

(a)
(b)
(c)

C 다음을 듣고 맞으면 T를, 틀리면 F를 고르세요. 🎧 060

1 The train is at Gravely Street Station now.   T F

2 The people missed their stop.   T F

Dictation

대화를 듣고 빈칸을 채우세요. 🎧 060

A: ① _____ , could I ask for your help?

B: Yeah, ② _____ _____ ?

A: We are ③ _____ _____ Gravely Street Station. Do you ④ _____ _____ we're close?

B: Yeah, it's in 3 ⑤ _____ _____ . Almost ⑥ _____ .

A: Oh, excellent. We were worried we had missed it.

B: Don't worry. It's coming up soon, and the doors will be on the ⑦ _____ .

* _____ 부분은 길 안내 시 자주 사용하는 표현입니다.

Situation II

Warm-up

대화를 듣고 대화와 관계 있는 사진을 고르세요. 🎧 061

(a) 　(b) 　(c)

Practice

A 대화를 듣고 질문에 알맞은 답을 고르세요. 🎧 061

Q Which station are the speakers at now?

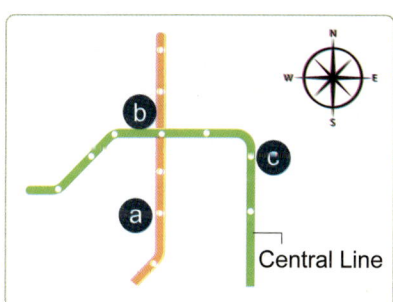

(a)　　　(b)　　　(c)

B 대화를 듣고 밑줄 친 부분에 해당하는 말을 따라 말하세요. 🎧 061

A: Excuse me, could you help us?

B: ① _____

A: We are looking for Splash Park Extreme, and we thought it was supposed to be right here at Exit 4.

B: ② _____

A: Oh no! Is it far from here?

B: ③ _____

Week 04
Transportation

Unit 04 Missing a Train

Listening 향상 팁

Listen for elision and contractions 소리 생략과 축약 듣기

소리 생략(Elision)이란?
- 발음할 때 모음이나 자음 또는 음절을 생략하는 것을 의미한다.

  예시 him → /im/   I love **him**. → I love **'im**.
       going to → /gənə/   It's **going to** leave soon. → It's **gonna** leave soon.
       want to → /wənə/   I **want to** take a walk. → I **wanna** take a walk.

축약(Contraction)이란?
- 흔히 구어체에서 두 단어를 한 단어로 줄이는 것을 의미한다.

  예시 He is → He's   There is → There's   I have → I've

A 다음을 듣고 소리 생략이 된 부분을 찾아 ○표 하세요. 🎧 062

1 Harry is my best friend. I love (him).
2 I'm going to take the next train.
3 I want to rebook the next available train.
4 I have a sweet tooth. I love chocolate.

B 다음을 듣고 축약이 된 부분을 찾아 ○표 하세요. 🎧 063

1 (You've) just missed the 3 o'clock train.
2 You can take the next one. It'll arrive 30 minutes later.
3 That'll cost a small rebooking fee.
4 I thought I could've made it.

C 맞으면 T를, 틀리면 F를 고르세요.

1 소리 생략은 자음이나 모음, 혹은 음절을 생략하는 것으로 going to가 /gənə/로 소리 나는 것이다. T F

2 축약은 두 단어를 한 단어로 줄이는 것인데, 문어체에서 흔히 볼 수 있다. T F

Situation I

Warm-up

대화를 듣고 들은 것에 ✓표 하세요. 🎧 064

- ☐ flustered
- ☐ on the next available train
- ☐ one hour later
- ☐ missed
- ☐ in 45 minutes
- ☐ original arrival time
- ☐ just left
- ☐ a slower train
- ☐ a rebooking fee

Practice

A 대화를 듣고 질문에 알맞은 답을 고르세요. 🎧 064

1 Why is the woman flustered?
   (a) She lost her ticket.
   (b) She can't find the platform.
   (c) She thinks she missed her train.

2 Why is the next train available arriving two hours later?
   (a) It is a high speed train.
   (b) It is a slow train.
   (c) It leaves in 35 minutes.

3 Why is there a rebooking fee?
   (a) The woman lost her ticket.
   (b) The woman missed her train.
   (c) She is an hour late.

B 대화를 듣고 내용에 알맞은 사진을 고르세요. 🎧 064

Q What did the woman miss?

(a)
(b)
(c)

C 다음을 듣고 맞으면 T를, 틀리면 F를 고르세요. 🎧 064

1 There are no more high speed trains on that day. T F

2 The right next train will arrive one hour later than the woman's original arrival time. T F

Dictation

대화를 듣고 빈칸을 채우세요. 🎧 064

A: Hi! I am so flustered. I think I just ①_____ my train. Here is my ticket.

B: Oh, yes, the train just ②_____. I can offer you a seat on the next train that leaves in ③_____. It is a slower train though, so it's ④_____ _____ arrive two hours later than you ⑤_____ originally. The next high speed train leaves in an hour, so it only arrives one hour ⑥_____ _____ your original arrival time. There is a ⑦_____ _____ of $35 either way.

* 　　 부분은 소리 생략(Elision)이나 축약(Contraction)이 일어나는 부분입니다.

Situation II

Warm-up

대화를 듣고 대화와 관계 있는 사진을 고르세요.

(a)    (b)    (c)

Practice

A 대화를 듣고 대화 내용과 맞도록 문장을 완성하세요.

1 The man is looking for (Platform 13 / the ticket counter).
2 The man plans to go to (New York / Boston).
3 The man (missed / caught up with) the train.
4 The woman told the man to go to (the ticket counter / the police office).

B 대화를 듣고 밑줄 친 부분에 해당하는 말을 따라 말하세요.

A: Excuse me, but where can we find Platform 13?

B: ① _____

A: Yes, we were. We're running so late!

B: ② _____

A: Oh no! That's terrible. What can we do?

B: ③ _____

Week 04 Transportation

Vocabulary

1	all stop	모든 역 정차
2	(bus / train) driver	(버스 / 열차) 운전사
3	bus stop	버스 정거장
4	cable car	케이블카
5	catch a train / bus	(기차 / 버스를) 따라잡다
6	conductor	(버스 / 기차의) 승무원
7	dining car	식당칸 차
8	dispatcher	(버스 / 열차 / 비행기 등) 운행 관리원
9	double-decker bus	이층 버스
10	express bus	고속버스
11	fare	(교통) 요금
12	first car	첫차
13	first class	일등칸, 특실
14	freight train	화물 열차
15	hail a taxi	택시를 잡다
16	high-speed train	고속열차
17	hire a car	자동차를 빌리다
18	last car	막차
19	limousine	리무진(대형 승용차)
20	miss a train / bus	(기차 / 버스를) 놓치다

Memo

21	nonstop	직통, 논스톱
22	overnight bus	심야 버스
23	passenger train	여객 열차
24	rental car	렌터카
25	rest stop	휴게소, 휴게 정차
26	round trip	왕복 여행
27	sleeper car	침대칸
28	sold out	(표) 매진, 품절
29	standard ticket	일반석 표
30	standing ticket	입석 표
31	station	역, 정거장, 정류소
32	steward	(여객기 / 여객선 / 기차의) 남자 승무원
33	subway	지하철
34	subway (route) map	지하철 노선도
35	taxi stand	택시 승강장
36	ticket machine	표 발매기
37	ticket office[counter]	매표소
38	tram	전차
39	transfer	환승, 갈아타기
40	trolley	전차

Memo

EBS 생수다
생생한 영어 수다

Week 05 At the Restaurant

- **Unit 01** Making a Reservation
- **Unit 02** Introducing a Restaurant
- **Unit 03** Advertising a New Product
- **Unit 04** Problems on Food

Week 05
At the Restaurant

Unit 01 Making a Reservation

Listening 향상 팁

Listen for specific purpose 특정 목적 듣기

식당 예약 상황을 이해하고 질문을 미리 예측하면 듣기에 도움이 된다.

- For which date do you want to make a reservation? 어느 날짜에 예약을 하고 싶으세요?
- How many will be in the party? 일행이 몇 명이세요?
- What name should I make a reservation under? 누구 이름으로 예약하시나요?
- A phone number where we can reach you, please. 연락 가능한 전화번호 부탁 드려요.
- I'd like to make a reservation for two this Friday. 이번 주 금요일에 2명 예약하고 싶습니다.
- Sorry. We're booked solid tonight. 죄송합니다. 오늘 밤은 예약이 다 찼습니다.
- Do you have any openings for Friday evening? 금요일 저녁에 자리 있나요?
- Can we have a table by the window in a non-smoking section? 금연석 창가 자리가 있나요?

A 다음 질문을 듣고 알맞은 답변을 골라 쓰세요. 🎧 067

(a) Party of 6.   (b) Jake Min. The last name is M-I-N as in Nick.
(c) 010-9876-5432.   (d) It's for Friday, the 12th, at 6:30 p.m.

1 _____   2 _____   3 _____   4 _____

B 다음을 듣고 빈칸에 알맞은 단어를 쓰세요. 🎧 068

1 I'd like to _____ ____ _____ for four tonight.
2 We're _____ _____ tonight.

C 맞으면 T를, 틀리면 F를 고르세요.

1 특정 상황에서 자주 활용되는 표현을 숙지하는 것은 듣기에 도움이 된다. [T] [F]

2 '오늘 저녁 영업하시나요?'는 'Do you have any openings tonight?'이라고 한다. [T] [F]

Situation I

Warm-up

다음을 듣고 들은 것에 ✓표 하세요. 🎧 069

- ☐ service staff
- ☐ occupied
- ☐ shortly
- ☐ make a reservation
- ☐ in your companion
- ☐ Valentine's Day
- ☐ Mother's Day
- ☐ the fourth Sunday
- ☐ last orders

Practice

A 다음을 듣고 질문에 알맞은 답을 고르세요. 🎧 069

1. Why did nobody answer the phone?
   (a) They are closed.   (b) They are busy.   (c) The call is over.

2. What information is NOT requested to make a reservation?
   (a) Date   (b) Time   (c) Phone number

3. When can a reservation NOT be made?
   (a) Lunch
   (b) New Year's Day
   (c) Second Sunday of a month

B 다음을 듣고 질문에 알맞은 그림을 고르세요. 🎧 069

Q By when can guests place an order at the restaurant?

(a)    (b)    (c)

C 다음을 듣고 맞으면 T를, 틀리면 F를 고르세요. 🎧 069

1 A waiter answered the phone. T F
2 The restaurant closes once a month. T F

Dictation

다음을 듣고 빈칸을 채우세요. 🎧 069

Thank you for calling Palace Garden Restaurant. The ① _____ _____ is currently ② _____, but your call will be answered shortly. If you are calling to ③ _____ _____, please be ready with the ④ _____, _____, and the number in your party. Please note that reservations are ⑤ _____ _____ for lunch, Valentine's Day, or Christmas. The restaurant is closed the ⑥ _____ Sunday of every month, and ⑦ _____ _____ are taken nightly at 10:30 p.m. Please continue to hold and someone will be with you shortly.

* ▢ 부분은 식당을 예약하는 특정 목적(Specific Purpose)을 나타내는 표현입니다.

Situation II

Warm-up

대화를 듣고 들은 것에 ✓표 하세요. 🎧 070

- ☐ make a reservation
- ☐ how many
- ☐ terribly sorry
- ☐ next Thursday
- ☐ what time
- ☐ don't accept reservations
- ☐ 17th
- ☐ 6 of us
- ☐ first served

Practice

A 대화를 듣고 여자가 예약하려고 하는 때를 골라 ○표 하세요. 🎧 070

(a) Day: (Tuesday / Thursday)
(b) Date: (7th / 17th)
(c) Time: (1 p.m. / 2 p.m.)

B 대화를 듣고 밑줄 친 부분에 해당하는 말을 따라 말하세요. 🎧 070

A: Thank you for waiting. Palace Garden Restaurant. How may I help you?

B: ① _____

A: Okay. That would be the 17th, correct? How many in your party and what time, ma'am?

B: ② _____

A: Oh, I am terribly sorry, but we don't take reservations for lunch. First come, first served.

B: ③ _____

Week 05
At the Restaurant

Unit 02 Introducing a Restaurant

Listening 향상 팁

Listen for transition words 전환어 듣기

전환어(Transition Words)란?
- 전환어를 사용하면 세련되고 간결하게 문장을 전달할 수 있다.
- 전환어는 다음에 오는 내용을 예측할 수 있도록 도와준다.
- 전환어의 종류

순서	first, second, finally	내용 전환	however, by the way
추가	also, in addition, moreover	결과	so, therefore, as a result
조건	in that case, as long as	강조	again, in particular
예시	for example, for instance	반대	on the other hand

A 다음을 듣고 알맞은 전환어를 고르세요. 🎧 071

1 This salad is fresh. (so / but) I'm sure you will enjoy it.
2 That bread is not fresh. (on the other hand / however) this is fresh.

B 다음 전환어를 아래 표에 알맞게 분류하여 쓰세요.

as a result   in particular   first   by the way   also   in that case

내용 전환	추가	결과	강조	조건	순서
by the way					

C 맞으면 T를, 틀리면 F를 고르세요.

1 전환어는 다음에 오는 내용을 예측할 수 있게 도와준다.

2 전환어는 앞에 나온 내용과 다른 내용이 나올 때만 사용한다.

Situation I

Warm-up

다음을 듣고 들은 것에 ✓표 하세요. 🎧 072

- ☐ hungry
- ☐ Ultra Bacon
- ☐ based on your order
- ☐ in that case
- ☐ double patties
- ☐ for a limited time
- ☐ come on down
- ☐ three strips of bacon
- ☐ at extra charge

Practice

A 다음을 듣고 질문에 알맞은 답을 고르세요. 🎧 072

1 What is being advertised?
   (a) A new restaurant   (b) A new hamburger   (c) A new dessert

2 What is included in the burger?
   (a) Two strips of bacon   (b) Two patties   (c) Four slices of cheese

3 What can you get for free if you buy the burger?
   (a) Fries and a drink   (b) Chicken nugget   (c) Sundae

B 다음을 듣고 질문에 알맞은 사진을 고르세요. 🎧 072

Q What is the advertisement mainly about?

(a)    (b)    (c)

C 다음을 듣고 맞으면 T를, 틀리면 F를 고르세요. 🎧 072

1 The burger is a brand-new menu item. T F

2 The burger all made before it is ordered. T F

Dictation

다음을 듣고 빈칸을 채우세요. 🎧 072

Are you hungry? Do you love bacon? ① _____ _____ _____, come on down to Jimmy's Fast Food Joint and try our new Ultimate Bacon Double Cheeseburger! It's ② _____ _____ topped with three strips of bacon and also covered in ③ _____. Each burger is made ④ _____ and based on your order, ⑤ _____ I know you won't be disappointed! For a limited time only, each order will come with fries and a drink ⑥ _____ _____ _____ charge! Be sure to come in to try it. ⑦ _____, it's for a limited time only!

* _____ 부분은 전환어(Transition Words)입니다.

Situation II

Warm-up

대화를 듣고 들은 것에 ✓표 하세요. 🎧 073

- ☐ take
- ☐ a cheeseburger combo
- ☐ offer
- ☐ free of charge
- ☐ cheaper
- ☐ regular
- ☐ $5.78
- ☐ ring one call up
- ☐ for to go

Practice

A 대화를 듣고 질문에 알맞은 사진을 고르세요.

Q What does the man order with the cheeseburger?

(a)  (b)  (c)

B 대화를 듣고 밑줄 친 부분에 해당하는 말을 따라 말하세요.

A: Welcome to Jimmy's Fast Food Joint. May I take your order, please?

B: ①＿＿＿＿＿＿＿＿＿＿＿＿＿＿＿＿＿＿＿＿＿

A: Okay, but there is a special for the new Ultimate Bacon Double Cheeseburger right now, and I can offer you a drink and fries for free.

B: ②＿＿＿＿＿＿＿＿＿＿＿＿＿＿＿＿＿＿＿＿＿

A: Yes, sir. It's $5.78. Shall I ring one up with a cola for you?

B: ③＿＿＿＿＿＿＿＿＿＿＿＿＿＿＿＿＿＿＿＿＿

Week 05 • Unit 02 97

Week 05
At the Restaurant

Unit 03 Advertising a New product

Listening 향상 팁

Listen for details 세부 사항 듣기

- 음식과 관련된 표현
  - How would you like that cooked/done? 그것을 어떻게 요리해[익혀] 드릴까요?
  - What size do you want? 어느 크기로 원하세요?
  - What side(s) do you want? 곁들임 요리[사이드 메뉴]는 무엇을 원하세요?
  - What type of bread would you like? 빵은 어떤 것을 원하세요?
  - What kind of dressing would you like? 소스는 어떤 것을 원하세요?

- 요리 관련 자주 쓰이는 어휘

meat	well-done 잘 익힌 medium 절반만 익힌 rare 살짝 익힌
bread	white/rye/whole wheat 흰/호밀/통밀 빵 bagel 베이글 bun 번
egg	over easy 양쪽 노른자를 살짝 익힌 over hard 완숙한 sunny-side up 한쪽 노른자만 익힌 boiled 삶은 scrambled 스크램블한
side-dish	steamed vegetables 찐 채소 baked potatoes 구운 감자 corn 옥수수 french fries 프렌치프라이
dressing	thousand island 사우전드아일랜드 oil and vinegar 오일앤비니거 Italian 이탈리안 French 프렌치 ranch 랜치

A 다음을 듣고 아래 질문의 대답이 될 수 없는 것을 고르세요. 🎧 074

1 How would you like the egg done? (a) (b) (c)
2 What kind of dressing would you like? (a) (b) (c)

B 다음을 듣고 빈칸에 알맞은 단어를 쓰세요. 🎧 075

1 I like my beef steak _____ with _____ vegetables.
2 A slice of _____ bread with an _____ _____ egg was all she had today.

C 맞으면 T를, 틀리면 F를 고르세요.

1 'sunny-side up egg'는 한쪽 노른자만 익힌 계란이다. T F
2 'How would you like your steak?'은 스테이크 고기 종류를 묻는 질문이다. T F

Situation I

Warm-up

다음을 듣고 들은 것에 ✓표 하세요. 🎧 076

- ☐ Sub Shop
- ☐ three new locations
- ☐ including
- ☐ stop in
- ☐ premade
- ☐ five different meats
- ☐ ten different fruits
- ☐ five kinds of sauces
- ☐ cookies

Practice

A 다음을 듣고 질문에 알맞은 답을 고르세요. 🎧 076

1 How many new locations were opened?
   (a) One   (b) Three   (c) Six

2 How many kinds of sauces do they have?
   (a) Five   (b) Six   (c) Ten

3 Why should park goers stop by?
   (a) There are free sandwiches at the shop.
   (b) They are having a sale this week.
   (c) The sandwiches are great for picnics.

B 다음을 듣고 질문에 알맞은 사진을 고르세요. 🎧 076

Q What is NOT served in the restaurant?

(a)  (b)  (c)

C 다음을 듣고 맞으면 T를, 틀리면 F를 고르세요. 🎧 076

1 There is a location of the store near a park. T F
2 There are six kinds of bread to choose from. T F

Dictation

다음을 듣고 빈칸을 채우세요. 🎧 076

Have you visited Shirley's Sub Shop yet? We just opened three new locations around town including one ① _____ _____ of Downtown Park! Our delicious subs make the perfect ② _____ _____, so stop by on your way into the park! All of our subs are made right in front of you, and you can choose from ③ _____ different kinds of bread, ④ _____ different meats, ten different ⑤ _____, and ⑥ _____ _____ _____ sauces! We also have all kinds of ⑦ _____, _____, and cookies. Looking forward to serving you soon.

* ▢ 부분은 광고에서 세부 사항(Details) 부분입니다.

Situation II

Warm-up

대화를 듣고 들은 것에 ✓표 하세요. 🎧 077

- ☐ something wrong
- ☐ reorder them
- ☐ turkey avocado
- ☐ breads and toppings
- ☐ at no charge
- ☐ bun
- ☐ mixed up
- ☐ ham and cheese
- ☐ lettuce

Practice

A 대화를 듣고 내용과 알맞은 문장을 모두 고르세요. 🎧 077

(a) The man visits the shop once again.
(b) The woman charges the man for this order.
(c) The man is buying two subs.
(d) The man needs to pick up his order when it's made.

B 대화를 듣고 밑줄 친 부분에 해당하는 말을 따라 말하세요. 🎧 077

A: Welcome back, sir. How can I help you?

B: ① _____

A: Oh, I'm sorry, sir. I'd be happy to remake them for you at no charge.

B: ② _____

A: I'll make them right away, sir. If you'd like to have a seat, I'll bring them to you when they are ready.

B: ③ _____

Week 05
At the Restaurant

Unit 04 Problems on Food

Listening 향상 팁

Listen for -(e)d ending sounds -(e)d로 끝나는 단어 듣기

-(e)d로 끝나는 단어들의 3가지 발음

- 대부분의 규칙동사는 '동사원형 + -(e)d'로 동사의 과거형과 과거분사형을 만든다.
- -ed는 어느 소리 뒤에 붙느냐에 따라 /t/, /d/, /id/ 세가지로 발음된다.

/k, p, s, sh, ch/ + -(e)d → /t/	/l, m, n, v/ 또는 모음 + -(e)d → /d/	/t, d/ + -(e)d → /id/
talked, stopped, kissed, washed, watched	called, steamed, cleaned, arrived, cried	waited, needed

A 다음을 듣고 -(e)d의 소리를 찾아 ○표 하세요. 🎧 078

1 chopped garlic   (/t/) /d/ /id/
2 sliced ham   /t/ /d/ /id/
3 fried chicken   /t/ /d/ /id/
4 roasted chicken   /t/ /d/ /id/
5 boiled egg   /t/ /d/ /id/
6 marinated beef   /t/ /d/ /id/

B -(e)d의 소리를 듣고, 그 소리를 갖는 단어를 찾아 ○표 하세요. 🎧 079

1 mashed   (grilled)   baked
2 broiled   steamed   diced
3 mixed   blended   sauteed

C 맞으면 T를, 틀리면 F를 고르세요.

1 -t, -d로 끝난 규칙동사에 -(e)d가 붙으면 -(e)d는 /id/ 소리가 난다.   T F
2 모음으로 끝난 규칙동사에 -(e)d가 붙으면 -(e)d는 /d/ 소리가 난다.   T F

Situation I

Warm-up

다음을 듣고 들은 것에 ✓표 하세요. 🎧 080

- ☐ your waiter
- ☐ look through
- ☐ today's specials
- ☐ New York strip steak
- ☐ roasted vegetables
- ☐ baked filet
- ☐ the salmon
- ☐ mashed turnips
- ☐ rosemary sauce

Practice

A 다음을 듣고 질문에 알맞은 답을 고르세요. 🎧 080

1 Who is Patrick?
   (a) A diner (b) A chef (c) A waiter

2 Which of the following is a special today?
   (a) Grilled steak (b) Mashed trout (c) Roasted vegetables

3 How is the fish cooked?
   (a) Roasted (b) Baked (c) Mashed

B 다음을 듣고 질문에 알맞은 사진을 고르세요. 🎧 080

Q Which is NOT a today's special?

(a)
(b)
(c)

C 다음을 듣고 맞으면 T를, 틀리면 F를 고르세요. 🎧 080

1 The steak is served with mashed turnips. T F

2 The fish on special is very fresh. T F

Dictation

다음을 듣고 빈칸을 채우세요. 🎧 080

Good evening, folks. My name is Patrick, and I'll be your server tonight. Before you ① _____ _____ the menus too much, I'd like to let you know about some specials that the chef is offering tonight. First, there is a New York strip steak ② _____ to order and ③ _____ with ④ _____ vegetables. Next, there is also a ⑤ _____ filet of trout. ⑥ _____ fresh this morning from the wharf, the trout is baked and served with ⑦ _____ turnips and rosemary sauce.

* _____ 부분은 동사에 -(e)d가 붙은 과거형이거나 과거분사형입니다.

Situation II

Warm-up

대화를 듣고 들은 것에 ✓표 하세요. 🎧 081

- ☐ drink order
- ☐ turnips
- ☐ roasted vegetables
- ☐ mashed potatoes
- ☐ broccoli soup
- ☐ vinaigrette
- ☐ garlic bread
- ☐ sesame oil
- ☐ garlic cream dressing

Practice

A 대화를 듣고 대화 내용과 맞도록 문장을 완성하세요. 🎧 081

1 The trout dish is (today's special / dessert).
2 The woman would like the (trout / beef steak).
3 The woman wants her dish served with (green salad / onion soup).
4 The woman chooses (vinaigrette / garlic cream dressing).

B 대화를 듣고 밑줄 친 부분에 해당하는 말을 따라 말하세요. 🎧 081

A: Here is your drink order. Are you ready to order?

B: ① _____

A: Certainly, you could have a green salad, roasted vegetables, mashed potatoes, or onion soup as an alternative.

B: ② _____

A: Would you like vinaigrette, garlic cream dressing, or oriental sesame dressing?

B: ③ _____

Week 05 • Unit 04

Week 05 At the Restaurant

Vocabulary

#	Term	뜻
1	appetizer	전채 요리
2	bar menu	(바에서 먹을 수 있는) 바 메뉴
3	bar seat	바 좌석
4	bartender	바텐더
5	booth	(식당의) 칸막이 자리
6	bus boy	(식당의) 테이블 정리 직원
7	casual dining	가벼운 식사, 일반 음식점
8	chef	(주로 호텔 / 식당의) 주방장
9	clear the table	테이블을 치우다
10	cook	(주방장보다 아래 급인) 요리사
11	deli	(미리 조제된 음식을 파는) 델리
12	dessert	디저트
13	diner	(식당의) 손님, (음식 값이 싼) 작은 식당
14	dish	요리, 접시
15	entrée	앙뜨레 (만찬의 주요리)
16	fine dining	고급 식당
17	food allergy	음식 알레르기
18	gourmet	미식가
19	hostess/host	(식당에서 자리 안내하는) 여자 안내원 / 남자 안내원
20	lunch menu	점심 메뉴

Memo

#	영어	한국어
21	maître d'	웨이터 주임, 호텔 지배인
22	party of two	2인 일행
23	place setting	자리 배치
24	private dining room	(식당에서 따로 구분된) 개별 방
25	send back (to the kitchen)	(부엌으로) 다시 보내다
26	server	서버, 웨이터, 웨이트리스
27	set menu	세트 메뉴
28	side dish	반찬
29	sommelier	(주로 포도주) 소믈리에(감별사)
30	soup du jour [soup of the day]	오늘의 수프
31	special	(식당의) 특선 요리
32	substitution	대체 요리; 대체하다
33	table for four	4인용 테이블
34	table side service	(식당 테이블 옆에서) 서빙하다
35	takeout [takeaway (영)]	포장 음식 전문점, 포장 음식
36	temperature preference	(음식) 온도 선호도
37	to go	(음식을) 포장하다
38	vegetarian	채식주의자
39	window seat	(식당 / 탈것의) 창가 좌석
40	wine and food pairing	포도주와 동반 음식

Memo

EBS 생수다
생생한 영어 수다

Week
06 At the Mall

Unit 01 Mall Opening

Unit 02 Sales Announcement

Unit 03 Announcement About Parking

Unit 04 Mall Closing

Week 06
At the Mall

Unit 01 Mall Opening

> **Listening 향상 팁**
>
> **Listen for meaningful chunks** 의미 덩어리로 듣기
>
> - 의미 덩어리(Meaningful Chunks)는 각각의 정보를 모아서 더 큰 단위로 묶는 과정을 나타낸다.
>
>   예시 Shops in the east wing / will not open / for another hour.
>   주어   동사   부사구(시간)
>
>   동쪽 별관의 상점들은 한 시간 뒤에 영업을 시작합니다.
>
> - 의미 덩어리는 정보를 더 빠르고 쉽게 이해하고 기억할 수 있게 도와준다.
>
>   예시 Her number is 010-1234-5678. 그녀의 전화번호는 010-1234-5678이다.
>   → 전화번호 숫자를 10개 따로따로 외우는 것보다 3자리-4자리-4자리씩 묶어 3개의 덩어리(chunks) 로 외우는 것이 더 쉽다.

A 다음을 듣고 의미 덩어리별로 표시하세요. 🎧 083

1. Please remember / to visit the new bakery, / Bread Factory, / on the first floor.
2. I heard an announcement about a sale, but I didn't catch the location.
3. If you will take the escalators behind you, then the café will be on your right.
4. I'm having a party at that restaurant next Saturday.

B 다음을 듣고 의미 덩어리가 바르게 표시되지 않은 곳을 골라 ○표 하세요. 🎧 084

1. As always, / there are maps / at the escalators on / each floor.
2. We have / to submit the proposal / by tomorrow / at all cost.

C 맞으면 T를, 틀리면 F를 고르세요.

1. 의미 덩어리는 각각의 정보를 더 큰 단위로 묶는 것을 의미한다. [T] [F]
2. 의미 덩어리는 덩어리로 묶어서 의미를 전달하기 때문에 듣는 사람의 이해를 도와준다. [T] [F]

Situation I

Warm-up

다음을 듣고 들은 것에 ✓표 하세요. 🎧 085

- ☐ the doors to the center
- ☐ shops in the west wing
- ☐ for another hour
- ☐ basement food court
- ☐ 10:30
- ☐ remember
- ☐ the new pet store
- ☐ on the fifth floor
- ☐ on all even floors

Practice

A 다음을 듣고 질문에 알맞은 답을 고르세요. 🎧 085

1 When was this announcement made?
  (a) Before the mall opened
  (b) As the mall opened
  (c) When the mall closed

2 Where are stores still closed?
  (a) In the main building (b) In the east wing (c) On the fourth floor

3 Where is the new store located?
  (a) In the basement (b) On the fourth floor (c) Near the central escalators

B 다음을 듣고 질문에 알맞은 그림을 고르세요. 🎧 085

Q When will the food court be open?

(a)    (b)    (c)

C 다음을 듣고 맞으면 T를, 틀리면 F를 고르세요. 🎧 085

1 Everything is open in the mall now.　　　　　　　　　　T　F

2 They are promoting a new clothing shop.　　　　　　　T　F

Dictation

다음을 듣고 빈칸을 채우세요. 🎧 085

Good morning, shoppers and welcome to Ridge Shopping Center. We are so happy to have you with us today. The doors ① _____ _____ _____ are now open, but shops in the east wing will not open ② _____ _____ _____. The basement food court will be open at 11:30. Please ③ _____ _____ _____ the new pet store, Paws In, ④ _____ _____ _____ _____. As always, ⑤ _____ _____ _____ at the escalators ⑥ _____ _____ _____, and there are information desks at the central escalators ⑦ _____ _____ _____ _____.

* _____ 부분은 의미 덩어리(Meaningful Chunks)이거나 그 일부입니다.

Situation II

Warm-up

대화를 듣고 들은 것에 ✓표 하세요. 🎧 086

☐ an announcement   ☐ a new pet shop   ☐ get the location
☐ on the fourth floor   ☐ direct route   ☐ elevators
☐ behind you   ☐ up two floors   ☐ on your left

Practice

A 대화를 듣고 대화 내용과 맞도록 문장을 완성하세요. 🎧 086

1 The man may be interested in (pets / the woman).

2 The man is now on the (2nd / 6th) floor.

3 The woman must be (a guest / an employee).

B 대화를 듣고 밑줄 친 부분에 해당하는 말을 따라 말하세요. 🎧 086

A: Excuse me. Can you help me?

B: ① _____

A: I heard an announcement about a new pet shop, but I didn't catch the location.

B: ② _____

A: What's the most direct route?

B: ③ _____

Week 06 • Unit 01

Week 06
At the Mall

Unit 02 Sales Announcement

> **Listening 향상 팁**
>
> **Listen for specific words** 특정 단어 듣기
>
> - 모든 단어를 다 듣지 않고, 주요 단어만 들어도 메시지를 이해할 수 있는 경우가 많다.
>
>   **[예시]** There is a **special sale** going on in the **Event Hall** on the **third floor** today.
>   오늘 3층의 이벤트 홀에서 특별 세일이 있습니다.
>   → 전체 문장을 다 듣지 못해도 special sale, Event Hall, third floor만 들어도 내용 파악이 가능하다.
>
> - 주로 내용어(Content Words)인 명사, 동사, 형용사를 중심으로 듣는 연습을 한다.
>
>   **[예시]** There is an **additional discount** on **V-neck sweaters** today.
>   오늘 브이넥 스웨터에 추가 할인이 있습니다.
>   → additional discount, V-neck sweaters만 들어도 내용 파악이 가능하다.
>
> - 구체적인 관련 어휘를 알고 있으면 듣기에 도움이 된다.
>
>   **[예시]** turtle-neck sweater 터틀넥 스웨터   hoodie 모자 달린 옷 ┐
>   crew-neck shirt 라운드 티셔츠   polo shirt 폴로 셔츠 ┘ 의복 관련 어휘

A 다음을 듣고 들은 문장을 고르세요. 🎧 087

1. (a) You can get an extra 30% off of blue jeans.
   (b) You'll find special clearance prices on hoodies.

2. (a) There's a special sale going on for vests in the Penny Plaza.
   (b) There's a Buy-One-Get-One-Free sale on polo shirts.

3. (a) Find the latest styles at affordable prices in the Men's Section.
   (b) Find the best deals with up to 70% off in the Kid's Section.

4. (a) Save big on women's fashion including V-neck sweaters and suits.
   (b) Pick from a range of trendy items including jackets and footwear.

B 맞으면 T를, 틀리면 F를 고르세요.

1. 모든 어휘를 들어야 문장을 이해할 수 있다.
2. 문장에서 동사, 명사, 형용사를 중심으로 들으면 내용 파악에 훨씬 효과적이다.

 생생한 영어 수다

Situation I

Warm-up

다음을 듣고 들은 것에 ✓표 하세요. 　088

- ☐ pleased
- ☐ the Event Hall
- ☐ kitchen tools
- ☐ decided to shop
- ☐ on the third floor
- ☐ additional discount
- ☐ a special sale
- ☐ special sale prices
- ☐ on specific fragrances

Practice

A 다음을 듣고 질문에 알맞은 답을 고르세요.

1 Why is this announcement being made?
   (a) To announce the closing time
   (b) To announce a sale
   (c) To announce a new store

2 Which of the following items would be found at the sale?
   (a) Plates　　　　(b) Sweaters　　　　(c) Jewelry

3 What department is NOT offering discounts?
   (a) Perfumes　　　(b) Make-up　　　　(c) Clothing

B 다음을 듣고 질문에 알맞은 사진을 고르세요.

Q Which of the following would NOT be offered on special clearance price?

(a) 　　(b) 　　(c)

C 다음을 듣고 맞으면 T를, 틀리면 F를 고르세요. 🎧 088

1 There is a sale on the third floor. [T] [F]

2 The sale items are all from different stores. [T] [F]

Dictation

다음을 듣고 빈칸을 채우세요. 🎧 088

Welcome to Deluxe Shopping Mall. We are so ①_____ you decided to ②_____ _____ _____ today. There is ③____ _____ _____ going on in the ④_____ _____ on the third floor today. At the sale, you'll find special ⑤_____ _____ on kitchenware and dishes from Trappings Department Store. There is also ⑥____ _____ _____ offered at Trappings on certain ⑦_____ and cosmetics. Enjoy your shopping today.

* 　　 부분은 세일과 관련된 특정 단어(Specific Words)입니다.

Situation II

Warm-up

대화를 듣고 들은 것에 ✓표 하세요. 🎧 089

- ☐ announcement
- ☐ perfumes
- ☐ for sale
- ☐ that way
- ☐ the selection
- ☐ by chance
- ☐ afraid not
- ☐ another designer
- ☐ some samples

Practice

A 대화를 듣고 질문에 알맞은 사진을 고르세요.

Q Which of the following items is on sale now?

(a)  (b)  (c)

B 대화를 듣고 밑줄 친 부분에 해당하는 말을 따라 말하세요. 🎧 089

A: Good morning, ma'am. How may I help you?

B: ① _____

A: Please follow me this way, and I'll show you the selection we have.

B: ② _____

A: Oh, I'm afraid not, but we have several others from the same designer on sale.

B: ③ _____

> Week 06
> At the Mall

Unit 03 Announcement About Parking

Listening 향상 팁

Listen for details 세부 사항 듣기

- 차량 종류처럼 구체적인 어휘를 숙지하면 듣기에 도움이 된다.

  예시 sedan 세단 SUV(Sport Utility Vehicle) SUV 차 compact car 소형차 convertible (지붕이 열리는) 컨버터블 station wagon (뒷문으로 짐을 실을 수 있는) 스테이션 왜건 minivan 미니밴 hatchback (뒷문이 있는) 해치백 hybrid (휘발유와 전기 병용의) 하이브리드 sports car 스포츠카

- 차량이나 주차 관련 예문

  - A red SUV is blocking the handicapped parking on Parking Level 3.
    빨간색 SUV가 주차장 3층의 장애인 구역을 막고 있습니다.
  - The emergency vehicle entrance is obstructed by a convertible.
    컨버터블이 응급차 입구를 막고 있습니다.
  - There is a blue sports car on Level 4 with its lights on.
    4층에 불이 켜진 파란색 스포츠카가 있습니다.
  - There is a compact car that will be towed soon from a handicapped space.
    장애인 주차구역에 주차한 소형차가 곧 견인될 예정입니다.

A 다음을 듣고 알맞은 해석을 고르세요. 🎧 090

(a) 응급차 입구를 불법 주차된 컨버터블이 가로 막고 있습니다.
(b) 갈색 스테이션 왜건 차량 운전자께서는 차로 와주세요. 불이 켜져 있습니다.
(c) 차량번호 7LP4868 흰 세단 운전자께서는 주차장으로 즉시 와 주시기 바랍니다.
(d) 불법 주차된 차량들은 즉시 견인될 예정입니다.

1 _____ 2 _____ 3 _____ 4 _____

B 맞으면 T를, 틀리면 F를 고르세요.

1 하이브리드는 수소를 연료로 이용하는 차량이다. T F

2 주차와 관련된 표현은 be blocking, a handicapped parking 등이 있다. T F

118 생생한 영어 수다

Situation I

Warm-up

다음을 듣고 들은 것에 ✓표 하세요. 🎧 091

- ☐ the patron
- ☐ parking lot
- ☐ parking deck
- ☐ a white convertible
- ☐ a handicapped space
- ☐ in 50 minutes
- ☐ DGC 785
- ☐ a tow truck
- ☐ again

Practice

A 다음을 듣고 질문에 알맞은 답을 고르세요. 🎧 091

1 Who is asked to come to the parking lot?
   (a) All the customers in the mall
   (b) An illegally parked customer
   (c) A blue convertible's owner

2 Where is the white convertible parked?
   (a) Outside the garage   (b) In a standing zone   (c) In a reserved parking space

3 What is going to happen in 15 minutes?
   (a) The car will be towed.
   (b) The patron will finish shopping.
   (c) The parking garage will close.

B 다음을 듣고 질문에 알맞은 사진을 고르세요. 🎧 091

Q Which of the following should be moved right away?

(a)

(b)

(c)

C 다음을 듣고 맞으면 T를, 틀리면 F를 고르세요. 🎧 091

1 The driver of the white convertible is going to the information desk. T F

2 The car may be going to be removed away soon. T F

Dictation

다음을 듣고 빈칸을 채우세요. 🎧 091

Attention, shoppers. Would the patron driving ① _____ _____ _____ with the license plate DGC ② _____ please come to the parking garage immediately? Your car is parked in a ③ _____ _____, and must be moved at once. A ④ _____ _____ is standing by, and the car will be removed from the parking deck in ⑤ _____ _____. Please come to the ⑥ _____ quickly to move your car. Again, white convertible with the license plate DGC 765 please come to the ⑦ _____ _____.

* ▢ 부분은 안내 방송에서 세부 사항(Details) 부분입니다.

Situation II

Warm-up

대화를 듣고 들은 것에 ✓표 하세요. 🎧 092

☐ the advertisement   ☐ my car   ☐ you'd better
☐ parking deck   ☐ right now   ☐ a handicapped spot
☐ hold   ☐ behind the register ☐ as soon as possible

Practice

A 대화를 듣고 내용과 알맞은 문장을 모두 고르세요. 🎧 092

(a) The car is the customer's.
(b) The woman parked in the right place.
(c) The woman decides not to buy the clothes.
(d) The man will deposit the items for the woman.

B 대화를 듣고 밑줄 친 부분에 해당하는 말을 따라 말하세요. 🎧 092

A: Oh my! I just heard that announcement. That's my car!

B: ① _____

A: I didn't realize it was a handicapped spot! Can you hold these items for me?

B: ② _____

A: Thank you so much. I'll be back as soon as possible to buy them.

B: ③ _____

Unit 04 Mall Closing

Week 06 At the Mall

Listening 향상 팁

Listen for meaningful chunks 의미 덩어리로 듣기

- 의미 덩어리(Meaningful Chunks)와 의미 덩어리 사이는 일반적으로 숨을 쉬는 휴지(Pause)를 두므로, 듣는 사람이 이해하기 쉽다.
- 장소나 시간 등 역할에 따라 의미 덩어리가 형성된다.
  예시 The shopping center will be closed / in 30 minutes. 쇼핑 센터가 30분 후에 폐점합니다.
- 접속사 앞, 전치사 앞에서 끊어 말하면서 의미 덩어리가 형성된다.
  예시 Please conclude your shopping / and make your way / to the exits.
  쇼핑을 마무리하시고 출구로 나가 주시기 바랍니다.
- 형용사구, 관계사절처럼 뒤에서 꾸미는 말이 올 때 의미 덩어리가 형성된다.
  예시 All of our registers / are already closed. 모든 계산대가 이미 종료되었습니다.

A 다음을 듣고 /로 의미 덩어리를 표시하세요. 🎧 093

1 The store around the corner / will open / at 10 a.m.

2 I am sorry. but all the stores close at 9 p.m.

3 Mr. Brown checked everything that he needed for the trip.

4 Please make sure that you have all your possessions with you as you exit.

B 맞으면 T를, 틀리면 F를 고르세요.

1 의미 덩어리와 의미 덩어리 사이에는 숨을 쉬어 의미 전달을 돕는다.

2 접속사, 전치사 다음에는 숨을 쉬어 의미 덩어리를 구별한다.

Situation I

Warm-up

다음을 듣고 들은 것에 ✓표 하세요. 🎧 094

- ☐ shopping center
- ☐ conclude
- ☐ possessions
- ☐ closing
- ☐ to the gates
- ☐ purchases
- ☐ in 50 minutes
- ☐ in 20 minutes
- ☐ at 10 a.m.

Practice

A 다음을 듣고 질문에 알맞은 답을 고르세요. 🎧 094

1 When is this announcement being made?
　(a) Before closing time　(b) After closing time　(c) After opening time

2 What will happen in 20 minutes?
　(a) The stores will all close.　(b) The doors will all lock.　(c) The mall will open.

3 What happens tomorrow at 9:30 a.m.?
　(a) The mall doors all lock.　(b) Customers may shop.　(c) The stores all close.

B 다음을 듣고 질문에 알맞은 그림을 고르세요. 🎧 094

Q What time will the shopping center open tomorrow?

(a) 　(b) 　(c)

C 다음을 듣고 맞으면 T를, 틀리면 F를 고르세요. 094

1 After 15 minutes, customers may not make purchases. T F

2 Customers can come to the mall tomorrow at 9 a.m. T F

Dictation

다음을 듣고 빈칸을 채우세요. 094

Attention, shoppers. The shopping center will be closing in 15 minutes. Please conclude your shopping ① _____ _____ your way ② _____ _____ _____. All stores will be closed ③ _____ _____ _____, and the mall doors ④ _____ _____ _____ in 20 minutes. ⑤ _____ _____ _____ that you have all your possessions and purchases with you ⑥ _____ _____ _____. Thank you for shopping with us today. We will be open tomorrow morning ⑦ _____ _____, and we hope to see you again soon!

* _____ 부분은 의미 덩어리(Meaningful Chunks)이거나 그 일부입니다.

Situation II

Warm-up

대화를 듣고 들은 것에 ✓표 하세요. 🎧 095

- ☐ closed
- ☐ our counters
- ☐ at 9 a.m.
- ☐ at 9 p.m.
- ☐ already locked
- ☐ gladly
- ☐ make a purchase
- ☐ tomorrow morning
- ☐ at that time

Practice

A 대화를 듣고 대화 내용과 맞도록 문장을 완성하세요. 🎧 095

1 It must be (before / past) 9 p.m. now.
2 The woman is (in time / late) for the shopping.
3 The man is a shopping mall (employee / customer).
4 The woman needs to come back (tonight / tomorrow).

B 대화를 듣고 밑줄 친 부분에 해당하는 말을 따라 말하세요. 🎧 095

A: Are you closed?

B: ① _____

A: Oh, no! I really needed to make a purchase tonight.

B: ② _____

A: What time do you open in the morning?

B: ③ _____

Week 06 At the Mall

Vocabulary

1	anchor store	(쇼핑몰이나 상가에서 고객을 끌어들이는) 중심 상점
2	announcement	구내 방송
3	atrium	(쇼핑몰 한가운데에 유리로 천장을 높게 한) 중앙 광장
4	basement	지하 1층, 지하실
5	brand-new	(완전) 새 것인; 신상품
6	clearance sale	창고[재고] 정리 세일
7	closing time	폐점 시간
8	clothing store	옷 가게
9	coupon	(할인) 쿠폰
10	customer service	고객 서비스
11	department store	백화점
12	east / west wing	동쪽 / 서쪽 별관
13	exchange	교환
14	final sale	(교환 / 환불이 안 되는) 마지막 세일
15	fitting room	(옷 가게의) 탈의실
16	food court	푸드 코트
17	free sample	무료 샘플, 무료 시식
18	gift certificate	상품권
19	gift receipt	(선물 받은 사람이 교환 / 환불할 때 쓸 수 있는) 영수증
20	gift wrap	선물용 포장

Memo

#	영어	한국어
21	greeter	(식당 / 상점 등에서) 고객맞이 직원
22	kiosk	(신문이나 음료를 파는) 가판대
23	limited time	한정 시간
24	mall cop	쇼핑몰 청원 경찰
25	music store	음악 가게, 음반 가게
26	operating hours	영업 시간
27	parking garage	(지상이나 지하에 여러 층이 있는) 주차장
28	parking deck	(여러 층이 있는) 지상 주차장
29	parking lot	(한 층짜리) 야외 지상 주차장
30	receipt	영수증
31	refund	환불
32	register	계산대
33	restroom	화장실
34	retail worker	소매점 직원
35	return	(상품) 반납
36	sales person [assistant]	(옷가게 등의) 판매 직원
37	security guard	경비원
38	security tag	(옷 등에 붙어 있는) 도난방지 꼬리표
39	stroller service	유모차 대여 서비스
40	window shopping	아이쇼핑

Memo

EBS 생수다
생생한 영어 수다

Week 07 On the Street

Unit 01 Getting Directions
Unit 02 Shopping for Souvenirs
Unit 03 Bargaining
Unit 04 Enjoying Street Food

Week 07 On the Street

Unit 01 Getting Directions

Listening 향상 팁

Listen for transition words 전환어 듣기

- 전환어(Transition Words)는 다음에 나올 내용을 예측하게 하는 매우 중요한 단서를 제공하고 앞뒤 문장 사이의 연관 관계를 더 명확히 보여 준다.

- 시간/순서를 나타내는 전환어(Time/Order Transition Words)는 일이 발생하는 순서를 나타낸다.

  예시 first 첫째   second 둘째   third 셋째   next 그 다음   then 그리고, 그 후
  above all 무엇보다도, 특히   in the beginning (맨)처음에   finally 마지막으로
  in conclusion 결론으로, 마지막으로   last but not least 마지막으로 그러나 앞에 말한 것과 같이 중요한

A 다음을 듣고 빈칸에 알맞은 단어를 쓴 다음 순서대로 번호를 쓰세요. 🎧 097

1 _____. go and buy a bus pass.   ①___
2 _____. show your pass to the driver as you enter.   ___
3 _____. go to the bus stop and wait.   ___

B 다음을 듣고 빈칸에 알맞은 단어를 쓰세요. 🎧 098

Okay, you'll go down this street and find the market. ①_____ _____ _____, there are a lot of food stalls. ②_____, the shops are all selling souvenirs and trinkets. ③_____, there are mostly clothing stores. ④_____, you'll find the jewelry shops you are looking for.

C 맞으면 T를, 틀리면 F를 고르세요.

1 first. second. finally는 일이 일어나는 시간이나 순서를 나타내는 전환어이다.   T F
2 전환어는 듣기에만 도움이 된다.   T F

Situation I

Warm-up

대화를 듣고 들은 것에 ✓표 하세요. 🎧 099

- ☐ lost
- ☐ first
- ☐ turn to the left
- ☐ the city
- ☐ then
- ☐ after that
- ☐ stranger
- ☐ at the third stop light
- ☐ not way

Practice

A 대화를 듣고 질문에 알맞은 답을 고르세요. 🎧 099

1. What is the man looking for?
   (a) A park (b) A city (c) A water park

2. What does the man need to do first?
   (a) Go straight (b) Turn right (c) Turn left

3. Where will the park be?
   (a) On the right (b) On the left (c) In front of the man

B 대화를 듣고 질문에 알맞은 곳을 고르세요. 🎧 099

Q The man is on the arrow now. Where is the place the man wants to go?

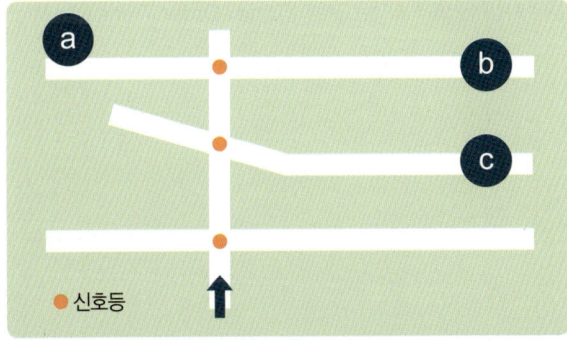

(a) (b) (c)

Week 07 • Unit 01 131

C 다음을 듣고 맞으면 T를, 틀리면 F를 고르세요. 🎧 099

1 The man knows the city very well.　　T　F

2 Neither speaker knows where the park is.　　T　F

Dictation

대화를 듣고 빈칸을 채우세요. 🎧 099

A: Excuse me, but I'm a bit ① _____ . I'm looking for Waterford Park. Do you know where it is?

B: Sure. Do you know the city well?

A: Sorry. I'm not ② _____ _____ _____ .

B: That's all right. Okay, here's what you do. ③ _____ , drive straight down this street about one kilometer. ④ _____ , at the third stop light, turn to the right.

A: What should I do ⑤ _____ _____ ?

B: Just drive straight for ⑥ _____ _____ _____ . The park will be right in front of you. There's ⑦ _____ _____ you can miss it.

* ▭ 부분은 시간/순서를 나타내는 전환어(Time / Order Transition Words)입니다.

Situation II

Warm-up

대화를 듣고 대화와 관계 있는 사진을 고르세요. 🎧 100

(a)  (b)  (c)

Practice

A 대화를 듣고 대화 내용과 맞도록 문장을 완성하세요. 🎧 100

1 The woman is (a resident / a stranger) on that area.
2 The woman is toward (the right / the wrong) direction now.
3 The woman has to (turn around / go straight) first.

B 대화를 듣고 밑줄 친 부분에 해당하는 말을 따라 말하세요. 🎧 100

A: Hello. Do you know where the Museum of Natural History is? I can't find it.

B: ① _____

A: Um … I don't know the city, so could you please give me directions there?

B: ② _____

A: Do you mean I just need to go straight?

B: ③ _____

Week 07 On the Street

Unit 02 Shopping for Souvenirs

Listening 향상 팁

Listen for specific purpose 특정한 목적 듣기

- 기념품 쇼핑처럼 특정 상황에 자주 사용되는 다양한 문장 형태를 알아두면 듣기에 도움이 된다.
- 판매를 권할 때 명령문이 자주 사용된다.

  [예시] Please come by quickly before we sell out. 품절이 되기 전에 빨리 오세요.
  Remember if you buy 3, the 4th one is 50% off. 3개를 구매하시면 4번째 것은 50% 할인해 드립니다.

- 판매 관련 자주 사용하는 표현

  [예시] We carry ... ~을 취급하다/팔다   There is an additional discount for ... ~에 추가 할인이 있다
  sold out 매진

A 다음을 듣고 빈칸에 알맞은 단어를 쓰세요. 🎧 101

1. (a) We've got all _____ ____ souvenirs for sale.
   (b) There are lots of gifts ____ _____ _____.

2. (a) _____ ____ some items for yourself in order to remember your trip.
   (b) _____ some special items here so you don't forget your time here.

3. (a) I'd like to tell you about a special sale we're having _____ _____.
   (b) Did you know we are having a _____ _____ super sale?

4. (a) Spend ____ ____ _____. and you'll get 20% off your entire purchase.
   (b) There is an additional discount for those spending _____ _____.

B 맞으면 T를, 틀리면 F를 고르세요.

1. 기념품 판매직원들은 손님들의 구매를 유도하기 위해 명령문을 자주 사용한다.

2. '~물품을 취급하다'라고 할 때 'There is …' 구문과 'We carry …' 구문을 자주 사용한다.

Situation I

Warm-up

다음을 듣고 들은 것에 모두 ✓표 하세요.

(a) 　(b) 　(c) 　(d)

Practice

A 다음을 듣고 질문에 알맞은 답을 고르세요.

1 Who is most likely the audience?
   (a) Gerald　　(b) Tourists　　(c) Bookstore owners

2 What is something you could buy at the shop?
   (a) Clothing　　(b) Music CD　　(c) Food

3 How can shoppers get a discount?
   (a) Visiting the shop early
   (b) Spending a certain amount
   (c) Bargaining with the staff

B 다음을 듣고 질문에 알맞은 그림을 고르세요.

Q How much is discounted for the purchase of souvenirs at $55?

(a) 　(b) 　(c)

C 다음을 듣고 맞으면 T를, 틀리면 F를 고르세요.

1 The shop specializes in selling gifts for tourists.　　T F
2 The sale is running all week.　　T F

Dictation

다음을 듣고 빈칸을 채우세요.

Welcome, shoppers, to Gerald's Souvenir Shop. We've got ① _____ _____ _____ souvenirs for sale. You can get postcards, T-shirts, stuffed animals, and books. We also have key chains and pictures. Pick up some ② _____ _____ _____ in order to remember your trip. Or buy some items ③ _____ _____ _____ and family members back home. Now, I'd like to tell you about a ④ _____ _____ we're having today only. Spend ⑤ _____ _____ _____, and you'll get ⑥ _____ _____ your entire purchase. That's a deal which simply ⑦ _____ _____ _____. Enjoy shopping here at Gerald's Souvenir Shop.

* _____ 부분은 할인 안내를 하는 특정한 목적(Specific Purpose)이 담긴 부분입니다.

Situation II

Warm-up

대화를 듣고 들은 것에 ✓표 하세요. 103

☐ in particular   ☐ at the gallery   ☐ souvenirs
☐ where to buy   ☐ postcards   ☐ to your family
☐ pictures   ☐ some books   ☐ exhibits

Practice

A 대화를 듣고 질문에 알맞은 사진을 고르세요. 103

Q Which of the following will the woman NOT show to the man?

(a) 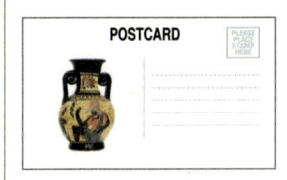   (b)    (c)

B 대화를 듣고 밑줄 친 부분에 해당하는 말을 따라 말하세요. 103

A: Good morning. Are you looking for anything in particular?

B: ① _____

A: Why don't you get a few postcards? We've got some really nice ones that you can mail to your friends from here.

B: ② _____

A: Yes. here. I can show you the postcards. And I'd like to show you some books about the museum's exhibits. You'll love them.

B: ③ _____

Unit 03 Bargaining

Week 07
On the Street

Listening 향상 팁

Listen for phrases 구 듣기

- 구(Phrase)는 단어 두 개 이상이 모여 하나의 의미를 나타내는 것이다.
- 구를 이루는 단어 각각을 알아도 구의 뜻을 모르면 그 의미 파악이 안 될 때가 종종 있으므로, 구는 하나의 단위처럼 한꺼번에 익히도록 한다.
- 관광지에서 기념품 등을 구매할 때 가격 흥정을 해야 하는 경우가 있다. 가격이나 흥정과 관련된 구를 정리해서 익히면 듣기와 말하기 때 유용하다.
  예시 meet + 사람 + halfway ~와 타협[절충]하다   have to pass 넘어가야/지나가야 하다
- 가격과 관련된 말을 할 때 Price와 함께 사용되는 표현들을 유의한다.
  예시 high price (○) 높은 가격   expensive price (×)
       low price   (○) 낮은 가격   cheap price   (×)

A 다음을 듣고 빈칸에 알맞은 단어를 쓰세요. 🎧 104

1 $30 seems ___ ___ ___.
2 Could you meet me _____?
3 Sorry. I think I'll ___ ___ ___.

B 구과 구를 바르게 연결하여 문장을 완성하세요.

1 How much is •   • (a) a package of postcards.
2 Interested in •   • (b) any sets of magnets?
3 I'm looking for •   • (c) this box of chocolates?

C 맞으면 T를, 틀리면 F를 고르세요.

1 구는 두 개 이상의 단어가 모여 하나의 의미를 나타내는 것이다.
2 '타협하다'는 'meet + 사람 + halfway'로 나타낼 수 있다.

Situation I

Warm-up

대화를 듣고 들은 것에 ✓표 하세요. 🎧 105

- ☐ blue wool coat
- ☐ 16 dollars
- ☐ make a profit
- ☐ my price range
- ☐ a reasonable price
- ☐ discount of
- ☐ how much
- ☐ that suggestion
- ☐ a deal

Practice

A 대화를 듣고 질문에 알맞은 답을 고르세요. 🎧 105

1. Where are the speakers?
   (a) At a restaurant   (b) At a bank   (c) At a clothing shop

2. Why does the woman NOT want to buy the item at first?
   (a) It is blue.   (b) It is expensive.   (c) It is made of wool.

3. How much of a discount does the woman receive?
   (a) $20   (b) $60   (c) $75

B 대화를 듣고 질문에 알맞은 사진을 고르세요.

Q What will the woman buy eventually?

(a)    (b)    (c)

C 다음을 듣고 맞으면 T를, 틀리면 F를 고르세요. 🎧 105

1 The woman is buying the sweater at the original price. T F

2 The woman doesn't buy the sweater in the end. T F

Dictation

대화를 듣고 빈칸을 채우세요. 🎧 105

A: Good afternoon, ma'am. Do you see anything that you like?

B: I think this blue wool sweater ① _____ _____, but it's a bit out of ② _____ _____ _____. I can't pay that much for it.

A: ③ _____ _____ would you like to pay?

B: ④ _____ _____ 60 dollars? I think that's a ⑤ _____ price.

A: I can't accept that offer. I won't ⑥ _____ _____ _____ at that price. What about paying 75 dollars for it? That's ⑦ _____ _____ _____ 20 dollars.

B: You've got a deal. Do you take cash?

* _____ 부분은 구(Phrases)를 이루는 부분입니다.

Situation II

Warm-up

대화를 듣고 들은 것에 ✓표 하세요. 🎧 106

- ☐ gold rings
- ☐ cost
- ☐ a special price
- ☐ too much money
- ☐ looking for
- ☐ half that amount
- ☐ a few another item
- ☐ the right thing
- ☐ what you get

Practice

A 대화를 듣고 내용과 알맞은 문장을 모두 고르세요. 🎧 106

(a) The woman asked about gold earrings first.
(b) The man is offering $10 off for the earrings.
(c) The woman wants to buy something at about 45 dollars.
(d) The woman will buy the gold earrings in the end.

B 대화를 듣고 밑줄 친 부분에 해당하는 말을 따라 말하세요. 🎧 106

A: Can I interest you in this pair of gold earrings?

B: ① _____

A: They cost one hundred dollars, but I can give you a special price. I can sell them to you for 90 dollars today.

B: ② _____

A: Shall I show you a few other items then? I've got just the right thing in mind for you.

B: ③ _____

Week 07 • Unit 03 141

Week 07 On the Street

Unit 04 Enjoying Street Food

Listening 향상 팁

Listen for tone and stress 어조와 강세 듣기

- 같은 어휘를 사용한 문장이더라도 어떤 어조(Tone)와 어느 부분에 강세(Stress)를 두느냐에 따라 의미가 달라진다.

  예시 He's eating fast food. = He, *not she*, is eating fast food. 바로 그가 패스트푸드를 먹고 있다.
  He's eating fast food. = He is still eating fast food, *not finished*. 그가 패스트푸드를 아직 먹고 있다.
  He's eating fast food. = He is eating fast food, *not something home-cooked*.
  그가 바로 패스트푸드를 먹고 있다.

A 다음을 듣고 강세가 주어진 부분을 표시하고, 같은 의미의 문장을 연결하세요. 🎧 107

1. I asked what he would order. • • (a) I DID ask what he would order.
2. I asked what he would order. • • (b) I asked what he, not she, would order.
3. I asked what he would order. • • (c) It was me that asked what he would order.
4. I asked what he would order. • • (d) I asked what, not when, he would order.

B 다음을 듣고 강세가 주어진 부분에 알맞은 뜻을 찾아 연결하세요. 🎧 108

1. He said the fish is fresh. • • (a) 그가 그 생선이야말로 싱싱하다고 말했다.
2. He said that fish is fresh. • • (b) 그가 생선이 정말 싱싱하다고 말했다.
3. He said the fish is fresh. • • (c) 바로 그가 생선이 싱싱하다고 말했다.

C 맞으면 T를, 틀리면 F를 고르세요.

1. 같은 문장이라도 어조와 강세를 달리하면 뜻이 달라진다.
2. 강세는 강조하고자 하는 말을 강하게 말하는 것이다.

Situation I

Warm-up

다음을 듣고 들은 것에 ✓표 하세요. 🎧 109

- ☐ interest you
- ☐ absolutely
- ☐ combine
- ☐ some of the food
- ☐ love them
- ☐ yummy
- ☐ the best hot dogs
- ☐ chili dogs
- ☐ feet-long hot dogs

Practice

A 다음을 듣고 질문에 알맞은 답을 고르세요.

1. Who is the speaker?
   (a) A pedestrian   (b) A street vendor   (c) A police officer

2. How many toppings does the man offer for regular hot dogs?
   (a) One   (b) Two   (c) Three

3. What is the other flavor that the man is offering?
   (a) Ketchup   (b) Mustard   (c) Chili

B 다음을 듣고 질문에 알맞은 사진을 고르세요.

Q Which of the following does the man NOT sell?

(a)  (b)  (c)

C 다음을 듣고 맞으면 T를, 틀리면 F를 고르세요. 🎧109

1 The man thinks his hot dogs are the best.   T F
2 There is only one size of hot dog available.   T F

Dictation

다음을 듣고 빈칸을 채우세요. 🎧109

Good evening, sir. Can I interest you in some of the food I'm selling? I'd like you to know that I have the ① _____ hot dogs in town. They're ② _____ delicious. You'll love them if you try them. I've got ketchup, mustard, and relish for you to put ③ ____ _____ _____ _____. And if you don't just want a regular hot dog, why don't you try one of ④ _____ _____ _____? The combination of the hot dog and chili will be something you'll ⑤ _____ _____. ⑥ _____! You can get regular-sized hot dogs or foot-long hot dogs. So what do you say? ⑦ _____?

* 　　 내용 강조를 위해 어조(Tone)와 강세(Stress)가 주어진 부분입니다.

144 생생한 영어 수다

Situation II

Warm-up

대화를 듣고 들은 것에 ✓표 하세요. 🎧 110

- ☐ hot dogs
- ☐ someone
- ☐ pay me nothing
- ☐ pretzels
- ☐ actually
- ☐ a deal
- ☐ mustard
- ☐ prefer to eat
- ☐ pretty good

Practice

A 대화를 듣고 대화 내용과 맞도록 문장을 완성하세요. 🎧 110

1. The woman is a (street vendor / passerby).
2. The man thought (chili / mustard) on a pretzel to be yucky.
3. The woman's pretzel is (more / less) tasty than the man expected.
4. The (pretzel / hot dog) costs $2.50.

B 대화를 듣고 밑줄 친 부분에 해당하는 말을 따라 말하세요. 🎧 110

A: Excuse me, but what are you selling?

B: ① _____

A: Mustard on a pretzel? Gross! How could anyone like that?

B: ② _____

A: It's a deal. Hey! This is pretty good. Thanks. How much do I owe you?

B: ③ _____

Week 07 On the Street

Vocabulary

#			Memo
1	across from	~의 맞은편에	
2	behind	~ 뒤에	
3	bus lane	버스 차선	
4	buy one get one free	1+1 할인	
5	corn dog	(꼬챙이에 낀 소시지를 옥수수 빵으로 감싼) 핫도그	
6	crosswalk	횡단보도	
7	crêpe	(얇은 밀가루판에 과일이나 햄 등을 넣어 싸먹는 일종의 팬케이크) 크레페	
8	crowded	(사람들이) 붐비는, 몰린, 혼잡한	
9	directions	길 안내	
10	discount	할인	
11	favorite spot	좋아하는[인기 있는] 장소	
12	fried	튀긴	
13	funnel cake	(재료를 깔때기로 소용돌이 모양으로 내뽑아 굽거나 튀긴) 퍼넬 케이크	
14	greasy	기름진	
15	gyro	(쇠고기 등을 마늘로 양념하여 빵에 얹어 먹는 그리스식 샌드위치) 자이로	
16	haggle	(물건 값을 두고) 흥정하다	
17	handmade	수제의; 수제품	
18	information center	안내 센터	
19	kebab	(밀가루 전병에 익힌 고기와 채소를 넣고 말은 일종의 롤 샌드위치) 케밥	
20	lane	차선	

21	local	지역의, 현지의; 현지 주민
22	market	시장
23	next to	~ 옆에
24	on a stick	꼬챙이에 끼운
25	pedestrian zone	보행자 전용 구역
26	pickpocket	소매치기
27	police stand	파출소
28	replica	(주로 박물관이나 기념품 점에서 파는) 복제품, 모형
29	sidewalk	보도, 인도
30	smoking area[section]	흡연 구역
31	specialty	특산품, 전문, 장기
32	spicy	매운, 톡 쏘는
33	stall	(시장의) 가판대, 좌판
34	straight	똑바로, 직진으로
35	street food	길거리 음식
36	street sign	(길거리) 표지판
37	tourist attractions	관광 명소
38	touristy	관광객의, 관광객에게 인기 있는
39	unique	독특한, 유일한
40	vendor	(길거리) 노점상

Memo

EBS 생수다
생생한 영어 수다

Week
08 At the Tourist Site

- **Unit 01** Purchasing Tickets
- **Unit 02** Booking a Tour
- **Unit 03** Rules at Tourist Sites
- **Unit 04** Touring a Site

Week 08
At the Tourist Site

Unit 01 Purchasing Tickets

Listening 향상 팁

Listen for selective information 선택적으로 정보 듣기

- 선택적으로 필요한 정보를 찾아 들을 때는 의문사(Who, What, When, Where, Which, How, Why 등)에 대한 답을 찾으며 듣는 것이 도움이 된다.

  예시 Q: **What times** is it showing today? 오늘 쇼가 몇 시에 있나요?
  A: There are four shows day: **2:00, 4:30, 6:00, and 8:00**. 2:00, 4:30, 6:00, 8:00에 쇼가 있습니다.

- 공연표를 구매할 때는 시간, 가격, 좌석 위치 등과 관련된 표현이 주로 사용된다

  예시 Q: Do you have any seats left for the 8 o'clock show today? 오늘 8시 공연에 남는 표가 있나요?
  A: I have an aisle seat in Row G open. G열 통로에 자리가 하나 있습니다.

A 다음 질문을 듣고 알맞은 답변을 고르세요. 🎧 112

1. (a) I have an aisle seat on the first floor and another on the second floor.
   (b) Floor seats are $30 each. and seats in the balcony are $18.

2. (a) I'm afraid there is a $10 fee for cancellations.
   (b) Yes. we have a reservation under your name.

3. (a) I prefer the matinee show.
   (b) I prefer to sit in the middle.

B 맞으면 T를, 틀리면 F를 고르세요.

1. 선택적인 정보에 대한 답을 구할 때 의문사를 염두에 두고 들으면 도움이 된다.
2. 공연표를 구매할 때 주로 시간, 좌석, 가격 등과 관련된 표현이 주로 사용된다.

Situation I

Warm-up

대화를 듣고 들은 것에 ✓표 하세요.

- ☐ tickets
- ☐ tomorrow's show
- ☐ performances
- ☐ prefer seeing
- ☐ in the theater
- ☐ a chair chart
- ☐ in the front
- ☐ you owe
- ☐ a total of

Practice

A 대화를 듣고 질문에 알맞은 답을 고르세요.

1 How many performances are there today?
  (a) 2 (b) 3 (c) 4

2 Which show does the woman select?
  (a) 4:00 (b) 6:30 (c) 8:00

3 How does the woman select her seats?
  (a) She buys two tickets. (b) She picks a time. (c) She looks at a chart.

B 대화를 듣고 질문에 알맞은 답을 고르세요.

Q Where are the most likely seats that the woman has chosen?

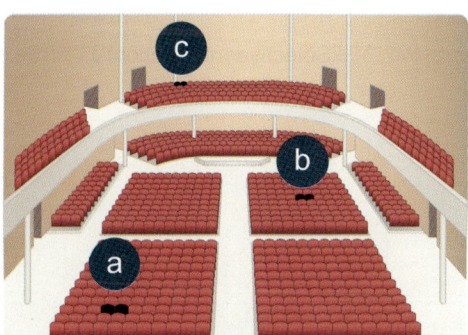

(a)   (b)   (c)

Week 08 • Unit 01

C 다음을 듣고 맞으면 T를, 틀리면 F를 고르세요.

1 The woman chooses the first performance of the day.　T　F
2 The tickets cost $50 each.　T　F

Dictation

대화를 듣고 빈칸을 채우세요.

A: Hi. I'd like to buy tickets for ① _____ _____.

B: There are ② _____ _____ _____ today.

　Which show would you like to see, the 4:00, 6:30, or 8:00 one?

A: Hmm…. I'd prefer to see ③ _____ _____ _____ _____.

B: No problem. Where in the theater do you want to sit?

　Here is a ④ _____ _____.

A: Let me see…. I'd like seats ⑤ _____ _____ _____. I need two

　tickets. How much do they cost?

B: ⑥ _____ _____ costs $25, so you owe ⑦ _____ _____ _____

　_____.

* _____ 부분은 선택적인 정보(Selective Information)을 나타내는 부분입니다.

Situation II

Warm-up

대화를 듣고 대화와 관계 있는 사진을 고르세요. 🎧 114

(a)    (b)    (c)

Practice

A 대화를 듣고 대화 내용과 맞도록 문장을 완성하세요. 🎧 114

1 The man (can / cannot) buy tickets for the show starting in 10 minutes.
2 There are less shows (on the weekdays / on the weekends).
3 The man will pay ($5 / $15) in total.

B 대화를 듣고 밑줄 친 부분에 해당하는 말을 따라 말하세요. 🎧 114

A: Excuse me. I want to purchase three tickets for the dolphin show starting in ten minutes.

B: ① _____

A: That's too bad. When is the next time the show will be performed?

B: ② _____

A: I'll take tickets for the 3:30 show. please. What do they cost?

B: ③ _____

Unit 02 Booking a Tour

Week 08 At the Tourist Site

Listening 향상 팁

Listen for intonation 억양 듣기

- 억양(Intonation)은 말의 높낮이를 뜻하며 크게 3가지 종류가 있다.
  - Falling Intonation: 문장의 끝을 내리는 경우이며, 주로 Wh-의문문에서 쓰인다.
    예시 What time is it? (↘) 몇 시인가요?
  - Rising Intonation: 문장의 끝을 올리는 경우이며, 주로 Yes/No의문문에서 쓰인다.
    예시 Is it 5 o'clock? (↗) 5시인가요?
  - Fall-Rise Intonation: 한 문장에 서로 다른 두개의 억양이 있는 경우이며, 주로 서로 다른 의미를 포함할 때 쓰인다.
    예시 I bought a present, (↗) but I didn't bring it. (↘) 선물을 샀는데, 가져 오지 않았어요.
- 부가 의문문은 일반적으로 상대방에게 동의를 구할 때 쓰며 문장 끝의 억양을 내린다.
  예시 We'll leave soon, won't we? (↘) 우리가 곧 떠날 거죠, 그렇죠?
- 부가 의문문의 끝을 올려 말하면 정말 몰라서 질문을 하는 경우이다.
  예시 The van is air-conditioned, isn't it? (↗) 밴에 에어컨이 있나요, 그런가요?

A 다음을 듣고 억양의 종류를 고르세요. 🎧 115

1 Do you have a brochure?   (Falling / Rising / Fall-Rise)
2 Where does the bus leave from?   (Falling / Rising / Fall-Rise)
3 I'm not hungry at the moment, but I'll be soon.   (Falling / Rising / Fall-Rise)

B 다음 부가의문문의 억양을 듣고 그 억양의 의도를 바르게 고르세요. 🎧 116

1 This is the office to book the walking tour, isn't it? •   • (a) 동의 구하기
2 You were the tour guide yesterday, weren't you?   •   • (b) 답변 구하기

C 맞으면 T를, 틀리면 F를 고르세요.

1 'Lunch is included, isn't it?'의 억양을 내리면 답을 몰라서 묻는 경우이다.   T F
2 'What are all the stops?'는 문장의 끝을 내려서 말한다.   T F

Situation I

Warm-up

대화를 듣고 들은 것에 ✓표 하세요. 🎧 117

- ☐ book
- ☐ semi-day one
- ☐ harbor area
- ☐ tours of the city
- ☐ more sights
- ☐ indefinitely
- ☐ full-day tour
- ☐ library
- ☐ how many tickets

Practice

A 대화를 듣고 질문에 알맞은 답을 고르세요. 🎧 117

1. What can the man book at this location?
   (a) Museum tickets (b) Tours of the city (c) Harbor cruises

2. What job does the woman likely have?
   (a) Taxi driver (b) Museum guide (c) Tourism official

3. What would be the most likely answer of the man to the woman's last question?
   (a) At 9:00. (b) Only one, please. (c) The full-day one.

B 대화를 듣고 질문에 알맞은 사진을 고르세요. 🎧 117

Q Where is the place that the man wants to go most?

(a)
(b)
(c)

C 다음을 듣고 맞으면 T를, 틀리면 F를 고르세요. 🎧 117

1 There are three types of tours available. T F
2 The full-day tour includes two more sites than the half-day one. T F

Dictation

대화를 듣고 빈칸을 채우세요. 🎧 117

A: Good morning, I can book tours of the city here, ① _____ _____ ?

B: That's correct. Are you interested in the ② _____ _____ or the half-day one?

A: I'm not sure. I'll get to see more sights on the full-day tour, ③ _____ ?

B: ④ _____ . The full-day tour takes you to the ⑤ _____ and the harbor area. The half-day tour doesn't do that.

A: Hmm…. I think I'd rather go on the full-day tour then. I ⑥ _____ want to visit the museum.

B: Excellent. How many tickets would you like to ⑦ _____ ?

*  부분은 억양(Intonation)을 주의해서 들어야 하는 부분입니다.

Situation II

Warm-up

대화를 듣고 대화와 관계 있는 그림을 모두 고르세요.

(a)    (b)    (c)

Practice

A 대화를 듣고 질문에 알맞은 그림을 고르세요.

Q What day is it today?

(a)    (b)    (c)

B 대화를 듣고 밑줄 친 부분에 해당하는 말을 따라 말하세요.

A: Hello. I need to book one of your tours. please.

B: ① _____

A: The walking tour of the historic district. You run that tour every day. don't you?

B: ② _____

A: Okay. Well…. Tomorrow is Wednesday. so… it's possible to take that tour. isn't it?

B: ③ _____

Week 08
At the Tourist Site

Unit 03 Rules at Tourist Sites

> **Listening 향상 팁**
>
> **Listen for vowel reduction** 모음 약화 듣기
>
> - 모음 약화(Vowel Reduction) 현상이 일어나는 경우
>   - 강조하는 말이 아니거나 기능어일 때
>   - 예시 Welcome **to** our city. 우리 시에 오신 걸 환영합니다.
>   → 전치사 to는 기능어이므로 모음이 약화된다.
>
> - 모음 약화 현상이 일어나지 않는 경우
>   - 내용어일 때
>   - 예시 I want **two** tickets. 표를 두 장 사고 싶어요.
>
> - Can과 Can't의 모음 약화
>   - 긍정문에서는 주동사에 강세가 주어지므로 조동사 can의 모음은 약화된다.
>   - 예시 I **can** do it. 나는 그것을 할 수 있다.
>   - 부정문에서는 주동사와 함께 can't에도 강세가 있으므로 can't의 모음이 약화되지 않는다.
>   - 예시 I **can't** do it. 나는 그것을 할 수 없다.

A 다음을 듣고 모음 약화 현상이 일어나는 부분을 빈칸에 쓰세요. 🎧 119

  1 You need _____ register _____ the tour.
  2 I would recommend you make _____ reservation _____ that.
  3 Would you like _____ go by train _____ bus?

B 다음을 듣고 can과 can't 중에서 올바른 것을 고르세요. 🎧 120

  1 I (can / can't) show you how to make a reservation.
  2 I (can / can't) make a reservation for them.

C 맞으면 T를, 틀리면 F를 고르세요.

  1 'I've walked for hours.'에서 for는 기능어이므로 모음 약화 현상이 일어난다.   T F
  2 'I've walked four hours.'에서 four는 내용어이므로 모음 약화 현상이 일어난다. T F

Situation I

Warm-up

다음을 듣고 들은 것에 ✓표 하세요. 🎧 121

- ☐ museum
- ☐ prohibited
- ☐ patrons
- ☐ first of all
- ☐ at the café
- ☐ furthermore
- ☐ photography
- ☐ at all times
- ☐ main entrance

Practice

A 다음을 듣고 질문에 알맞은 답을 고르세요. 🎧 121

1 Who most likely is the speaker?
   (a) An artist
   (b) A tourist
   (c) A guide

2 What can be purchased at the museum?
   (a) Camera flashes
   (b) Copies of artwork
   (c) Mobile phones

3 When should guests go to the main lobby?
   (a) When they are ready to start the tour
   (b) When they want to meet others
   (c) When they have to take a call

B 다음을 듣고 질문에 알맞은 사진을 고르세요. 🎧 121

Q What is completely prohibited in this place?

(a)
(b)
(c)

C 다음을 듣고 맞으면 T를, 틀리면 F를 고르세요.

1 It's important to be quiet in the galleries.   T F
2 Everyone should turn their phones off.   T F

Dictation

다음을 듣고 빈칸을 채우세요.

Before we enter the gallery, I need ①_____ tell you a few things. First of all, photography is strictly prohibited. Camera flashes ②_____ harm the paintings. Fortunately, you ③_____ purchase postcards ④_____ pictures of the artwork ⑤_____ the souvenir shop. Next, please keep ⑥_____ voices down ⑦_____ all times. Many of our patrons like to observe the art in silence. Therefore, you should try not to disturb them. Furthermore, we request that you turn off your mobile phones. If you need to speak on your phone, you may leave the gallery and go to the main lobby.

* _____ 부분은 모음 약화(Vowel Reduction)가 일어나는 부분입니다.

Situation II

Warm-up

대화를 듣고 들은 것에 ✓표 하세요. 🎧 122

- ☐ something to eat
- ☐ against
- ☐ cafeteria
- ☐ from my bag
- ☐ prohibited
- ☐ three more rooms
- ☐ not supposed
- ☐ historic building
- ☐ of interest

Practice

A 대화를 듣고 내용과 알맞은 문장을 모두 고르세요. 🎧 122

(a) They are in the museum.

(b) The woman needs to go to the restroom right now.

(c) Eating snack is prohibited in here.

(d) The woman has decided to wait by the end of touring.

B 대화를 듣고 밑줄 친 부분에 해당하는 말을 따라 말하세요. 🎧 122

A: Hold on a minute. I want to get something to eat from my bag.

B: ① _____

A: Why not?

B: ② _____

A: Hmm…. I guess I can wait a few minutes. We've almost finished touring the building, haven't we?

B: ③ _____

Week 08 • Unit 03 161

Unit 04 Touring a Site

**Week 08
At the Tourist Site**

Listening 향상 팁

Listen for details 세부 사항 듣기

- 세부 사항을 들을 때 의문사(Who, What, Where, When, How, Why)와 관련된 내용에 유의하여 듣는다.

  예시 Q: What can we see on the third floor? 3층에서 무엇을 볼 수 있나요?
  A: We can see art works from European, Asian, and American masters.
  유럽, 아시아, 미국의 대가들의 작품을 볼 수 있습니다.

- 내용 중 언급된 숫자, 날짜, 장소 등을 바꿔 말하는(Paraphrasing) 연습을 하면 듣기뿐 아니라 말하기에도 도움이 된다.

  예시 We are open 365 days a year. = We are never closed. 우리는 일년 365일 내내 문을 엽니다.
  There are no other poetry collections as extensive as these works here.
  = We have the largest poetry collection in the world. 여기가 세상에서 가장 많은 시 작품을 가지고 있습니다.

*패러프레이징(Paraphrasing)이란? 사용된 말이나 글을 다른 어휘나 구문을 사용해서 다시 표현하는 것

A 다음을 듣고 같은 의미의 문장을 고르세요. 🎧 123

1. (a) We are open daily from 9 in the morning to 7 in the evening.
   (b) We are open 7 days.

2. (a) The tour is guided in four languages.
   (b) There are many visitors from England, France, China, and Spain.

3. (a) The museum is closed every other Mondays.
   (b) The museum is closed every Monday.

B 맞으면 T를, 틀리면 F를 고르세요.

1. Wh-의문문에 대해 답할 때 그 세부 사항은 주로 의문사와 관련된 내용이다. T F

2. 패러프레이징(Paraphrasing)을 연습하면 듣기와 말하기가 향상될 수 있다. T F

Situation I

Warm-up

다음을 듣고 들은 것에 ✓표 하세요. 🎧 124

- ☐ museum
- ☐ sculptures
- ☐ make sure to check
- ☐ our collection
- ☐ Greek and Roman artifacts
- ☐ dinosaur fossils
- ☐ four floors
- ☐ on loan
- ☐ next two

Practice

A 다음을 듣고 질문에 알맞은 답을 고르세요. 🎧 124

1 How many floors are there in the museum?
   (a) 1　　　　　(b) 2　　　　　(c) 3

2 What is located on the first floor?
   (a) Works of art　　(b) Ancient relics　　(c) Fossils of dinosaurs

3 How much time do the guests have to explore?
   (a) One hour　　(b) Two hours　　(c) Three hours

B 다음을 듣고 질문에 알맞은 사진을 고르세요. 🎧 124

Q What can you see on the second floor?

(a) 　(b) 　(c)

C 다음을 듣고 맞으면 T를, 틀리면 F를 고르세요. 🎧 124

1 There are different types of exhibits on each floor.

2 Some of the items are being borrowed from another museum.

Dictation

다음을 듣고 빈칸을 채우세요. 🎧 124

Welcome to the Peabody Museum. We hope you enjoy viewing our collection. There are ① _____ _____ here. The third floor contains ② _____ _____ _____. You can view art from ③ _____, _____, and _____ masters. I'm sure you'll love the paintings and sculptures. On the second floor, you can see our collection of ④ _____ _____ and _____ relics. We have some special items ⑤ _____ _____ from the Athens Museum. Be sure to check them out. Finally, on the first floor, as you can see, we have ⑥ _____ _____. Now, please have a great time for ⑦ _____ _____ _____ _____.

* 🟨 부분은 주의해서 들어야 할 세부사항(Details)입니다.

Situation II

Warm-up

대화를 듣고 들은 것에 ✓표 하세요. 🎧 125

- ☐ palace
- ☐ the throne room
- ☐ king's family
- ☐ various occasions
- ☐ wealthy
- ☐ its kings
- ☐ the royal quarters
- ☐ antique furniture
- ☐ throne jewels

Practice

A 대화를 듣고 대화 내용과 맞도록 문장을 완성하세요. 🎧 125

1 They are in (a museum / a palace).
2 The throne room is decorated with (sculptures / paintings).
3 There are many (old furniture / antique sculptures) in the royal quarters.
4 The crown jewels are in the (throne room / royal quarters).

B 대화를 듣고 밑줄 친 부분에 해당하는 말을 따라 말하세요. 🎧 125

A: Which room in the palace is this?

B: ① _____

A: I like the artwork on the walls. When were these paintings made?

B: ② _____

A: What are we going to see next?

B: ③ _____

Week 08 • Unit 04

Week 08 At the Tourist Site

Vocabulary

1	age restriction	나이 제한
2	ancient remains [ruins]	유적지
3	artifacts [relics]	유물
4	beginning / ending time	개막/폐막 시간
5	burial [grave] goods	부장품
6	cancelation policy	취소 규정
7	castle	성
8	city tour [sightseeing]	시내 관광
9	city tour [sightseeing] bus	시내 관광 버스
10	confirmation number	(예약) 확인 번호
11	curator	(박물관/미술관의) 전시 책임자
12	discount ticket	할인표
13	docent	(박물관의) 해설사
14	dress code	(때/장소에 맞춰 격식을 차려 입는) 드레스 코드, 복장 규정
15	excavate	발굴하다
16	excavation	발굴, 발굴터, 출토, 출토지
17	historic	역사적으로 중요한, 역사적인
18	historic site	유적지
19	itinerary	(여행) 일정
20	littering	쓰레기 투기

Memo

#	English	Korean
21	local customs	현지 세금[관세]
22	local guide	현지 안내인[가이드]
23	monastery	수도원
24	monument	(건물 / 동상 등의) 기념물, 역사적 건축물
25	mummy	미라
26	museum leaflet	박물관 안내장
27	non-refundable	환불이 안 되는
28	observatory	전망대
29	opera house	오페라 하우스[극장]
30	performance	공연, 실적
31	photography	사진술, 사진 촬영
32	prehistory	선사 시대
33	restoration	복원
34	temple	절, 사원
35	theater	극장
36	ticket agent	매표원
37	ticket booth	매표소
38	time allowed [allotted]	허용 시간
39	tipping	팁 주기
40	tour details	관광 세부 정보

Memo

EBS 생수다
생생한 영어 수다

Week 09 On the Phone

- **Unit 01** Arranging a Meeting
- **Unit 02** Getting a Complaint Call
- **Unit 03** Transferring a Call
- **Unit 04** Changing a Project Schedule

Week 09
On the Phone

Unit 01 Arranging a Meeting

Listening 향상 팁

Predict what language will come next 다음에 오는 말 예측하기

- 전화 영어에서 상황별로 유용한 표현들을 단계별로 정리해 두면 다음 내용을 예측하기 쉽다. 아래는 약속을 변경하는 경우의 예시이다.
  - 1단계: 약속을 바꿔야만 한다는 것을 먼저 밝힌다.
    어쩔 수 없이 바꾼다는 느낌이 전달되도록 afraid, sorry, have to 등을 사용한다.
  - 2단계: 약속을 바꿔야 하는 이유를 설명한다.
    구체적인 이유를 밝히는 것이 예의이다. 이때 sudden(ly), unexpected(ly), unfortunately, apologize 등이 유용하다.
  - 3단계: 시간/장소를 다시 정한다.
    자신이 제시하거나 상대방에게 물어 정한다. available, free, okay 등이 유용하다.
  - 4단계: 다시 한 번 감사한 마음을 전하고 변경된 시간/장소를 언급하면서 통화를 마무리한다.
    예시 What a relief! Then I'll see you at 4:00 at your office.
    정말 다행입니다. 그러면 당신 사무실에서 4시에 뵙겠습니다.

A 다음을 듣고 알맞은 단계를 고르세요. 🎧 127

(a) 약속을 바꿔야 하는 상황을 알리기   (b) 약속을 바꿔야 하는 이유를 설명하기
(c) 감사한 마음을 전하며 통화를 마무리하기   (d) 약속 변경을 이해한다고 말하기

1 _____   2 _____   3 _____   4 _____

B 맞으면 T를, 틀리면 F를 고르세요.

1 약속을 변경할 때 단계별로 유용한 표현을 알면 다음 내용을 예측하고 말하는데 유용하다.   T F

2 약속 변경을 할 때 suddenly, unexpectedly 등의 표현이 좋다.   T F

Situation I

Warm-up

다음을 듣고 들은 것에 ✓표 하세요. 🎧 128

- ☐ received your e-mail
- ☐ Tuesday
- ☐ another meeting
- ☐ would like to have
- ☐ 10 p.m.
- ☐ directions
- ☐ unfortunately
- ☐ visit your office
- ☐ calling me back

Practice

A 다음을 듣고 질문에 알맞은 답을 고르세요. 🎧 128

1 Why is Mr. Thompson calling?
   (a) He tries to reschedule the meeting.
   (b) He wants to meet Ms. Eastwood today.
   (c) He e-mailed Ms. Eastwood.

2 When does Mr. Thompson suggest meeting?
   (a) That afternoon   (b) Wednesday morning   (c) Wednesday afternoon

3 What does Mr. Thompson need to meet Ms. Eastwood?
   (a) Another meeting   (b) Her phone number   (c) Directions to her office

B 다음을 듣고 질문에 알맞은 답을 고르세요. 🎧 128

Q When would Mr. Thompson NOT most likely to have a meeting?

WEEKLY SCHEDULE

TIME	MONDAY	TUESDAY	WEDNESDAY	THURSDAY	FRIDAY	SATURDAY	SUNDAY
morning		a	b				
afternoon			c				

(a)   (b)   (c)

C 다음을 듣고 맞으면 T를, 틀리면 F를 고르세요. 🎧 128

1 Ms. Eastwood works at Dynamic Systems.   T F
2 Ms. Eastwood's office is in Springfield.   T F

Dictation

다음을 듣고 빈칸을 채우세요. 🎧 128

Good morning, Ms. Eastwood. This is Cedric Thompson calling from Dynamic Systems. I received ① _____ _____ and would love to have a meeting with you. ② _____, I cannot meet today because I am ③ _____ _____. But I am free on Wednesday in the morning. ④ _____ _____ _____ at 10 a.m.? I can ⑤ _____ _____ _____ in Springfield because I have another meeting there in the afternoon. I ⑥ _____ _____ to your office though. How about ⑦ _____ _____ _____ at 457-3934? Talk to you soon. Goodbye.

* 부분은 다음에 오는 말을 예측할 수 있도록 돕는 부분입니다.

Situation II

Warm-up

대화를 듣고 들은 것에 ✓표 하세요. 🎧129

- ☐ a staff meeting
- ☐ Friday
- ☐ a bunch of pizzas
- ☐ merger
- ☐ the CEO
- ☐ an e-mail
- ☐ training session
- ☐ during lunch
- ☐ right away

Practice

A 대화를 듣고 대화 내용과 맞도록 문장을 완성하세요. 🎧129

1 The (CEO / CFO) will visit the office this week.

2 All staff will have (a training session / a staff meeting) tomorrow.

3 The staff will have lunch (during / after) the meeting today.

B 대화를 듣고 밑줄 친 부분에 해당하는 말을 따라 말하세요. 🎧129

A: We need to have a staff meeting to talk about the merger with the Dolson Corporation.

B: ① _____

A: No. the training session for the computer software is being held all day. And Thursday is no good because the CEO is coming here.

B: ② _____

A: All right. I'll call Sal's Deli right now and have a bunch of sandwiches and chips delivered. You send an e-mail to everyone.

B: ③ _____

Week 09
On the Phone

Unit 02 Getting a Complaint Call

> **Listening 향상 팁**
>
> **Listen for complaints 불평 듣기**
>
> - 불평을 할 때도 예의를 갖추고 공손한 표현으로 시작하는 것이 좋다.
>   - 예시 I'm sorry to have to say this, but ...
>   - Don't get me wrong, but I think we should ...
>   - Don't take it personal, but ...
> - 주문한 물품에 대해 불평하는 경우
>   - 부품 일부나 상품 자체가 분실되었을 때
>   - 예시 My order is missing one item. 주문한 상품 중 하나가 빠졌어요.
>   - 다른 물품이 배송 되었을 때
>   - 예시 I just got my order and it's incorrect. 주문한 것을 막 받았는데, 틀린 것이 왔어요.
>   - 물품이 파손되었을 때
>   - 예시 The items you sent me are damaged. 보내주신 물품이 파손되었어요.

A 다음을 듣고 빈칸에 알맞은 단어를 쓰세요. 🎧 130

1. I wanted to call to _____ about a _____ package.
2. I didn't get _____ that I _____ .
3. I haven't _____ my _____ item.

B 다음 대화를 듣고 어느 것에 관해 불평하는지 고르세요. 🎧 131

1. (a) 분실   (b) 파손
2. (a) 결제 카드 변경   (b) 카드 재발급 요청

C 맞으면 T를, 틀리면 F를 고르세요.

1. 불평 사항을 정확히 전달하기 위해서 반드시 큰소리로 상대방에게 항의해야 한다.   T F
2. 주문한 물품에 관해 전화로 항의할 때 분실, 오배송, 파손 중 문제점이 무엇인지 밝히고 구체적인 내용을 전해야 한다.   T F

Situation I

Warm-up

대화를 듣고 들은 것에 ✓표 하세요. 🎧 132

- ☐ speaking
- ☐ of assistance
- ☐ on your homepage
- ☐ the shirts
- ☐ the right size
- ☐ the pants
- ☐ order number
- ☐ arrange to send
- ☐ the wrong items

Practice

A 대화를 듣고 질문에 알맞은 답을 고르세요. 🎧 132

1. Where does Janet work?
   (a) In a call center
   (b) In a clothing store
   (c) In a delivery company

2. Who is Brian Washington?
   (a) A customer
   (b) A vendor
   (c) A service representative

3. What information does Janet need?
   (a) Brian's sizes
   (b) Brian's order number
   (c) Brian's phone number

B 대화를 듣고 질문에 알맞은 사진을 고르세요. 🎧 132

Q Which of the following will Mr. Washington NOT get?

(a)
(b)
(c)

C 다음을 듣고 맞으면 T를, 틀리면 F를 고르세요. 🎧 132

1 Janet is calling Mr. Washington. T F
2 Janet is going to send Mr. Washington new items. T F

Dictation

대화를 듣고 빈칸을 채우세요. 🎧 132

A: Hello. This is customer service. Janet speaking. How may I be of assistance?

B: Hello. My name is Brian Washington. I ① _____ some clothes on your website, and they were just ② _____ _____ me. But there are ③ _____ _____ _____ _____.

A: What's the matter with them, sir?

B: One of the shirts is ④ _____ _____ _____, and the pants I ordered ⑤ _____ _____, either.

A: I'm terribly sorry about that. Can I have your order number, please? Then, I can ⑥ _____ _____ _____ you the right items.

B: Sure. My ⑦ _____ _____ is CR5403M1.

* _____ 부분은 불평(Complaints)과 관련된 부분입니다.

Situation II

Warm-up

대화를 듣고 대화와 관계 있는 사진을 고르세요. 🎧 133

(a)  (b)  (c)

Practice

A 대화를 듣고 질문에 알맞은 사진을 고르세요. 🎧 133

Q Where will the woman make sure to visit tomorrow?

(a)  (b)  (c)

B 대화를 듣고 밑줄 친 부분에 해당하는 말을 따라 말하세요. 🎧 133

A: Hi. I bought a vacuum cleaner at your store a couple of hours ago, but it won't work.

B: ① _____

A: When I plugged it in, it wouldn't turn on.

B: ② _____

A: I don't have time to return the vacuum cleaner today. I guess I can do that tomorrow morning.

B: ③ _____

Week 09 • Unit 02 177

Week 09
On the Phone

Unit 03 Transferring a Call

> **Listening 향상 팁**
>
> **Listen for gist** 요지 파악하여 듣기
>
> - 전화 영어에서 상황별로 유용한 표현들을 정리해 두면 요지를 파악하기 쉽다. 아래는 전화로 약속을 정하는 경우이다.
>   - 1단계: 전화 건 목적이 약속 정하기임을 밝히기
>   - 예시) I'm calling to arrange a meeting. 회의 시간을 정하기 위해 전화 드렸습니다.
>   - 2단계: 시간/장소 정하기
>   - 예시) How does 3:00 sound to you? 3시 어떠세요?
>   What day would be convenient for you? 무슨 요일이 편하세요?
>   I'm pretty much booked solid all day on Monday. 월요일은 일정이 거의 잡혀 있습니다.
>   Tuesday is wide open for me. 화요일은 언제라도 가능합니다.
>   - 3단계: 시간/장소를 다시 확인하면서 통화를 마무리하기
>   - 예시) Let's meet at 10:00 on Tuesday at my office. 제 사무실에서 화요일 10시에 봅시다.

A 대화를 듣고 빈칸에 알맞은 단어를 쓰세요. 🎧 134

1. A: I'm just calling to _____ _____ our appointment.
   B: Sure. When do you _____ _____ _____ ?

2. A: _____ does Tuesday morning _____ to you?
   B: Tuesday is _____ _____ for me. How about 10:00 at my office?

3. A: Yes. 10:00 _____ _____ me.
   B: Wonderful. Let's meet Wednesday _____ 10:00 _____ my office.

B 맞으면 T를, 틀리면 F를 고르세요.

1. 약속 정하기는 전화 영어의 대표적인 상황 중 하나이다.

2. '선약이 꽉 잡혀 있다'라는 표현은 'I'm booked solid.'로 하면 된다.

Situation I

Warm-up

대화를 듣고 들은 것에 ✓표 하세요. 🎧 135

- ☐ no longer
- ☐ my loan
- ☐ paying off
- ☐ the terms
- ☐ accounts
- ☐ treated by
- ☐ transfer
- ☐ hold on
- ☐ one second

Practice

A 대화를 듣고 질문에 알맞은 답을 고르세요. 🎧 135

1 Who is calling?
   (a) Jason Cartwright   (b) A borrower   (c) Janet Morgan

2 What did Jason Cartwright and the caller do?
   (a) Played basketball   (b) Worked on a loan   (c) Attended the same college

3 What does the caller want to do?
   (a) Pay off the loan
   (b) Apply for a new loan
   (c) Change the terms of the loan

B 대화를 듣고 질문에 알맞은 사진을 고르세요. 🎧 135

Q Who is most likely to pick up the call next?

(a)  (b)  (c)

C 다음을 듣고 맞으면 T를, 틀리면 F를 고르세요. 🎧 135

1 Jason Cartwright has quit the company. [T] [F]

2 Janet Morgan is handling Jason Cartwright's accounts. [T] [F]

Dictation

대화를 듣고 빈칸을 채우세요. 🎧 135

A: Hello. May I ① _____ _____ Jason Cartwright, please?

B: I'm sorry, but he ② _____ _____ _____ here. What do you need to speak with him about?

A: He was the person who ③ _____ _____ _____. I need to speak to him ④ _____ _____ it. I'd like to ⑤ _____ _____ _____ a bit.

B: Ah, okay. All of Mr. Cartwright's accounts are ⑥ _____ _____ by Janet Morgan. Would you like me to ⑦ _____ you to her?

A: Yes, please. That would be great.

B: All right. Hold on just one moment, please.

* _____ 부분은 전화를 건 요지(Gist)에 해당하는 부분입니다.

Situation II

Warm-up

대화를 듣고 대화와 관계있는 사진을 고르세요. 🎧 136

(a) 　(b) 　(c)

Practice

A 대화를 듣고 내용과 알맞은 문장을 모두 고르세요. 🎧 136

(a) The man is calling about the advertisement on TV.
(b) The woman works in the Sales Department.
(c) The man has to hang up his current call.
(d) The man will speak with Steve shortly.

B 대화를 듣고 밑줄 친 부분에 해당하는 말을 따라 말하세요. 🎧 136

A: Hello. Thank you for calling Swanson's. This is Marcia. How may I help you?

B: ① _____

A: You need to speak with someone in the Sales Department.

B: ② _____

A: Of course. It's 54. But if you wait a minute, I can transfer your call. I'll put you on the line with Steve.

B: ③ _____

Week 09
On the Phone

Unit 04 Changing a Project Schedule

Listening 향상 팁

Listen for transition words 전환어 듣기

구분	내용 전환	결과
기능	내용의 흐름이 바뀌는 것을 나타내어 듣는 사람의 이해를 돕는다.	앞뒤 문장 사이의 응집력을 높여준다.
예시	however, on the other hand, otherwise, although, even if 등	however, so, as a result, consequently 등
예문	Whales breathe through lung like other mammals. **However**, they live in oceans. 고래는 다른 포유류처럼 폐로 숨을 쉰다. **그렇지만**, 바다에 산다.	There was a car crash around the post office; **consequently**, we were late. 우체국 부근에서 자동차 사고가 있었다. **그래서** 우리가 늦었다.

A 다음을 듣고 빈칸에 알맞은 단어를 쓰세요. 🎧 137

1 Half the team was out sick. _____ we finished the project on time.

2 It will not be profitable; ____ _____ _____ _____, there is lots of future potential.

3 I think he will finish today. _____ it'll be done in the morning.

4 The product was super popular. _____ ____ _____ sales soared.

5 His computer crashed. _____ he had to start from scratch.

6 It was being greatly discounted. _____ it sold out quickly.

B 맞으면 T를, 틀리면 F를 고르세요.

1 however, on the other hand는 내용이 서로 다른 문장이 자연스럽게 연결되도록 돕는다.

2 therefore, so 다음에 오는 내용은 앞 문장의 결과를 나타낸다.

Situation I

Warm-up

다음을 듣고 들은 것에 ✓표 하세요. 🎧 138

- ☐ apparently
- ☐ as a result
- ☐ in the final stages
- ☐ the blueprints
- ☐ final due date
- ☐ however
- ☐ later than
- ☐ November 5th
- ☐ next two months

Practice

A 다음을 듣고 질문에 알맞은 답을 고르세요. 🎧 138

1. What does Johnson Construction need to start doing as soon as possible?
   (a) Planning a building   (b) Starting to build   (c) Finishing blueprints

2. When is the new final date?
   (a) November 15th   (b) December 1st   (c) December 15th

3. What are the workers expected to do?
   (a) Stay late every night
   (b) Work on two weekends
   (c) Both of the above

B 다음을 듣고 질문에 알맞은 사진을 고르세요. 🎧 138

Q What kind of company is it?

(a)    (b)    (c)

C 다음을 듣고 맞으면 T를, 틀리면 F를 고르세요. 🎧 138

1 Blueprints no longer need to be finished. T F

2 Only two more weeks are left to complete everything. T F

Dictation

다음을 듣고 빈칸을 채우세요. 🎧 138

All right, everyone, I have some news. ①_____, Johnson Construction needs to start building as soon as possible. ②_____ we have to finish the blueprints faster than we had planned. ③_____ _____, the final due date is no longer December 1st. It's been moved up to ④_____ _____. I realize this only gives us two more weeks to complete everything. ⑤_____ please remember that we're already in the final stages. ⑥_____, we're going to have to work plenty of overtime, ⑦_____ expect to stay late every night and to come in on the next two weekends.

* _____ 부분은 전환어(Transition Words)입니다.

Situation II

Warm-up

대화를 듣고 들은 것에 ✓표 하세요. 🎧 139

- ☐ delay
- ☐ shut off
- ☐ positive
- ☐ delivery
- ☐ assembly lines
- ☐ require costing
- ☐ the original plan
- ☐ needs to repair
- ☐ this contract

Practice

A 대화를 듣고 대화 내용과 맞도록 문장을 완성하세요. 🎧 139

1 They are supposed to send items by (this Friday / this coming Tuesday).

2 They have to shut down one of the (factories / assembly lines).

3 They will (be off / work) this weekend.

4 They have to pay (more / less) than they expected.

B 대화를 듣고 밑줄 친 부분에 해당하는 말을 따라 말하세요. 🎧 139

A: Susan. we've got to delay our delivery of items to Sherman Motors.

B: ① _____

A: That was the original plan. but we had to shut down one of the assembly lines. It needs to be repaired.

B: ② _____

A: I'm positive we can do that by next Tuesday. However. we'll have to operate the assembly lines over the weekend.

B: ③ _____

Week 09 • Unit 04

Week 09 On the Phone

Vocabulary

1	apology	사과
2	appointment	(만날) 약속
3	arrangement	(모임이나 약속) 준비, 채비
4	available	(통화가) 가능한
5	away from one's desk	(사람이) 자리에 없는
6	be on the phone	(사람이) 통화 중이다
7	behind schedule	일정보다 늦은
8	better than expected	예상보다 더 좋은
9	busy	(전화가) 통화 중인
10	call waiting/forwarding/blocking	통화 중 대기/착신 전환/통화 차단
11	caller	발신자
12	caller ID service	발신자 표시 서비스
13	cancel	취소하다
14	change	바꾸다, 변경하다
15	conference call	3자 통화, 전화 회의
16	direct number	직통 번호
17	disconnected	(전화가) 끊긴
18	discrepancy	차이
19	engaged	(전화가) 통화 중인
20	expect a call	전화를 기다리다

Memo

21	frustration	불만, 좌절감
22	get the wrong number	전화를 잘못 걸다
23	give a ring	전화를 걸다
24	hang up	전화를 끊다
25	have a bad connection	(전화 통화 품질이) 안 좋다
26	hold	(전화를 끊지 않고) 기다리다
27	leave / take a message	메시지를 남기다 / 받다
28	make a call	전화를 걸다
29	make ... better	~이 더 좋아지다
30	mortgage	담보 대출
31	phase	단계
32	pick up	(전화기를 들어) 전화를 받다
33	postpone	연기하다, 미루다
34	return a call	못 받은 전화를 걸다
35	run out of battery	배터리가 다 되어가다
36	time-consuming	시간이 걸리는
37	timeline	시각표, 연대기
38	unexpected problem	예기치 않은 문제, 돌발 문제
39	video call	영상 통화
40	voicemail	음성사서함

EBS 생수다
생생한 영어 수다

Week
10 At the Office

Unit 01 Introducing the New Manager
Unit 02 Announcing a Training Session
Unit 03 Announcing a Conference
Unit 04 Overcoming Problems

Week 10
At the Office

Unit 01 Introducing the New Manager

> **Listening 향상 팁**
>
> **Listen for phrases 구 듣기**
> - 두 개 이상의 단어가 모여서 한 가지 의미를 나타낼 때 '구(Phrase)'라고 한다.
> - 단어를 하나씩 듣지 않고, 빈출 어구를 한 덩어리로 들으면 이해도를 높일 수 있다.
> - get, make, take, do, have 등의 기본 동사를 활용한 어구를 잘 정리하는 것이 도움이 된다.
>   예시 get acquainted with ~와 친숙해지다   make quite an impression on ~에게 깊은 인상을 주다
>   count on ~를 의지하다   count + 사람 + in ~를 끼워주다
>   count + 사람 + out ~를 제외시키다

A 다음을 듣고 빈칸에 알맞은 단어를 쓴 후, 그 뜻을 고르세요. 🎧 141

1 Please count me _____ this time. _____

2 He _____ a good impression on me. _____

3 You can always _____ _____ me. _____

4 Help him _____ _____ _____ everyone. _____

> (a) 그는 나에게 좋은 인상을 주었다.   (b) 당신은 항상 나에게 의지해도 좋다.
> (c) 이번에 나는 안 하겠다.   (d) 그가 모든 사람과 친해지도록 도와줘라.

B 맞으면 T를, 틀리면 F를 고르세요.

1 두 개 이상의 단어가 모여 한 가지 의미를 나타낼 때 '구(Phrase)'라고 한다. T F

2 구를 이루는 단어 하나만 달라져도 구의 뜻이 달라진다. T F

Situation I

Warm-up

다음을 듣고 들은 것에 ✓표 하세요. 🎧 142

- ☐ attention
- ☐ made a decision
- ☐ the new director
- ☐ the Accounting Department
- ☐ the choice we took
- ☐ best of all
- ☐ one of the hardest working
- ☐ get the best out of
- ☐ a big round of hands

Practice

A 다음을 듣고 질문에 알맞은 답을 고르세요. 🎧 142

1. Which department is getting a new director?
   (a) HR (b) Accounting (c) Purchasing

2. Where was the new director found?
   (a) Outside the company
   (b) Within the company
   (c) From the HR department

3. How much experience does the new director have?
   (a) Very little (b) The same as others (c) More than others

B 다음을 듣고 질문에 알맞은 사진을 고르세요. 🎧 142

Q What will the audience do right after the announcement?

(a)  (b)  (c)

C 다음을 듣고 맞으면 T를, 틀리면 F를 고르세요. 🎧 142

1 Sabrina Wilson is the new director of the HR Department. T F
2 Sabrina Wilson works very hard for the company. T F

Dictation

다음을 듣고 빈칸을 채우세요. 🎧 142

May I have your attention, please? We made a decision on ① _____ _____ _____ of the Accounting Department. We couldn't be happier with ② _____ _____ _____ _____. ③ _____ _____ _____, we didn't have to go outside the company. We found her right here. So it's my great pleasure to tell you that Sabrina Wilson is your new boss. Sabrina is one of ④ _____ _____ _____ _____ at the company. She's got ⑤ _____ _____ _____ almost anyone here, and I'm sure she'll ⑥ _____ _____ _____ _____ _____ all of you. How about ⑦ _____ _____ _____ _____ _____ for Sabrina?

* ___ 부분은 단어 2개 이상이 모여 구(Phrases)를 이루는 부분입니다.

Situation II

Warm-up

대화를 듣고 들은 것에 ✓표 하세요. 🎧 143

- ☐ a new supervisor
- ☐ interview
- ☐ quite an impression
- ☐ upper management
- ☐ definitely
- ☐ candidate
- ☐ next week
- ☐ get acquainted with
- ☐ count on him

Practice

A 대화를 듣고 대화 내용과 맞도록 문장을 완성하세요. 🎧 143

1. The new supervisor is (Karen / Jason).
2. The woman (met / didn't meet) the new supervisor before.
3. The (woman / man) will help the new supervisor to settle down.

B 대화를 듣고 밑줄 친 부분에 해당하는 말을 따라 말하세요. 🎧 143

A: Karen. you should know that we have a new supervisor in the office.

B: ① _____

A: It's Jason Carter. I believe that you met him when he came here to interview. He made quite an impression on upper management.

B: ② _____

A: Well. he's going to be starting here next Monday. I'd like for you to help him get acquainted with everyone here.

B: ③ _____

Week 10 At the Office

Unit 02 Announcing a Training Session

Listening 향상 팁

Listen for sentence stress 문장의 강세 듣기

- 영어는 '강세 박자 언어(Stress-timed Language)'라고 하여 문장을 말할 때 걸리는 시간이 모든 음절의 수만큼 늘어나는 것이 아니라, 강세(stress)를 받는 음절의 수만큼 걸린다는 뜻이다.
- 즉 강세가 있는 음절과 그 다음 강세가 있는 음절이 나올 때까지의 시간 간격을 한 박자로 하고 그 나머지 강세가 없는 음절은 삼키듯이 약하게 말하게 된다.

  예시 One,   two,   three,   four.
        One and,   two and,   three and, four and.
        One and a, two and a, three and a, four and a.
  → 예시 두 번째 줄의 and, 세 번째 줄의 and a를 말하는 사람이 삼키는 것처럼 정확히 발음하지 않고 빨리 발음하므로 위 예시를 말하는 데 걸리는 시간은 서로 비슷하다.

- 강세가 없는 단어는 거의 기능어에 속한다.
- 강세를 받지 않는 부분은 약하고 빠르게 발음을 하여 잘 들리지 않으므로 이에 주의하여 듣기 연습을 하는 것이 좋다.

A 다음을 듣고 강세가 있는 부분에 ◯표 하세요. 🎧 144

1 (People) watch (movies).

2 The people are watching movies.

3 Men read books.

4 The men read books.

B 맞으면 T를, 틀리면 F를 고르세요.

1 우리말은 음절 박자 언어인 반면, 영어는 강세 박자 언어이다. T F

2 영어는 전체 음절의 개수가 아니라, 강세가 있는 음절의 개수가 발음되는 시간에 영향을 받는다. T F

Situation I

Warm-up

다음을 듣고 들은 것에 ✓표 하세요. 🎧 145

- ☐ some great news
- ☐ complaining about
- ☐ the new software
- ☐ has agreed to give
- ☐ a training session
- ☐ all day long
- ☐ lead four sessions
- ☐ up to half of you
- ☐ the sign-up sheets

Practice

A 다음을 듣고 질문에 알맞은 답을 고르세요. 🎧 145

1 What has everyone been complaining about?
   (a) A training session   (b) New hardware   (c) New software

2 When is the training session?
   (a) In two hours   (b) Tomorrow   (c) Next week

3 How many training sessions will there be?
   (a) One   (b) Two   (c) Three

B 다음을 듣고 질문에 알맞은 사진을 고르세요. 🎧 145

Q What will the training session be on?

(a)    (b)    (c)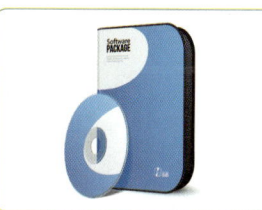

C 다음을 듣고 맞으면 T를, 틀리면 F를 고르세요. 🎧 145

1 The speaker has bad news. [T] [F]

2 Each training session will be three hours long. [T] [F]

Dictation

다음을 듣고 빈칸을 채우세요. 🎧 145

I've got ① _____ _____ _____, everyone. I know you've all been complaining about ② _____ _____ _____ we started using. Well, the company that sold it to us has agreed to send someone here ③ _____ _____ _____ _____ _____. Isn't that welcome news? He's going to be here ④ _____ _____ _____ tomorrow. He's going to lead three sessions, each of which will be two hours long. ⑤ _____ _____ _____ _____ _____ can be in one session. I've got the sign-up sheets here, so ⑥ _____ _____ _____ _____ come up here and choose ⑦ _____ _____ you'd like to get your training?

* _____ 부분은 강세 문장(Sentence Stress)의 일부분입니다.

Situation II

Warm-up

대화를 듣고 들은 것에 ✓표 하세요. 🎧 146

- ☐ training session
- ☐ new employees
- ☐ this Thursday
- ☐ assist
- ☐ exactly
- ☐ introductory speech
- ☐ their basic duties
- ☐ four times before
- ☐ actually

Practice

A 대화를 듣고 내용과 알맞은 문장을 모두 고르세요. 🎧 146

(a) The woman got a call from Mr. Wright.
(b) The woman wanted the training session on Friday.
(c) The man will deliver an introductory speech on the session.
(d) The woman has ever taught the workers on the duties.

B 대화를 듣고 밑줄 친 부분에 해당하는 말을 따라 말하세요. 🎧 146

A: Mr. Wright called to tell me that the training session for new employees is this Friday.

B: ① _____

A: And he said that he wants you to assist with it.

B: ② _____

A: You're going to give the introductory speech and also train the workers on their basic duties.

B: ③ _____

Week 10 • Unit 02 197

Week 10 At the Office

Unit 03 Announcing a Conference

Listening 향상 팁

Listen for specific words 특정 단어 듣기

- 새로운 단어나 특정 단어를 더 잘 들으려면 이미 알고 있는 단어로 그 뜻을 이해하면 듣기와 암기에 도움이 된다.
  예시 accommodation: food and lodging 숙박   annual: happening every year 해마다 일어나는

- 두 개 이상의 의미를 가진 단어는 문맥에 따라 그 의미를 찾고 동의어나 동의 표현으로 패러프레이징 (Phraphrasing)을 하는 연습을 하면 도움이 된다.
  예시 **cover** travel expenses: pay for travel expenses 여행 비용을 **대다**
  cover the window: block the window 창문을 **가리다**
  cover the presentation: be responsible for the presentation 발표를 **책임지다**

A 다음을 듣고 같은 의미의 문장을 고르세요. 🎧 147

1. (a) Do you like Jazz? (b) Are you a musician?
2. (a) The offer is effective next week. (b) This offer expires next week.
3. (a) We have to make reports every three months.
   (b) We write these reports every other month.
4. (a) Use the non-stop bus to get there quickly.
   (b) Maybe I didn't express my desires clearly.
5. (a) The decision was fair to all the people involved.
   (b) She paid the cost of the taxi for the group.

B 맞으면 T를, 틀리면 F를 고르세요.

1. 새로운 단어를 익힐 때 대표적인 뜻 한 가지만 알면 된다. T F
2. 새로 익히는 어려운 단어를 이미 알고 있는 단어로 그 의미를 이해하면 암기가 쉽다. T F

Situation I

Warm-up

다음을 듣고 들은 것에 ✓표 하세요. 🎧 148

- ☐ the semi-annual conference
- ☐ mechanical engineers
- ☐ last
- ☐ keynote speech
- ☐ workshops
- ☐ brochures
- ☐ registration fee
- ☐ travel costs
- ☐ worthwhile

Practice

A 다음을 듣고 질문에 알맞은 답을 고르세요. 🎧 148

1. When will the annual conference be held in San Diego?
   (a) Next week
   (b) Next month
   (c) Next year

2. Who will pay the registration fee?
   (a) There is no fee.
   (b) The participant
   (c) The company

3. Who will pay for the travel expenses?
   (a) There are no expenses.
   (b) The participant
   (c) The company

B 다음을 듣고 질문에 알맞은 사진을 고르세요. 🎧 148

Q Who of the following will be interested in the conference?

(a)  (b)  (c)

Week 10 • Unit 03 199

C 다음을 듣고 맞으면 T를, 틀리면 F를 고르세요. 🎧 148

1 The annual conference for mechanical engineers will be held from July 19th to 22nd. T F

2 There will be only workshops at the conference. T F

Dictation

내용을 듣고 빈칸을 채우세요. 🎧 148

There is one more thing to mention before we finish this meeting. Next month, ① _____ _____ _____ for mechanical engineers will be held in San Diego. It's going to last from July 19th to 22nd. There are several great speakers, workshops, and other ② _____ _____ _____ . If you're interested, talk to Sylvia. She has ③ _____ _____ for the conference. You can attend the event, and we'll pay ④ _____ _____ _____ . However, the company won't be able to ⑤ _____ your ⑥ _____ _____ _____ _____ while you're there. Still, it might be ⑦ _____ _____ _____ to go.

*  부분은 특정 단어(Specific Words)에 해당하는 부분입니다.

Situation II

Warm-up

대화를 듣고 들은 것에 ✓표 하세요. 🎧 149

- ☐ website
- ☐ seriously
- ☐ Tuesday
- ☐ sponsoring
- ☐ keynote speaker
- ☐ get authorization
- ☐ a conference
- ☐ the top name values
- ☐ inquiry

Practice

A 대화를 듣고 내용과 알맞은 문장을 모두 고르세요. 🎧 149

(a) The woman found the information about the conference.
(b) Tina Struthers will give a keynote speech at the conference.
(c) The conference will be held from August 4th to 6th.
(d) Mr. Jenkins will go to the conference with them.

B 대화를 듣고 밑줄 친 부분에 해당하는 말을 따라 말하세요. 🎧 149

A: I saw on Marino Enterprises' website that the firm is sponsoring a conference next week.

B: ① _____

A: Well, the keynote speaker is Tina Struthers. She's one of the top names in the industry.

B: ② _____

A: On August 4th and 5th. That's Tuesday and Wednesday. We'll need to receive authorization from Mr. Jenkins to attend.

B: ③ _____

Week 10 • Unit 03 201

Week 10
At the Office

Unit 04 Overcoming Problems

Listening 향상 팁

Listen for gist 요지 파악하여 듣기

- 주요 내용(Main Idea, Key Points)을 소개하는 표현을 귀 기울여 듣도록 한다.
  - 예시 The purpose of my speech is… 제 연설의 목표는 ~
  - The important thing is… 중요한 것은 ~
  - The main point is… 요점은 ~
- 중요한 것은 반복하는 경우가 많으므로 반복되는 내용을 파악하면서 듣는다.
- 중요한 내용은 천천히 명확하게 말하는 경우가 많으므로 속도에 유의하여 듣는다.

A 다음을 듣고 알맞은 내용끼리 연결하여 문장을 완성하세요. 🎧 150

1. The purpose of my speech is •   • (a) that we have a new client.
2. The main point is •   • (b) we finish on time.
3. The important thing is •   • (c) to help you understand our policies.

B 다음을 듣고 문제가 무엇인지 고르세요. 🎧 151

(a) 샘플을 엉뚱한 주소로 보냈다.
(b) 상품들이 품질 관리 과정을 통과하지 못하고 있다.
(c) 고객 수가 줄고 있어 그 이유를 알아내야만 한다.

1 _____   2 _____   3 _____

C 맞으면 T를, 틀리면 F를 고르세요.

1. 요지는 항상 맨 앞에 말하므로 맨 처음만 잘 들으면 된다. T F
2. 주요 내용을 말할 때는 명확히 말하는 경우가 많으므로 속도에 유의하여 듣도록 한다. T F

Situation I

Warm-up

다음을 듣고 들은 것에 ✓표 하세요. 🎧 152

- ☐ announcement
- ☐ a crisis
- ☐ enough contracts
- ☐ unfortunately
- ☐ bidding on
- ☐ due
- ☐ by the end of next week
- ☐ financially stable
- ☐ meet your co-workers

Practice

A 다음을 듣고 질문에 알맞은 답을 고르세요. 🎧 152

1. What does the company lack to be profitable now?
   (a) Projects   (b) Contracts   (c) Customers

2. How many bids need to be won in order to become profitable again?
   (a) At least one   (b) At least two   (c) At least three

3. When is all bidding finished?
   (a) By the middle of next week
   (b) By the end of this month
   (c) By the beginning of next month

B 다음을 듣고 질문에 알맞은 사진을 고르세요. 🎧 152

Q Where can the team list be found?

(a)    (b)    (c)

C 다음을 듣고 맞으면 T를, 틀리면 F를 고르세요. 🎧 152

1 There are several projects for the company to bid on. T F
2 The projects can save the company financially. T F

Dictation

다음을 듣고 빈칸을 채우세요. 🎧 152

I've got an important ①_____ to make. We're in a bit of ②____ _____ because we don't have enough contracts to be profitable. Fortunately, there are several projects we're bidding on. Each bid ③____ _____ _____ the middle of next week. If we win at least two, we'll become ④_____ _____ again. But it's going to ⑤_____ _____ _____ by everyone to make sure that happens. I've assigned each of you to a team to work ⑥_____ _____ _____. I e-mailed the list to you now. So ⑦_____ _____ _____ and meet your teammates, and then let's get to work.

* 부분은 글의 요지(Gist)에 해당하는 부분입니다.

Situation II

Warm-up

대화를 듣고 들은 것에 ✓표 하세요. 🎧 153

- ☐ the sales report
- ☐ the wrong sales figures
- ☐ rewrite
- ☐ pretty happy
- ☐ June
- ☐ before afternoon
- ☐ apparently
- ☐ fix
- ☐ treat

Practice

A 대화를 듣고 대화 내용과 맞도록 문장을 완성하세요. 🎧 153

1 Ms. Powell is not happy with (the man's / the woman's) report.

2 The man inserted the (March / May) sales figures.

3 The (man / woman) will help to fix the sales report.

4 The man will (pay for / cook) lunch for the woman.

B 대화를 듣고 밑줄 친 부분에 해당하는 말을 따라 말하세요. 🎧 153

A: Jeremy. I got the sales report you wrote from Ms. Powell. She's pretty unhappy about it.

B: ① _____

A: Apparently. you inserted the wrong sales figures. The ones you used were for March. but you were supposed to put the May figures in the file.

B: ② _____

A: Yes. that's why Ms. Powell wanted me to speak with you. Let's go to my office and rewrite the report. We need to finish before noon.

B: ③ _____

Week 10 At the Office

Vocabulary

#		
1	address	연설; (문제를) 해결하다
2	agenda	(토론) 의제, 안건 (목록)
3	annual / quarterly report	연간 / 분기 보고서
4	balance sheet	대차대조표
5	bulletin board	알림판, 게시판
6	employee	직원[종업원]
7	employee morale	직원[종업원] 사기
8	employee of the month	이달의 직원[종업원]
9	experienced	경험이 많은
10	expert	전문가
11	financial statement	재무제표
12	gross income	총수입, 총연봉
13	human resources [HR]	인적 자원, 인사부
14	immediate boss [superior, supervisor]	직속 상관
15	income statement	손익계산서
16	in person	(사람이) 직접
17	join	합류하다
18	layoff	(주로 불경기로 인한) 정리 해고
19	manufacturing / production department	제작부
20	memorandum	메모, 회람

Memo

#	단어	뜻
21	motivation	동기, 동기 부여
22	notice	공지
23	online training	온라인 교육
24	on-the-job training	(실무) 현장 교육
25	operating profit	영업 이익
26	overcome	(부상 / 어려움을) 극복하다
27	paycheck	급여
28	payroll	급여 대상자 명단
29	pay stub	(미국식) 급여 명세서
30	pink slip	해고 통지서
31	presentation	발표
32	product demonstration	제품 시연
33	public relations department	홍보부
34	recruit	채용하다
35	relocation	(직원들) 발령, 전보
36	resolution	(문제 / 불화) 해결, 결의안
37	short notice	갑작스런 통지[통보]
38	solve	(문제를) 해결하다
39	unforeseen	예기치 않은
40	warm welcome	따뜻한 환영

Memo

EBS 생수다
생생한 영어 수다

Week 11 Business Trips

Unit 01 Renting a Car
Unit 02 At a Meeting Place
Unit 03 Business Lunch
Unit 04 Accepting Invitations

Week 11
Business Trips

Unit 01 Renting a Car

Listening 향상 팁

Listen for selective information 선택적으로 정보 듣기

- 선택적으로 정보를 잘 들으려면 그에 해당하는 질문을 하면서 듣는 습관이 필요하다. 특히 의문사를 활용한 질문에 답을 구하는 연습을 하면 도움이 된다.

  예시 I am calling to... ⋯▸ Why? 왜 전화 할까?
  I'll need a car from then to... ⋯▸ When? 언제까지 필요할까?
  Please call me back at... ⋯▸ What number? 몇 번으로 전화를 해야 할까?

- 주요 정보를 얻기 위해 장소, 시간과 같은 부사와 목적어가 되는 명사, to부정사, 동명사 등의 내용어를 중심으로 들으면 도움이 된다.

A 다음을 듣고 삐 소리가 나는 부분의 답을 얻기 위한 알맞은 의문사를 고르세요. 🎧 155

1 (a) who   (b) when   (c) where
2 (a) who   (b) when   (c) where
3 (a) who   (b) when   (c) where
4 (a) what   (b) why   (c) how
5 (a) how far   (b) how much   (c) how often

B 맞으면 T를, 틀리면 F를 고르세요.

1 구체적인 정보를 얻기 위해서는 문장의 모든 단어를 빠짐없이 들어야 한다.

2 필요한 정보를 얻기 위해 '언제, 어디서, 누가, 무엇을, 어떻게' 등과 같이 의문사로 시작하는 질문의 답을 구하면서 들으면 듣기 실력을 향상시킬 수 있다.

Situation I

Warm-up

다음을 듣고 들은 것에 ✓표 하세요.

- ☐ make a reservation
- ☐ flying to New Jersey
- ☐ January 12th
- ☐ good gas mileage
- ☐ easy to park
- ☐ accompanying
- ☐ a midsized car
- ☐ plenty of legroom
- ☐ any available vehicles

Practice

A 다음을 듣고 질문에 알맞은 답을 고르세요.

1 Why is Ms. Bryant calling?
   (a) To reserve a flight
   (b) To reserve a taxi
   (c) To reserve a car

2 When will Ms. Bryant return the car?
   (a) January 12th
   (b) January 19th
   (c) January 22nd

3 How many are there in Ms. Bryant's party?
   (a) One
   (b) Three
   (c) Four

B 다음을 듣고 질문에 알맞은 사진을 고르세요.

Q What type of car does Ms. Bryant want?

(a)

(b)

(c)

C 다음을 듣고 맞으면 T를, 틀리면 F를 고르세요. 🎧 156

1 Ms. Bryant will be driving very little.   T F
2 Ms. Bryant would like a car with plenty of legroom.   T F

Dictation

다음을 듣고 빈칸을 채우세요. 🎧 156

Hello. My name is Claudia Bryant. I'm calling to ① _____ _____ _____ for a car. I'm flying to ② _____ _____ _____ on January 12th. I'll need a car from then ③ _____ _____ _____. I'm going to be driving a lot, so I'd like a vehicle that gets ④ _____ _____ _____ and is ⑤ _____ _____ _____. In addition, there will be three people accompanying me. Therefore, we need a midsized car with ⑥ _____ _____ _____. Could you please call me back at 954-9404 to let me know if you have ⑦ _____ _____ _____ then? Thank you. Goodbye.

* _____ 부분은 차를 렌트하는 데 중요한 선택적인 정보(Selective Information)의 일부분입니다.

Situation II

Warm-up

대화를 듣고 대화와 관계 있는 사진을 고르세요. 🎧 157

(a)    (b)    (c)

Practice

A 대화를 듣고 대화 내용과 맞도록 문장을 완성하세요. 🎧 157

1 The man wants to rent (an economy car / an SUV).

2 The man needs the car for the next (three / five) days.

3 The man has to pay (as much as / more than) $75 if he wants an insurance.

B 대화를 듣고 밑줄 친 부분에 해당하는 말을 따라 말하세요. 🎧 157

A: ① _____

B: Yes, we do. What kind of car do you need?

A: ② _____

B: We've got one of those available. It will seat that many people in addition to your luggage.

A: ③ _____

B: We charge $75 a day to rent our SUV. If you need insurance, that will cost extra.

Week 11
Business Trips

Unit 02 At a Meeting Place

> **Listening 향상 팁**
>
> **Predict the purpose by the context** 문맥으로 목적 예측하기
>
> - 상황이나 문맥을 알면 어떤 내용인지 예측하는 것이 용이해진다. 예를 들어, TV에서 일기 예보를 보며 들으면 날씨와 관련된 표현을 예측할 수 있다.
>   예시 Temperatures are in the mid-20's ℃. 기온이 섭씨 20도 중반입니다.
>   We're expecting a thunderstorm. 뇌우가 예상됩니다.
>   It's going to freeze tonight. 오늘밤에는 기온이 영하가 되겠습니다.
>
> - 목적을 나타내는 표현이 들어간 문장을 유의하여 듣는다.
>   예시 (in order) to... ~하기 위해, ~하려고   so that... can/may ~ …가 ~하기 위해

A 다음을 듣고 빈칸에 알맞은 단어를 쓰세요. 🎧 158

1 Let's stay a little late this week _____ _____ we can finish this week.

2 ____ _____ _____ increase profits, we need to come up with a new plan.

B 다음을 듣고 내용에 알맞은 사진을 고르세요. 🎧 159

(a)    (b)    (c)

1 _____   2 _____   3 _____

C 맞으면 T를, 틀리면 F를 고르세요.

1 상황과 문맥을 이해하는 것은 듣기에 도움이 된다.

2 목적을 나타내는 표현으로는 in order to …, so that … may/can 등이 있다.

Situation I

Warm-up

다음을 듣고 들은 것에 ✓표 하세요. 🎧 160

- ☐ negotiations
- ☐ the merger
- ☐ executives
- ☐ CEO
- ☐ business cards
- ☐ make the lead
- ☐ the most knowledgeable
- ☐ speak out
- ☐ nothing else

Practice

A 다음을 듣고 질문에 알맞은 답을 고르세요. 🎧 160

1. Why are they travelling to Symington Manufacturing?
   (a) To discuss a contract
   (b) To negotiate a merger
   (c) To have a party

2. Why is Carter going to take a lead?
   (a) Because he knows about the merger very well.
   (b) Because he is the head of the delegation.
   (c) Because he is in charge of the merger.

3. What should the audience provide to the man when asked?
   (a) Their bags
   (b) Facts
   (c) Their opinions

B 다음을 듣고 질문에 알맞은 사진을 고르세요. 🎧 160

Q What will they exchange with the company they are visting?

(a)  (b)  (c)

C 다음을 듣고 맞으면 T를, 틀리면 F를 고르세요. 🎧 160

1 Everyone should introduce themselves and pass out business cards. T F

2 Everyone should share their opinions. T F

Dictation

다음을 듣고 빈칸을 채우세요. 🎧 160

Everyone, please listen carefully. We're about to arrive at Symington Manufacturing to ① _____ _____ _____ regarding ② _____ _____. We'll be met at the front desk by a couple of executives. Be sure to introduce yourselves and to pass out ③ _____ _____. Now, when the meeting starts, Carter is going to ④ _____ _____ _____ because he's the most knowledgeable on the topic. As for the rest of you, ⑤ _____ _____ _____ unless I ask you a question. In that case, I'd like you to provide the ⑥ _____ ____ _____ and nothing else. Just give facts, ⑦ _____ _____ .

* _____ 부분은 문맥으로 목적을 예측할 수 있는 부분입니다.

Situation II

Warm-up

대화를 듣고 대화와 관계 있는 사진을 고르세요.

(a)

(b)

(c)

Practice

A 대화를 듣고 내용과 알맞은 문장을 모두 고르세요.

(a) The woman is the guest for FTR productions.
(b) The woman wants to drink coffee.
(c) The woman will borrow a laptop from the man.
(d) The woman will let the man know the Wi-Fi password.

B 대화를 듣고 밑줄 친 부분에 해당하는 말을 따라 말하세요.

A: ① _____

B: Thank you very much.

A: ② _____

B: Coffee would be great.

A: ③ _____

B: Yes, please. I would.

Week 11 • Unit 02 217

Unit 03 Business Lunch

Week 11 Business Trips

Listening 향상 팁

Listen for discourse markers 담화 표지 듣기

- 담화 표지(Discourse Markers)는 구어에서 대화 내용의 이동을 나타내는 어구를 의미한다. 전환어(Transition Words)가 대표적인 담화 표지이다.
- 담화 표지의 의미와 역할을 이해하면 듣기와 말하기에 크게 도움이 된다.

상황	예시
대화를 시작할 때	Let's get started.
대화를 마무리 지을 때	so, to sum up
대화 주제로 다시 돌아올 때	anyway
앞에 한 말을 다시 한 번 더 반복할 때	what I mean is, in other words
상대방의 의견에 동의하거나 응대할 때	certainly, absolutely, definitely, exactly, great, sure, awful
상대방에게 자신의 생각을 제안할 때	Let's..., How/What about...? Why don't you...? Shall we...?

A 다음을 듣고 알맞은 담화 표지를 골라 문장을 완성하고, 그 역할을 고르세요. 🎧 162

(a) 대화를 마무리 지을 때 (b) 앞에 말한 내용을 다시 반복할 때
(c) 상대방 의견에 동의할 때 (d) 자신의 생각을 제안할 때

1 (Certainly! / Exactly!) That's the way it should be.　　_____
2 (How about / What about) 10 o'clock?　　_____
3 (In other words / What I mean is) we need to do it again.　　_____
4 (To sum up / So), that covers all I want to say.　　_____

B 맞으면 T를, 틀리면 F를 고르세요.

1 Why don't you...? 는 상대방에게 왜 안 하는지 이유를 물어보는 담화 표지이다.　T F

2 상대방에게 제안할 때 사용할 수 있는 표현으로 Shall we...? What about...? 등이 있다.　T F

Situation I

Warm-up

대화를 듣고 들은 것에 ✓표 하세요. 🎧 163

☐ agreeing to meet ☐ for lunch ☐ do some business
☐ shall you ☐ in that case ☐ why don't you
☐ several times before ☐ recommend ☐ seafood pizza

Practice

A 대화를 듣고 질문에 알맞은 답을 고르세요. 🎧 163

1 What meal will they be sharing?
   (a) Breakfast (b) Lunch (c) Dinner

2 How many times has the man been there before?
   (a) Never (b) Once (c) Several

3 Who recommends the seafood pasta?
   (a) The man (b) The woman (c) The waiter

B 대화를 듣고 질문에 알맞은 사진을 고르세요.

Q Where is the dialogue taking place?

(a)  (b)  (c)

C 다음을 듣고 맞으면 T를, 틀리면 F를 고르세요. 🎧 163

1 Only one of them has been there before. T F

2 They will discuss business after placing the order. T F

Dictation

대화를 듣고 빈칸을 채우세요. 🎧 163

A: Thank you for agreeing to meet me for lunch today. We can ① _____ _____ _____ while we eat.

B: It's no problem at all. ② _____ _____ look at the menu? I've never been here before.

A: In that case, ③ _____ _____ _____ let me order? I've been here several times in the past.

B: Sounds good. What do you recommend?

A: ④ _____ _____ the seafood pasta. I'll ⑤ _____ _____ _____ _____ so that I can order.

B: Great. After you order, ⑥ _____ _____ _____ to business then. We have ⑦ _____ _____ _____ _____ today.

* _____ 부분은 담화 표지(Discourse Markers)에 해당하는 부분입니다.

220 생생한 영어 수다

Situation II

Warm-up

대화를 듣고 들은 것에 ✓표 하세요. 🎧 164

- ☐ a bit more time
- ☐ entrée
- ☐ overall
- ☐ hoping to buy
- ☐ lowering
- ☐ a guarantee
- ☐ a specific number
- ☐ discuss the quantity
- ☐ all with that

Practice

A 대화를 듣고 내용과 알맞은 문장을 모두 고르세요. 🎧 164

(a) They are waiting for dessert.
(b) The price is higher than the man's expectation.
(c) The man will buy a certain amount of products every month.
(d) The number of products to purchase will be fixed at the next meeting.

B 대화를 듣고 밑줄 친 부분에 해당하는 말을 따라 말하세요. 🎧 164

A: I think we've got a bit more time until the entrée arrives. So what do you think of our offer?

B: ① _____

A: We can probably do that, but we'd need a guarantee that you'd buy a specific number of products every month.

B: ② _____

A: Excellent. Well, why don't we discuss the numbers that will satisfy both of us after we eat?

B: ③ _____

Week 11 • Unit 03   221

Week 11
Business Trips

Unit 04 Accepting Invitations

Listening 향상 팁

Listen for details 세부 사항 듣기

- 세부 사항은 주로 의문사 Who, What, When, Where, How, Why 등에 대한 답을 찾을 때가 많으므로 숫자, 장소, 시간 등을 나타내는 명사, 형용사, 부사에 유의해서 듣는 연습을 하도록 한다.
- 수락과 거절을 나타내는 표현을 미리 익혀 두고, 그 다음에 이어지는 세부 사항을 파악하도록 한다.

수락	거절
Sure.	No, thanks.
Sounds like a good idea.	Sounds good, but I can't...
Yes, I would.	I'd love to, but I can't...
I'd like to...	No, but thanks for V+-ing
I'd love to...	I'm afraid I can't...
Definitely	I'm sorry, but I can't accept.

A 다음을 듣고 알맞은 것끼리 연결하여 문장을 완성하세요. 🎧 165

1 Sure. •   • (a) I am so full now.
2 No, thanks. •   • (b) I will join you for lunch.
3 I'd love to. •   • (c) I will be there by noon.
4 Certainly. •   • (d) I have a deadline to meet.
5 I'm afraid I can't. •   • (e) How can I help you?

B 맞으면 T를, 틀리면 F를 고르세요.

1 상대방의 제안을 거절할 때 I'm sorry나 I'm afraid로 시작하면 공손하게 거절할 수 있다.

2 I'd like to는 상대방의 제안을 수락할 때, I'd like to, but...은 거절할 때 사용한다.

Situation I

Warm-up

다음을 듣고 들은 것에 ✓표 하세요. 🎧 166

- ☐ responding
- ☐ the e-mail
- ☐ inviting me
- ☐ for a conference
- ☐ a presentation
- ☐ newest products
- ☐ drop by
- ☐ three hours to show
- ☐ afterward

Practice

A 다음을 듣고 질문에 알맞은 답을 고르세요. 🎧 166

1 Why is the man responding to the e-mail?
   (a) To decline an invitation
   (b) To reschedule a meeting
   (c) To accept an invitation

2 What time does the man propose to stop by?
   (a) At 10 a.m.   (b) At 11 a.m.   (c) At noon

3 What does the man suggest doing after the demonstration?
   (a) Having lunch   (b) Having a meeting   (c) Taking a walk

B 다음을 듣고 질문에 알맞은 사진을 고르세요. 🎧 166

Q What most likely will the man do tomorrow at 11 a.m.?

(a)  (b)  (c)

C 다음을 듣고 맞으면 T를, 틀리면 F를 고르세요. 🎧 166

1. Mr. Stratford is excited to demonstrate some new products to Ms. Carpenter. T F

2. The meeting will take around two hours. T F

Dictation

다음을 듣고 빈칸을 채우세요. 🎧 166

Hello, Ms. Carpenter. This is Jerry Stratford responding to the e-mail you sent me this morning. Thank you for inviting me ① _____ _____ _____ _____ for a meeting. I'd be more than happy to give you ② _____ _____ _____ my firm's ③ _____ _____. It just so happens that I'm in Springfield right now, so I can drop by your office ④ _____ _____. How does ten in the morning sound? I'll need ⑤ _____ _____ _____ to show you everything. So I imagine I'll finish ⑥ _____ _____. Perhaps we can ⑦ _____ _____ _____ afterward. I'll see you tomorrow. Goodbye.

* _____ 부분은 시연에 관한 세부 사항(Details)에 해당하는 부분입니다.

Situation II

Warm-up

대화를 듣고 들은 것에 ✓표 하세요. 🎧 167

- ☐ interested
- ☐ our factory
- ☐ products
- ☐ technique
- ☐ in action
- ☐ about ten minutes
- ☐ absolutely
- ☐ impossible
- ☐ as well

Practice

A 대화를 듣고 대화 내용과 맞도록 문장을 완성하세요. 🎧 167

1. The man will arrive at (the factory / the lab) of a company.
2. Jason Schmidt works for (the man's / the woman's) company.
3. The company uses the new (machines / technique) now.

B 대화를 듣고 밑줄 친 부분에 해당하는 말을 따라 말하세요. 🎧 167

A: Mr. Porter, would you be interested in seeing our factory? I can show you how we manufacture our products.

B: ① _____

A: If you're not busy, we can go there right now.

B: ② _____

A: It sure does. You can see it in action in about five minutes. Shall we go?

B: ③ _____

Week 11 • Unit 04 225

Week 11 Business Trips

Vocabulary

#	Term	의미
1	agreement	협정, 합의, 합의서
2	annual general meeting [AGM]	연차 주주 총회
3	associate	(직장·사업) 동료; 결부하다
4	attire	의복, 복장
5	automatic transmission	(자동차의) 자동변속기
6	be at a standstill	교착 상태에 있다
7	business trip	출장
8	call a meeting	회의를 소집하다
9	car rental company [agency]	렌터카 회사
10	client	고객
11	collision damage waiver	(렌터카의) 충돌 파손에 관한 보험
12	compromise	절충하다; 절충, 절충안
13	contact information	연락처 정보
14	drop-off time / date	(렌터카) 반납 시간 / 일자
15	fuel policy	(렌터카의 기름의 채움 정도에 따른) 연료 규정
16	full to full	(렌터카의 기름을) 가득 채운 상태로 받아 다시 가득 채워 반납하는
17	get down to business	일을 착수[시작]하다
18	head count	인원수
19	hire	(단기간) 빌리다, 세내다, 고용하다
20	improve	향상하다

Memo

#	영어	한국어
21	inspection/observation tour	시찰 여행
22	item	(목록의) 항목
23	keep to the point	요점을 벗어나지 않다
24	leave ... open	~을 결정하지 않고 두다
25	mergers and acquisitions [M&A]	(기업) 인수 합병
26	minutes	회의록
27	move on to	(새로운 주제/일로) 넘어가다
28	option	선택 사항
29	pick-up location	(렌터카) 수령지
30	pick-up time / date	(렌터카) 수령 시간 / 일자
31	productive	생산성이 좋은
32	proposal	제안, 제안서
33	purpose of rental	(렌터카) 렌트[임대] 목적
34	request	요청하다; 요청
35	RSVP	(초대장에서) 회답 요망
36	share	(의견을) 나누다
37	surcharge	추가요금
38	travel expenses	출장 경비
39	travel on business	출장 가다
40	workshop	워크숍

EBS 생수다
생생한 영어 수다

Week 12 Speech / Presentation

- **Unit 01** Opening and Closing a Presentation
- **Unit 02** Linking Ideas
- **Unit 03** Emphasizing Important Points
- **Unit 04** Describing Graphs / Charts

Week 12
Speech / Presentation

Unit 01 Opening and Closing a Presentation

Listening 향상 팁

Listen for specific words 특정 단어 듣기

비즈니스 프레젠테이션 각 단계에서 유용한 표현

단계	예시
인사	Good morning! 좋은 아침입니다! Ladies and gentlemen, it's an honor to be here. 신사숙녀 여러분, 이 자리에 서게 되어 영광입니다. Thank you for coming. 와 주셔서 감사합니다.
발표자 소개	My name is Paul Edwards, the Director at Englishunt. 저는 잉글리시헌트 사의 부장인 폴 에드워즈입니다.
발표 제목 / 주제 소개	Today, I'd like to talk to you about... 오늘, 저는 여러분에게 ~에 관해 말하고 싶습니다. I'm going to speak about... ~에 관해 말하겠습니다. The purpose of this presentation is... 이 발표의 목적은 ~입니다. Today's topic is... 오늘의 주제는 ~입니다. The focus of my presentation is... 제 발표의 중심은 ~입니다. Today, I'm here to say... 오늘 저는 ~을 말하려고 왔습니다.
발표 마무리	That completes my presentation. 이렇게 제 발표를 마칩니다. That covers all I wanted to say today. 이렇게 오늘 발표하고 싶은 모든 것을 했습니다.

A 다음을 듣고 발표의 어느 단계인지 골라 ○표 하세요. 🎧 169

1 (a) 인사하기 (b) 마무리하기 2 (a) 주제 소개하기 (b) 소속 밝히기

3 (a) 주제 소개하기 (b) 이름 밝히기 4 (a) 주제 소개하기 (b) 마무리하기

B 맞으면 T를, 틀리면 F를 고르세요.

1 'It's an honor to be here...'는 발표를 마무리 지을 때 적합한 표현이다.

2 'I'm going to speak about...'은 발표 제목이나 주제를 소개하는 표현이다.

Situation I

Warm-up

다음을 듣고 들은 것에 ✓표 하세요. 🎧 170

- ☐ brand-new
- ☐ get it approving
- ☐ effects
- ☐ pharmaceutical
- ☐ suffering from
- ☐ dramatic
- ☐ next week
- ☐ heart diseases
- ☐ until the end

Practice

A 다음을 듣고 질문에 알맞은 답을 고르세요. 🎧 170

1 What type of products does Johnson Labs manufacture?
   (a) Medicine   (b) Computers   (c) Artificial hearts

2 When will Proximal be available for sale?
   (a) Next week   (b) Next month   (c) In 10 years

3 How many years did it take Johnson Labs to develop and get Proximal approved?
   (a) 5 years   (b) 10 years   (c) 15 years

B 다음을 듣고 질문에 알맞은 사진을 고르세요. 🎧 170

Q What body part does Proximal affect?

(a) 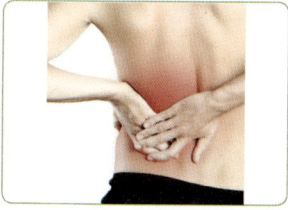   (b) 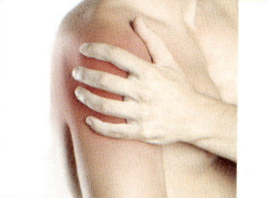   (c)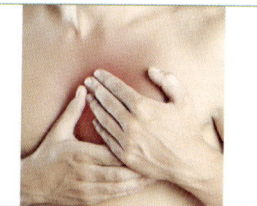

C 다음을 듣고 맞으면 T를, 틀리면 F를 고르세요. 🎧 170

1 Malorie Smith is speaking on behalf of Johnson Labs.　　T　F

2 Questions should be asked immediately.　　T　F

Dictation

다음을 듣고 빈칸을 채우세요. 🎧 170

Thank you for coming this morning. My name is Malorie Smith, and I represent Johnson Labs. Today, I'm going to speak about a brand-new ① _____ which my company will begin selling next month. It took us ten years to develop and ② ____ ____ _____, but I believe that time was well spent. This medicine, which we call Proximal, will be used by ③ _____ _____ _____ various ④ _____ _____. ⑤ ____ _____ of Proximal are dramatic. I'll tell you all about them ⑥ ____ ____ _____. If you would ⑦ _____ _____ until the end, I'd appreciate it. Now, let me begin.

*　　부분은 약품 관련 특정 단어(Specific Words)입니다.

Situation II

Warm-up

대화를 듣고 대화와 관계 있는 사진을 고르세요. 🎧 171

(a) 　(b) 　(c)

Practice

A 다음을 듣고 내용과 맞도록 문장을 완성하세요. 🎧 171

1 The woman is about to (begin / finish) her presentation.

2 The woman is (introducing / considering) what the R&D Department does.

3 Some of the products that the R&D Department is working on would be (profitable / costly).

B 다음을 듣고 밑줄 친 부분에 해당하는 말을 따라 말하세요. 🎧 171

And that brings me to the end of my presentation.

① _____

While we have several products that should be able to be marketed this year, we also have many others in the pipeline.

② _____

Now, since I have concluded my remarks, I'd like to allow everyone here to speak up.

③ _____

Unit 02 Linking Ideas

Week 12 Speech/Presentation

Listening 향상 팁

Listen for collocations 연어로 듣기

- 연어(Collocation)는 'co (함께) + location (위치)'이라는 단어의 조합처럼, 특정한 뜻을 나타낼 때 흔히 함께 쓰이는 단어들의 결합을 의미한다.
- 원어민들은 일상 대화에서 2~3,000개의 단어로 크게 불편하지 않게 의사소통을 하는데, 이는 단어들을 적절히 조합하여 연어를 많이 활용하기 때문이다.
- 연어의 예시

형용사 + 명사	동사 + 명사
brief introduction 간단한 소개	wear shoes 신발을 신다
brief summary 간략한 요약	wear glasses 안경을 쓰다
brief overview 간단한 개요	wear a watch 시계를 차다
brief meeting 간단한 회의	wear perfume 향수를 뿌리다

A 다음 연어의 예를 듣고 빈칸에 알맞은 공통 단어를 쓰세요. 🎧 172

1. (a) short-term _____ 단기 목표   (b) main _____ 주요 목표
2. (a) _____ project 진행 중인 프로젝트   (b) _____ conflict 지속적인 분쟁
3. (a) _____ research 광범위한 연구   (b) _____ knowledge 해박한 지식
4. (a) _____ money 돈을 모금하다   (b) _____ a child 아이를 기르다

B 맞으면 T를, 틀리면 F를 고르세요.

1. 특정한 뜻을 나타낼 때 흔히 함께 쓰이는 단어들의 결합을 연어라고 한다
2. 연어는 '형용사 + 명사,' '명사 + 동사' 등 다양한 형태의 결합이 가능하다.

Situation I

Warm-up

다음을 듣고 들은 것에 ✓표 하세요. 🎧 173

- ☐ opening remarks
- ☐ the heart of the matter
- ☐ private investment
- ☐ expand our equipment
- ☐ popularity
- ☐ purchase requests
- ☐ the high supply
- ☐ raise
- ☐ attainable aim

Practice

A 다음을 듣고 질문에 알맞은 답을 고르세요. 🎧 173

1 What is the main problem?
   (a) The demand is too high.
   (b) The demand is too low.
   (c) The machines are broken.

2 How much money do they need to raise?
   (a) $500,000
   (b) $50,000,000
   (c) $500,000,000

3 What would the group most likely discuss right after the man's remark?
   (a) How to raise the money
   (b) How to train employees
   (c) How to sell products more

B 다음을 듣고 질문에 알맞은 사진을 고르세요. 🎧 173

Q What do they want to expand?

(a) 　(b) 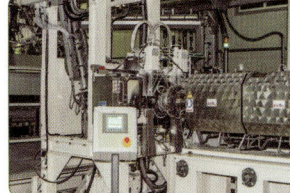　(c)

C 다음을 듣고 맞으면 T를, 틀리면 F를 고르세요. 🎧 173

1 Their products are extremely popular.   T F

2 Speaker has no idea how to raise the money needed.   T F

Dictation

다음을 듣고 빈칸을 채우세요. 🎧 173

Now that I've ① _____ my opening remarks, I'd like to get to the heart of the matter. We need to come up with ② _____ _____ _____ so that we can ③ _____ _____ _____ this year. ④ _____ _____ the popularity of our products, we're getting more and more purchase requests than ever. But we're not able to ⑤ _____ _____ _____ _____ for our items right now. I've come up with a few ideas on how we can ⑥ _____ _____ _____ we need. It won't be easy to raise half a billion dollars, but I believe it's ⑦ _____ _____ _____.

*  부분은 연어(Collocation)를 이루는 부분입니다.

Situation II

Warm-up

다음을 듣고 들은 것에 ✓표 하세요. 🎧 174

- ☐ considerable
- ☐ fortunately
- ☐ the solutions
- ☐ feasible
- ☐ come up with
- ☐ create a task project
- ☐ this ongoing project
- ☐ extensive research
- ☐ let her discuss

Practice

A 다음을 듣고 내용과 알맞은 문장을 모두 고르세요. 🎧 174

(a) Their client likes the results of the Washington Project.

(b) The woman's company needs to make a new solution.

(c) April Devine is the client who is not happy with the solutions.

(d) April Devine will continue to lead the meeting.

B 다음을 듣고 밑줄 친 부분에 해당하는 말을 따라 말하세요. 🎧 174

We've spent a considerable amount of time on the Washington Project.

① _____

He claims they're both expensive and unfeasible. We therefore need to come up with some new ideas.

② _____

It's going to be led by April Devine, who has done extensive research on this type of situation.

③ _____

Unit 03 Emphasizing Important Points

Week 12 Speech/Presentation

Listening 향상 팁

Listen for stressed words 강세어 듣기

- 강세(Stress)를 받는 부분이 다르면 같은 문장이라도 그 의미가 달라진다.
    예시 It SOUNDS LIKE rain. 빗소리 같다.
    → 물 떨어지는 소리가 마치 빗소리 같다는 의미 (진짜로 비가 오는 게 아니다)
    It sounds like RAIN. 비가 오는 것 같다.
    → 물 떨어지는 소리가 비 오는 소리라는 의미 (진짜로 비가 오는 중이다)

- 강세를 받는 부분은 크고 길게 발음되므로 강세를 받는 부분만 들어도 그 문장을 이해할 수 있다.
    예시 Will you WALK my DOG to the PARK? 내 개를 공원에 산책시켜 주실래요?
    → WALK, DOG, PARK만 들어도 개를 공원에 산책시켜 달라는 의미를 쉽게 유추할 수 있다.

강세를 받을 수 있는 것	일반적으로 강세를 받지 않는 것
내용어(Content Words) : 동사, 명사, 형용사, 부사	기능어(Function Words) : 전치사, 관사, 대명사

A 다음을 잘 듣고 강세를 받는 부분에 유의하여 알맞은 해석을 고르세요. 🎧 175

1 I called Tom yesterday.   •   • (a) 바로 내가 톰에게 어제 전화를 했다.

2 I CALLED Tom yesterday. •   • (b) 나는 어제 존이 아니라 톰에게 전화를 했다.

3 I called TOM yesterday.   •   • (c) 나는 어제 톰을 찾아간 것이 아니라 전화를 했다.

B 다음을 잘 듣고 강세를 받는 부분을 모두 ○표 하세요.

1 Do you like to watch a movie?   2 Did she give her presentation yesterday?

C 맞으면 T를, 틀리면 F를 고르세요.

1 중요한 정보를 전달하는 명사, 형용사, 부사, 동사는 강세를 받는다.   T F

2 강세를 받는 부분은 더 강하고 길게 읽는다   T F

Situation I

Warm-up

다음을 듣고 들은 것에 ✓표 하세요. 🎧 176

- ☐ projections
- ☐ make a profit
- ☐ reiterate
- ☐ half a billion dollars
- ☐ the first profit
- ☐ an enormous one
- ☐ this sudden turnaround
- ☐ our newest toothbrush
- ☐ naturally

Practice

A 다음을 듣고 질문에 알맞은 답을 고르세요. 🎧 176

1 Why is $500,000 significant?
   (a) It is a loss.   (b) It is an investment.   (c) It is their first profit.

2 What caused the change?
   (a) A popular ad   (b) The sales team   (c) Good prices

3 How old is the company?
   (a) Less than one year old   (b) 3 years old   (c) 5 years old

B 다음을 듣고 질문에 알맞은 사진을 고르세요. 🎧 196

Q What is advertised in the ad?

(a) 　(b) 　(c)

C 다음을 듣고 맞으면 T를, 틀리면 F를 고르세요. 🎧 176

1 This company never had a profit before.　　　　　　　　　　T F

2 The sales doubled.　　　　　　　　　　　　　　　　　　　T F

Dictation

다음을 듣고 빈칸을 채우세요. 🎧 176

According to our projections, we're set to make a profit of $500,000 this year. Let me reiterate. That's ① _____ ___ _____ dollars ② ____ _____. We're going to make ③ ____ _____ _____ in our five-year history. And we're going to make ④ ____ _____ _____. So what's the reason for this sudden turnabout? It's simple. One of our ads ⑤ _____ _____ on the Internet, so that ⑥ _____ _____ _____ us. The ad was for our newest toothpaste, so sales went up. How far up? They went up ⑦ _____. Naturally, sales of other products increased, so everything started selling well.

* 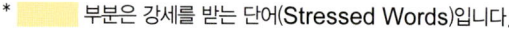 부분은 강세를 받는 단어(Stressed Words)입니다.

Situation II

Warm-up

대화를 듣고 들은 것에 ✓표 하세요. 🎧 177

- ☐ the audience
- ☐ developed
- ☐ a fast computer chip
- ☐ 15% faster
- ☐ on the market
- ☐ serious
- ☐ absolutely
- ☐ revolution
- ☐ on your arms

Practice

A 대화를 듣고 내용과 알맞은 문장을 모두 고르세요. 🎧 177

(a) They are mainly talking about a computer chip.
(b) The computer chip is 50% faster and cheaper than its old model.
(c) The computer chip costs less than most of the chips now.
(d) The man's company started a revolution.

B 대화를 듣고 밑줄 친 부분에 해당하는 말을 따라 말하세요. 🎧 177

A: Now that I've concluded my remarks, does anyone in the audience have a question?

B: ① _____

A: It's more than 50% faster than anything available on the market.

B: ② _____

A: Absolutely. Not only is it that much quicker than anything else, but we can manufacture it for a cheaper price than most of the chips on the market today.

B: ③ _____

Week 12
Speech / Presentation

Unit 04 Describing Graphs / Charts

Listening 향상 팁

Listen for details 세부 사항 듣기

- 그래프나 도표를 묘사할 때 쓰는 단어

그래프나 도표 모양	단어
상향, 증가할 때	expand, go up, grow, increase, rise
하향, 감소할 때	decline, decrease, drop, fall, go down
증가/감소하다가 차츰 평평해질 때	flatten out, level off
변화가 없을 때	remain/stay constant/stable
변화의 정도를 나타낼 때	considerably, dramatically, moderately, significantly, slightly
변화의 속도를 나타낼 때	gradually, quickly, rapidly, slowly, steadily, suddenly

A 다음을 듣고 알맞은 그래프를 고르세요. 🎧 178

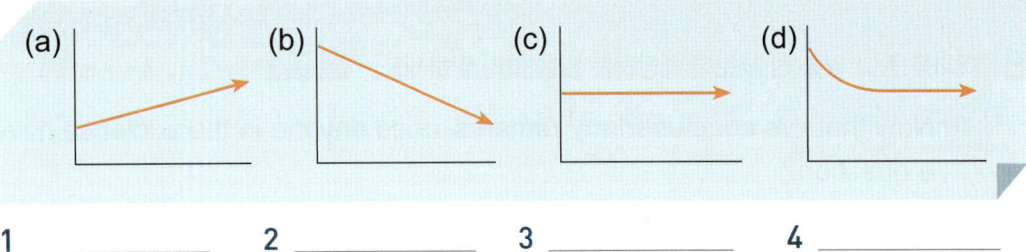

1 _____   2 _____   3 _____   4 _____

B 맞으면 T를, 틀리면 F를 고르세요.

1 매출액이나 이익이 증가할 때 사용할 수 있는 표현은 **decrease, fall** 등이 있다.   T F

2 급격하게 증가하거나 감소할 때 **moderately, slightly** 등을 사용할 수 있다.   T F

Situation I

Warm-up

다음을 듣고 들은 것에 ✓표 하세요. 🎧 179

- ☐ pie chart
- ☐ at 35%
- ☐ remainder
- ☐ marketing share
- ☐ in third place
- ☐ bar graph
- ☐ top position
- ☐ at 10%
- ☐ has been changing

Practice

A 다음을 듣고 질문에 알맞은 답을 고르세요. 🎧 179

1. What is the group looking at?
   (a) A graph (b) A chart (c) A picture

2. What place is this company in?
   (a) 1st (b) 2nd (c) 3rd

3. What is the visual aid demonstrating?
   (a) It shows market share.
   (b) It shows profit share.
   (c) It shows price chart.

B 다음을 듣고 질문에 알맞은 사진을 고르세요. 🎧 179

Q What kind of industry does the man's company belong to?

(a)
(b)
(c)

C 다음을 듣고 맞으면 T를, 틀리면 F를 고르세요. 🎧 179

1 Everyone is invited to look at a flow chart.　　　　T　F

2 Fourth position has 10% of the overall market share.　　　　T　F

Dictation

다음을 듣고 빈칸을 채우세요. 🎧 179

Please take a look at ① _____ _____ _____ up on the screen. This shows ② _____ _____ _____ for businesses in ③ _____ _____ _____ industry. As you can see, Anderson Construction has the top position ④ _____ _____. However, we're right behind ⑤ _____ _____ _____ at 25%, and we've been ⑥ _____ _____ _____ _____ lately. In third place, at 14%, is Kelly Construction, and the JT Company is in fourth place at 10%. Several smaller companies are getting the remainder of the business. Now, here's a graph that shows how each company's market share ⑦ _____ _____ _____ this year.

* _____ 부분은 발표에 관한 세부 사항(Details)에 해당하는 부분입니다.

Situation II

Warm-up

대화를 듣고 대화와 관계 있는 그림을 고르세요. 🎧 180

(a) 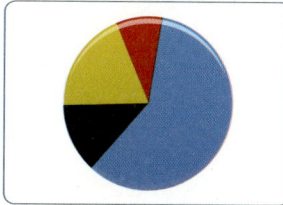 (b) 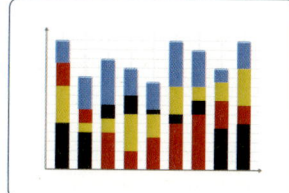 (c)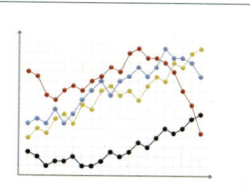

Practice

A 대화를 듣고 대화 내용과 맞도록 문장을 완성하세요. 🎧 180

1 The spending of their company has (increased / decreased) over the last six months.

2 The company's revenue is (ramaning steady / going up) lately.

3 The company's spending is getting (under / out of) control now.

B 대화를 듣고 밑줄 친 부분에 해당하는 말을 따라 말하세요. 🎧 180

A: This is a line graph showing spending in the past six months.

B: ① _____

A: That's correct. Since January. our spending has increased 77% on a monthly basis. That's simply unsustainable.

B: ② _____

A: I've got another graph here. Revenue has been holding steady at around $2 million per month.

B: ③ _____

Week 12 Speech / Presentation

Vocabulary

#	단어	뜻
1	adapt	(새로운 용도/상황에) 적응하다, 맞추다
2	accurate	정확한
3	anticipate	예상하다
4	audio-visual aids	시청각 자료[교구]
5	bar graph	막대 그래프
6	cost-effective	비용 효율이 높은[가성비가 좋은]
7	creativity	창의성, 창조력
8	customer survey	고객 설문
9	decline	(수/가치/실적이) 감소하다, 떨어지다, 하락하다
10	efficiency	효율성
11	emphasize	강조하다
12	figure	수치, 숫자
13	finish up	끝내다, 마치다, (결국) ~에 이르다
14	follow-up	후속의, 후속 조치
15	forecast	예측하다, 전망하다
16	go over	~을 검토하다
17	handout	유인물
18	illustrate	(삽화/도해를) 넣다, (삽화/도해를 넣어) 설명하다
19	in brief	간단히 말해
20	increase	(수/가치/실적이) 증가하다, 늘어나다

Memo

#	영어	한국어
21	innovation	혁신, 혁신책
22	objective	목표, 목적
23	outline	개요를 보여주다; 개요
24	overview	개관, 개요
25	pie chart	파이 차트
26	pointer	포인터
27	profitable	이익이 되는, 돈이 되는
28	projector	프로젝터, 영사기
29	put it another way	그것을 바꾸어 말하다
30	relevant	(논의 중인 주제와) 관련 있는, 적절한
31	run out of time	시간이 부족하다
32	slide	슬라이드
33	statistics	통계, 통계학
34	strategy	전략
35	strength	장점
36	summarize	요약하다
37	time frame	(어떤 일에 쓰이는 / 쓸 수 있는) 기간
38	USB Flash Drive	USB 메모리
39	visual	시각의; 시각 자료
40	weakness	단점

정답 및 스크립트

Answer Key & Script

Week 01 At the Airport
Unit 01 Checking In

Listening 향상 팁 p.10

A 1 Come on in.   2 He's the tallest of all.
   3 What's up?   4 He's on another line.
   5 How much is it?   6 I'm not tired at all.

B 1 of   2 it an old   3 in   4 it, all

C 1 T   2 T

Situation I pp. 11-12

Attention passengers. To ensure speedy service, please remember to have all your travel documents ready before you reach the check-in counter. Two forms of ID are required, or one form of ID plus an e-ticket. Self check-in kiosks are available for passengers with their travel documents and flight numbers ready. We encourage you to use the kiosks for speedier service.

승객 여러분께 안내 말씀 드립니다. 빠른 서비스를 위해 체크인 카운터에 가기 전에 모든 여행 서류를 준비하는 것을 잊지 마세요. 두 종류의 신분증이나, 신분증 하나와 e-티켓이 필요합니다. 무인 탑승 수속기에서 하는 셀프 체크인은 여행 서류와 항공편 번호가 준비된 승객이 이용하실 수 있습니다. 더욱 빠른 수속을 위해서는 무인 탑승 수속기 이용을 권장합니다.

Warm-up

passengers, ensure, speedy service, remember, travel documents, flight numbers

Practice

A 1 (b)   2 (a)   3 (b)   **B** (b)   **C** 1 T   2 T

Dictation

① have all   ② ready   ③ check-in   ④ forms of
⑤ an e-ticket   ⑥ encourage you   ⑦ speedier

Situation II p. 13

A: Hello. Good morning, sir. Where are you flying to today?
B: I'm on my way to Vancouver. I was trying to use the kiosks, but I couldn't get it to load.
A: Well, we can check you in here. Do you have your IDs or an e-ticket?
B: Here are my IDs, but I didn't bring an e-ticket with me.
A: No problem, sir. This will be fine. Any bags to check?
B: Yes, just this one, please.

A: 안녕하세요. 좋은 아침입니다. 오늘 어디로 비행 가시나요?
B: 밴쿠버로 가는 중입니다.
   무인 탑승 수속기를 이용하려고 했는데 잘 되지 않았어요.
A: 그럼 여기서 체크인 해드리겠습니다.
   신분증이나 e-티켓 있으신가요?
B: 여기 제 신분증입니다. 그런데 e-티켓은 가져오지 않았어요.
A: 문제 없습니다. 이걸로도 괜찮아요. 부칠 가방 있으십니까?
B: 네. 이거 하나 부탁드려요.

Warm-up

flying, on my way, the kiosks, IDs, e-ticket, bags to check

Practice

A (a), (c)

B ① I'm on my way to Vancouver. I was trying to use the kiosks, but I couldn't get it to load.
   ② Here are my IDs, but I didn't bring an e-ticket with me.
   ③ Yes, just this one, please.

Unit 02 Security Checkpoint

Listening 향상 팁 p. 14

A 1 (a)   2 (c)

There will be two machines: an X-ray machine and a metal detector. The X-ray machine has a conveyor belt that you put your bags on. Lay your bags flat, but take out your laptop. Please do not put your passport and boarding pass in your bag; the staff needs to see them. You should use the plastic bins for small items like your phone, keys, or coins. Please make sure that you take coins, keys, or anything metal out of your pockets. If you need to remove your belt or shoes, the security staff will tell you. Then, walk through the metal detector.

엑스레이기와 금속탐지기, 이렇게 두 종류의 기계가 있습니다. 엑스레이기에 있는 컨베이어 벨트에 가방을 누세요. 가방을 놓혀 두는데, 그 안의 노트북은 꺼내세요. 여권과 탑승권을 가방 안에 두지 마세요. 직원들이 그것들을 봐야 합니다. 플라스틱 통에 전화기, 열쇠, 동전과 같이 조그만 물품을 두세요. 동전, 열쇠, 혹은 다른 금속 종류는 반드시 주머니에서 꺼내세요. 여러분이 허리띠나 구두를 벗어야만 한다면, 보안 요원이 지시를 할 것입니다. 그리고 금속탐지기를 통과하세요.

B 1 conveyor belt **2** metal detector **C 1** T **2** F

Situation I
pp. 15-16

All liquids must be together in one clear bag with 100ml or less of each liquid. No exceptions will be made. No lighters, knives, or other items that may be considered weapons will be allowed beyond the security checkpoint. Empty your pockets and remove all coats, shoes, and belts before passing through the scanning machine. If you are carrying a laptop or tablet PC, please take it out of your bag and place it in a bin on the conveyor belt.

모든 액체류는 반드시 100ml 또는 그 이하의 액체 각각을 투명한 가방 하나에 함께 담아야 합니다. 예외는 없습니다. 라이터, 칼, 또는 무기로 간주되는 다른 물품들은 보안 검색대 너머로 가져가실 수 없습니다. 보안 검색대를 통과하기 전에 주머니를 비우시고, 코트와 신발과 벨트를 모두 벗어 주세요. 노트북이나 태블릿 PC를 소지하신 분은 가방에서 꺼내어 컨베이어 벨트 위에 있는 통에 넣어주세요.

Warm-up

liquids, exceptions, knives, scanning machine, tablet PC, conveyor belt

Practice

A 1 (b) **2** (c) **3** (c) **B** (b) **C 1** F **2** T

Dictation

① together ② 100ml or less ③ No exceptions
④ lighters, knives ⑤ Empty ⑥ coats, shoes
⑦ out of

Situation II
p. 17

A: Hello, sir. Please empty your pockets.
B: Do I need to remove my jacket, shoes, and belt, too?
A: Yes, sir. No exceptions I'm afraid.
B: It's okay. Just checking.
A: Do you have any items off the banned item list in your luggage such as lighters and knives?
B: Oh, I do have a lighter in my pocket. Can you throw this away for me, please?

A: 안녕하세요. 주머니를 비워주세요.
B: 제 재킷과 신발, 벨트를 모두 벗어야 하나요?
A: 네, 죄송하지만 예외는 없습니다.
B: 괜찮아요. 그냥 확인한 거예요.
A: 라이터나 칼과 같이 금지 품목 리스트에 있는 물건이 수하물에 있습니까?
B: 아, 주머니에 라이터가 있어요. 이것을 대신 버려 주시겠어요?

Warm-up

(a), (b), (d), (f)

Practice

A 1 security checkpoint **2** something
3 a lighter

B ① Do I need to remove my jacket, shoes, and belt, too?
② It's okay. Just checking.
③ Oh, I do have a lighter in my pocket. Can you throw this away for me, please?

Unit 03 Waiting to Board

Listening 향상 팁
p. 18

A 1 (c) **2** (b)

A: Excuse me. I couldn't quite hear the announcement. What did you say?
B: I'm very sorry, but we've had a gate change. The flight will leave from Gate C50 now.
A: Oh, okay. Where is it?
B: It's 5 gates down from here. Just please keep going this way.
A: Has the departure time changed then?
B: No sir, it will depart on time at 4:25 and boarding will begin in 15 minutes.

A: 실례합니다. 안내 방송을 제대로 못 들어서요. 뭐라고 했죠?
B: 죄송합니다만, 탑승구가 변경되었습니다. 비행기는 C50 탑승구에서 출발할 것입니다.
A: 아, 그렇군요. 그게 어디죠?
B: 여기에서부터 탑승구 다섯개를 지나면 있습니다. 그냥 이 길로 쭉 가세요.
A: 그러면 출발 시간이 바뀌었나요?
B: 아니요.. 4:25 제시간에 떠날 것이므로 탑승은 15분 후에 시작할 겁니다.

B 1 (b)　2 (a)　3 (a)　4 (b)

1 20　2 14　3 3:30　4 5:45

C 1 F　2 T

Situation I
pp. 19-20

Attention passengers on flight 30 bound for New York with a stop in Atlanta. The departure gate has been changed to 18B. The gate change has caused a boarding delay of 15 minutes. Boarding will begin at 4:50. Again, please note that the boarding gate for flight 30 to New York has changed to 18B. Boarding will begin 15 minutes late at 4:50.

애틀란타를 경유하는 뉴욕행 비행기 30편을 타시는 승객 여러분께 안내 말씀 드립니다. 출발 탑승구가 18B로 변경되었습니다. 탑승구 변경으로 인해 탑승이 15분 지연되었습니다. 탑승은 4시 50분에 시작될 예정입니다. 다시 한번 말씀 드립니다. 뉴욕행 비행기 30편의 탑승구가 18B로 변경되었음에 유의하시기 바랍니다. 탑승은 15분 늦은 4시 50분에 시작될 예정입니다.

Warm-up
flight 30, New York, the departure gate, 18B, boarding gate, 4:50

Practice
A 1 (b)　2 (a)　3 (c)　　B (b)　　C 1 F　2 F

Dictation
① flight 30　② 18B　③ delay　④ 15　⑤ 4:50
⑥ note　⑦ late

Situation II
p. 21

A: Excuse me, is the gate for flight 30 bound for New York changed?
B: Yes, the gate has been changed from 10B to 18B.
A: Has the boarding time changed too then?
B: Yes, boarding has been delayed 15 minutes and will start at 4:50.
A: Okay, good. Which way is Gate 18B?
B: It's in the same terminal, so just continue walking that way.

A: 실례합니다. 뉴욕행 비행기 30편의 탑승구가 변경되었나요?
B: 네. 탑승구가 10B에서 18B로 변경되었습니다.
A: 탑승 시간도 변경되었나요?
B: 네. 탑승은 15분 지연되어 4시 50분에 시작될 예정입니다.
A: 네, 좋아요. 18B 탑승구는 어느 쪽인가요?
B: 같은 터미널에 있으니, 그냥 저 길로 쭉 걸어가시면 됩니다.

Warm-up
flight 30, New York, 10B, changed, boarding time, Gate 18B

Practice
A (b)

B ① Yes, the gate has been changed from 10B to 18B.
　② Yes, boarding has been delayed 15 minutes and will start at 4:50.
　③ It's in the same terminal, so just continue walking that way.

Unit 04 Immigration Control

Listening 향상 팁

A 1 (b)　2 (b)　3 (a)

1 (a) It is a very long trip. 정말 긴 여행이었어요.
　(b) For a week 일주일이요.
2 (a) None of your business. 상관 마세요.
　(b) At my cousin's 사촌 집에요.
3 (a) To visit my relatives 친척들을 방문하려고
　(b) I had a great time. 좋은 시간 보냈어요.

B **1** (d) **2** (c) **3** (b)

1 Do you have any seating preference for an aisle or a window seat?
복도 자리와 창가 자리 중에 선호하시는 좌석이 있으신가요?

2 Will you please put your bag in the overhead bin?
당신의 가방을 객석 위에 있는 짐칸에 좀 넣어주시겠어요?

3 Where are you flying to today?
오늘 비행기를 타고 어디 가시나요?

C **1** F **2** T

Situation I
pp. 23-24

Please be sure you have all your immigration documents ready. Immigration officials will need to see your passport, boarding pass, and visa documentation. Those with return or forwarding flights need to show all of their onward travel documents to officers. Please wait behind the yellow line for the next available officer. Only one person at a time is allowed to approach the immigration desk.

반드시 모든 입국 서류들을 준비하도록 하십시오. 입국 심사관은 여러분의 여권, 탑승권, 비자 서류를 확인해야 합니다. 왕복 또는 차후 비행기편을 이용하시는 분들은 향후 여행 서류들을 모두 입국 심사관에게 보여 주셔야 합니다. 노란 선 뒤에 서서 이용 가능한 다음 입국 심사관을 기다리시죠. 입국 심사대에는 한 번에 한 사람만 허용됩니다.

Warm-up (a), (c)

Practice

A **1** (c) **2** (c) **3** (b)   **B** (b)   **C** **1** T **2** T

Dictation

① ready ② passport, boarding pass
③ behind the yellow ④ available ⑤ one
⑥ a time ⑦ immigration

Situation II
p. 25

A: Next passenger, please step forward with all your immigration documents.
B: Good morning. Here is my passport and boarding pass.
A: Thank you. How long will you be traveling?
B: My wife and I are going to be in Europe for two weeks.
A: Ma'am. Please wait behind the yellow line. Only one person at a time.
B: It's my wife. She's just excited.

A: 다음 승객분, 입국 심사 서류를 모두 가지고 앞으로 오세요.
B: 안녕하세요. 여기 제 여권과 탑승권입니다.
A: 감사합니다. 얼마나 오랫동안 여행하실 건가요?
B: 아내와 저는 유럽에 2주 동안 있을 예정입니다.
A: 손님, 노란 선 뒤에서 기다려주세요. 한 번에 한 사람입니다.
B: 제 아내예요. 그냥 좀 신이 났나 봐요.

Warm-up (a)

Practice

A (a), (c)

B ① Good morning. Here is my passport and boarding pass.
② My wife and I are going to be in Europe for two weeks.
③ It's my wife. She's just excited.

Week 02 On the Plane
Unit 01 Emergency Procedures on the Plane

Listening 향상 팁
p. 30

A 1 There is a life vest / under your seat.
2 I am sorry I can't, / but I can give you a blanket.
3 She tried her best / to succeed.
4 Unfortunately, / it was delayed.

B **1** 3개 **2** 2개

1 I left my cell phone / in my room / this morning.
오늘 아침 나는 내 방에 핸드폰을 두고 왔습니다.

2 The plane for Chicago / was delayed.
시카고 행 비행기가 지연되었습니다.

C **1** T **2** F

Situation I

pp. 31-32

Please pay attention to the safety video and the cabin crew as we begin our safety demonstration. Take a moment to notice the cabin crew indicating where the exits are. In the case of an emergency landing, please assume the position shown on the screen. Should a water landing occur, there is a life vest under your seat. Please follow the instructions of the cabin crew at all times.

안전 시범 교육을 시작하오니 안전 비디오와 승무원을 주목해 주시기 바랍니다. 출구의 위치를 가리키고 있는 승무원을 잠시 주의해서 보십시오. 비상 착륙의 경우에는 화면에 보이는 자세를 취해 주십시오. 바다에 불시착하는 경우가 발생하면 좌석 밑에 구명조끼가 있습니다. 항상 승무원의 지시를 따라 주십시오.

Warm-up

cabin crew, demonstration, indicating, in the case of, under your seat, at all times

Practice

A 1 (a) 2 (b) 3 (b)   **B** b   **C** 1 T 2 T

Dictation

① as ② Take a moment ③ indicating
④ In the case of ⑤ please assume
⑥ under your seat ⑦ at all times

Situation II

p. 33

A: Yes, ma'am. You rang for service?
B: Yes, I'm afraid I find it very cold in here. Can you turn down the air conditioning?
A: I'm sorry you are feeling cold. Unfortunately the air circulation system is what makes it feel cold.
B: So you can't adjust it?
A: I'm sorry I can't, but I can offer you a blanket. Would you like one?
B: Oh yes, please. That would be great.

A: 네, 손님. 서비스 벨 누르셨습니까?
B: 네, 여기가 아주 추운 것 같아서요. 바람 좀 약하게 해 주실 수 있으신가요?
A: 추우셨다니 죄송합니다. 안타깝게도 공기순환 장치 때문에 춥게 느끼신 것 같습니다.
B: 그럼 조절할 수 없다는 건가요?
A: 조절이 안 되는 점 죄송합니다. 하지만 담요를 드릴 수 있습니다. 담요 가져다 드릴까요?
B: 네, 그래 주세요. 그래 주시면 좋겠습니다.

Warm-up   (a), (b)

Practice

A (b), (c)

B ① Yes, I'm afraid I find it very cold in here. Can you turn down the air conditioning?
② So you can't adjust it?
③ Oh yes, please. That would be great.

Unit 02 Captain's Greetings

Listening 향상 팁

p. 34

A 1 expected 2 seated, lavatory 3 stay, turned off

B 1 (a) 2 (a) 3 (b)

1 Please pay attention to the safety video and the cabin crew as we begin our safety demonstration.
안전 교육을 시작하오니 안전 교육 비디오와 승무원을 주목해 주십시오.

2 We will be flying at a height of around 30,000 feet today with a ground speed of around 580 mph.
오늘 시속 580마일의 속도로 3만 피트 상공을 비행하고 있습니다.

3 The captain has turned on the fasten seat belt sign.
기장이 안전 벨트 표시등을 켰습니다.

C 1 T 2 F

Situation I

pp. 35-36

Good morning, ladies and gentlemen. This is your captain speaking. We will be flying at a height of around 30,000 feet today with a ground speed of around 580 mph. That's 9,140 meters and about 930 km/h in metric. The outside air temperature is currently -60 ℉, or -51 ℃. We are looking at about a four-hour flight today. We are expecting some turbulence during portions of the flight. As such, please be sure to keep your seat belt fastened when seated.

좋은 아침입니다 여러분. 저는 여러분을 모시고 있는 기장입니다. 우리는 오늘 약 시속 580마일로 30,000피트 상공을 비행할 것입니다. 미터법으로는 9,140미터와 약 시속 930킬로미터입니다. 현재 바깥 기온은 화씨 -60도, 즉 섭씨 -51도 입니다. 오늘은 약 4시간 비행을 할 것으로 예상하고 있습니다. 비행 도중 간간이 난류가 있을 것으로 예상됩니다. 그러므로, 앉아계실 때에는 안전벨트를 꼭 착용하시기 바랍니다.

Warm-up (b)

Practice
A 1 (b) 2 (c) 3 (c)   B (c)   C 1 T 2 F

Dictation
① captain ② at a height ③ a ground speed
④ metric ⑤ air temperature ⑥ turbulence
⑦ fastened

Situation II   p. 37

A: Welcome aboard, sir. May I see your boarding pass, please?
B: Yes, here it is.
A: You are in seat 8K, so please go through the galley and take a right.
B: It's a window seat, right?
A: Yes, sir. You'll pass through the first class cabin, and then it will be the 4th row window seat.
B: Thank you very much.

A: 탑승을 환영합니다. 탑승권 좀 보여 주시겠습니까?
B: 네, 여기 있습니다.
A: 8K 좌석이시네요. 갤리를 통과하셔서 오른쪽입니다.
B: 창가 쪽 좌석이죠?
A: 네, 그렇습니다. 일등석을 지나 4번째 열 창가 좌석입니다.
B: 정말 감사합니다.

Warm-up
boarding pass, seat 8K, window seat, galley, first class cabin, 4th row

Practice
A 1 a passenger 2 a galley 3 a window
B ① Yes, here it is.
  ② It's a window seat, right?
  ③ Thank you very much.

Unit 03 Duty Free Sales

Listening 향상 팁   p. 38

A 1 water   2 metal   3 computer
  4 better   5 item   6 Saturday
  7 bottle   8 title   9 catalogue
  10 idiot   11 matter 12 Seattle
B 1 right away 2 What else 3 how to 4 out of
C 1 T 2 F

Situation I   pp. 39-40

Attention, ladies and gentlemen. We are pleased to announce that we will begin the sale of duty free items shortly. Please take a moment to look through the duty free catalogue. You will find great savings on a wide variety of products including perfumes, liquor, jewelry, and other pretty little accessories. If you have any questions, please ask any of the cabin crew members.

여러분, 주목해 주시기 바랍니다. 면세 상품 판매를 곧 시작함을 알려드립니다. 잠시 면세 상품 카탈로그를 훑어보십시오. 향수, 술, 보석, 기타 작고 예쁜 액세서리들을 포함한 다양한 상품들을 할인된 가격으로 찾아보실 수 있을 것입니다. 궁금한 점이 있으시면 어느 승무원에게든 물어보시기 바랍니다.

Warm-up
announce, duty free items, look through, catalogue, a wide variety, perfumes

Practice
A 1 (b) 2 (c) 3 (c)   B (b)   C 1 F 2 T

Dictation
① announce ② duty ③ items ④ catalogue
⑤ variety ⑥ pretty ⑦ cabin crew

Situation II p. 41

A: Did you start the sale of duty free items yet?
B: We will begin in a little while. Please look through this duty free catalogue.
A: Are there any good deals right now?
B: We always have great prices, but accessories are an additional 10% off right now.
A: Oh, wow. I hope I can find a pretty necklace for my wife.
B: I'll be back in a few minutes to see if you have any questions.

A: 아직 면세 판매 시작 안 했나요?
B: 곧 시작할 것입니다. 이 면세품 카탈로그를 훑어 보세요.
A: 가격 괜찮은 게 지금 좀 있나요?
B: 항상 좋은 가격에 제공해드리고 있지만 액세서리가 지금 10% 추가 할인됩니다.
A: 오. 제 아내에게 사 줄 예쁜 목걸이를 발견할 수 있으면 좋겠네요.
B: 더 필요한 것이 있으신지 여쭤보러 몇 분 후에 다시 오겠습니다.

Warm-up
sale, duty free items, good deals, additional 10% off, necklace, wife

Practice
A 1 (b)   2 (a)

B ① We will begin in a little while. Please look through this duty free catalogue.
   ② We always have great prices, but accessories are an additional 10% off right now.
   ③ I'll be back in a few minutes to see if you have any questions.

Unit 04 Take-off and Landing Announcements

Listening 향상 팁 p. 42

A 1 (d)   2 (c)   3 (b)   4 (a)
C 1 F   2 T

Situation I pp. 43-44

Good afternoon, ladies and gentlemen. This is the captain speaking. We are just approaching JFK International Airport and preparing for landing. Please be sure that your seats are in their upright positions and that your seat belts are securely fastened. Please also open all the window shades and return your tray tables to their original positions. After landing, would you please remain seated with your seat belts fastened until the aircraft comes to a complete stop and the seat belt sign is turned off? Thank you, and I hope you enjoyed your flight.

안녕하십니까, 여러분. 저는 여러분을 모시고 있는 기장입니다. 우리는 막 JFK 국제공항에 접근하면서 착륙을 준비 중입니다. 좌석 등받이를 똑바로 올려주시고 안전벨트를 단단히 매주시기 바랍니다. 또한 모든 창문 가리개를 열어주시고 간이 테이블을 원위치 해주시기 바랍니다. 착륙 후에 비행기가 완전히 멈추고 안전벨트 등이 꺼질 때까지 계속 안전벨트를 착용하고 앉아 계시겠습니까? 고맙습니다. 즐거운 비행 보내셨기를 바랍니다.

Warm-up (a), (c)

Practice
A 1 (b)   2 (c)   3 (c)   B (c)   C 1 F   2 T

Dictation
① captain   ② that your   ③ fastened   ④ would you
⑤ remain   ⑥ stop   ⑦ turned off

Situation II p. 45

A: Excuse me, ma'am. I need to ask you to put your seat in an upright position.
B: Oh? Are we preparing for landing already?
A: Yes, we are approaching JFK right now. Please also open the window shade and put your tray table up.
B: Okay, I will. Would you please put my bag in the overhead bin, too?
A: Certainly. Please remember after we land to remain seated with your seat belt fastened.
B: Okay. Thank you.

A: 실례합니다. 좌석을 똑바로 올려 주시길 부탁드립니다.
B: 아? 벌써 착륙을 준비하고 있나요?

A: 네. 지금 JFK 공항에 접근하고 있습니다.
또한 창문 가리개를 열어 주시고 간이 테이블을
올려주시기 바랍니다.
B: 네, 그럴게요. 제 가방을 머리 위 선반에 올려 주시겠어요?
A: 물론이죠. 착륙한 이후에도 잊지 말고 안전벨트를 계속 착용하고 앉아 계시길 바랍니다.
B: 네. 고맙습니다.

Warm-up
upright position, landing, approaching, my bag, overhead bin, remain seated

Practice
A 1 a cabin crew member 2 land
  3 window shade 4 the woman's

B ① Oh? Are we preparing for landing already?
  ② Okay, I will. Would you please put my bag in the overhead bin, too?
  ③ Okay. Thank you.

Week 03 At the Hotel
Unit 01 Reserving Rooms

Listening 향상 팁
p. 50

A 1 How long, nights 2 rate, per

B 1 (b) 2 (a) 3 (c)

1 What's the name of the card holder?
  카드 소지자의 이름이 무엇입니까?
2 What type of rooms would you like?
  어떤 방을 원합니까?
3 What's the rate on weekends?
  주말 요금이 어떻게 되나요?

C 1 T 2 T

Situation I
pp. 51-52

Thank you for calling Sunny Day Inn. All lines are currently busy, but we will answer your call as soon as possible. Room rates start at $125 for weekdays and $165 for weekends and holidays. All room categories include a complimentary continental breakfast. There is also a complimentary shuttle to the airport every hour. Please continue to hold and we will be with you shortly.

써니 데이 인에 전화 주셔서 감사합니다. 현재 모든 전화가 통화 중이지만 가능한 한 빨리 응답하겠습니다. 숙박 요금은 주중에 125 달러부터 주말과 공휴일에 165 달러까지 있습니다. 모든 방 유형은 유럽식 무료 조식을 포함하고 있습니다. 또한 매 시간마다 공항까지 무료 셔틀버스도 운행합니다. 잠시 대기하시면 곧 연결됩니다.

Warm-up
lines, busy, room rates, for weekdays, room categories, continental breakfast

Practice
A 1 (b) 2 (c) 3 (a)   B c   C 1 F 2 T

Dictation
① All lines ② Room rates ③ holidays
④ room categories ⑤ complimentary
⑥ shuttle ⑦ continue to hold

Situation II
p. 53

A: Sorry we missed your call. How can I help you?
B: Oh, I finally got through. I need to make a reservation.
A: What date do you want to make a reservation for?
B: Next Saturday the 8th. How much is it?
A: Weekend rates are $165.
B: Perfect. Please put the room in the name of Melinda Littleton.

A: 전화를 받지 못해서 죄송합니다. 무엇을 도와드릴까요?
B: 오, 드디어 연결되었네요. 예약을 하려고 하는데요.
A: 며칠로 예약을 원하시나요?
B: 다음 주 토요일 8일이요. 얼마예요?
A: 주말 가격은 165달러입니다.
B: 좋네요. 멜린다 리틀턴이라는 이름으로 예약해 주세요.

Warm-up
missed, reservation, Saturday, 8th, weekend rates, in the name of

Practice

A 1 F 2 T 3 F

B ① Oh, I finally got through. I need to make a reservation.
② Next Saturday the 8th. How much is it?
③ Perfect. Please put the room in the name of Melinda Littleton.

Unit 02 Checking In

Listening 향상 팁   p. 54

A 1 715 2 1005 3 2157

1 Room number 715
2 Room number 1005
3 Room number 2157

B 1 (b) 2 (a) 3 (c)

1 Just dial 0 to reach the front desk.
프런트 데스크에 전화하시려면 0번을 누르세요.

2 In-room breakfast is available at an extra charge. 추가 요금을 내시면 조식 룸서비스가 가능합니다.

3 Room service and housekeeping are available around the clock.
룸서비스와 하우스키핑은 24시간 가능합니다.

C 1 T 2 T

Situation I   pp. 55-56

I found your reservation, and I'll just need to see some ID and a credit card for a deposit, please. I'll let you know that breakfast is in the lobby restaurant from 6:30 to 10:30 a.m. Room service is 24 hours, and housekeeping is also available around the clock. The pool on the 5th floor is available to you free of extra charge. Please note that checkout is at noon on your final day.

고객님의 예약을 확인하였고, 예치금을 위해 신분증과 신용카드를 보여주시겠습니까? 조식은 아침 6시 30분부터 10시 30분까지 로비 식당에서 제공됨을 알려드립니다. 룸 서비스는 24시간 동안, 방 청소 또한 24시간 내내 이용 가능합니다. 5층에 있는 수영장 이용은 무료입니다. 체크아웃은 마지막 날 정오라는 점에 유의하시기 바랍니다.

Warm-up (a), (c)

Practice

A 1 (a) 2 (b) 3 (c)   B (c)   C 1 T 2 T

Dictation

① for a deposit ② lobby restaurant
③ Room service ④ housekeeping
⑤ around the clock ⑥ free of ⑦ checkout

Situation II   p. 57

A: Hello, sir. Checking in? Can I see some ID, please?
B: Yes, I have a standard room reserved, but I was hoping to change to an ocean view.
A: Let me see here. I have had an eleventh hour cancellation, so I can change your room for a small rebooking fee.
B: Oh, I don't mind paying the fee. Might as well get the best view, vacations like this aren't exactly a dime a dozen.
A: If you want my two cents' worth, I'd suggest that you move to the corner suite.
B: Oh why not, let's go the whole nine yards!

A: 안녕하세요, 체크인하시겠습니까? 신분증을 보여 주시겠어요?
B: 네, 일반 객실로 예약을 했는데, 오션뷰(바다가 보이는 객실)로 바꿨으면 합니다.
A: 알아보겠습니다. 막판에 취소된 것이 있어서 약간의 재예약 수수료를 받고 변경해 드릴 수 있습니다.
B: 아, 비용 내는 것은 상관없어요. 최고의 전망에서 보내는 것이 훨씬 더 낫죠. 이런 휴가는 흔한 일이 아니니까요.
A: 제 의견을 말씀드리자면, 코너 스위트 룸으로 옮기는 것을 추천해 드립니다.
B: 오, 좋지요. 무엇이든 다 해 보죠!

Warm-up

checking in, standard room, an ocean view, eleventh hour, rebooking fee, a dime a dozen

Practice

A (a)

B ① Yes, I have a standard room reserved, but I was hoping to change to an ocean view.

② Oh, I don't mind paying the fee. Might as well get the best view, vacations like this aren't exactly a dime a dozen.

③ Oh why not, let's go the whole nine yards!

Practice

A 1 (b)   2 (a)   3 (a)   **B** (c)   **C** 1 T   2 T

Dictation

① would like   ② work for   ③ family suite
④ city view   ⑤ king bed   ⑥ suite   ⑦ available

Unit 03 Complaining

Listening 향상 팁   p. 58

A 1 (c)   2 (a)

1 (a) your birthday   (b) your victory
  (c) your inconvenience
2 (a) care of it   (b) the number
  (c) him to the concert

B 1 forgot   2 afraid   **C** 1 F   2 T

Situation I   pp. 59-60

A: Hello, sir. How may I help you?
B: I would like to change my room immediately! I just went to the room you gave me, and it's not going to work for us at all. I booked an ocean view family suite, but we have a city view with only one king bed. I am here with my wife and kids, so we need the suite that has a king bed and two twin beds. Do you have another room available for us?

A: 안녕하세요. 어떻게 도와드릴까요?
B: 당장 방을 바꾸고 싶어요! 당신이 주신 방으로 막 들어왔는데 이건 우리가 원한 것이 전혀 아니에요.
오션뷰(바다를 볼 수 있는 전망의) 패밀리 스위트 룸을 예약했는데, 시내 전망에 킹사이즈 침대 하나만 달랑 있네요. 여기에 아내, 아이들과 같이 와서 킹 사이즈 침대 하나에 트윈 사이즈 침대 2개가 필요합니다. 우리가 이용 가능한 다른 방이 있나요?

Warm-up

change, immediately, work, booked, a king bed, available

Situation II   p. 61

A: Hello? Housekeeping. How may I help you?
B: Yes, we just came back to our room. It's 4 p.m. and housekeeping hasn't visited yet.
A: Oh, I'm terribly sorry for that, ma'am. You are in room 417, correct?
B: Yes, that's right. I'd like for the linens to be changed and we will need fresh towels.
A: Yes, ma'am. Right away. I will call the floor manager for the fourth floor right away and someone will come to your room immediately.
B: Thank you. Please send them right away.

A: 안녕하세요? 객실 청소 서비스입니다. 어떻게 도와드릴까요?
B: 네. 방금 막 우리 방으로 돌아왔는데요. 오후 4시인데 객실 청소 서비스가 아직 안 왔었네요.
A: 아이고, 대단히 죄송합니다. 고객님. 417호에 묵으시는 거 맞으시죠?
B: 네, 맞아요. 침구 세트를 바꿔주셨으면 좋겠고, 새 수건들도 필요해요.
A: 네, 고객님. 즉시 처리해드리겠습니다. 지금 바로 4층 담당 매니저에게 전화하면, 직원이 즉시 고객님의 객실로 갈 것입니다.
B: 고맙습니다. 지금 바로 보내주세요.

Warm-up   (a)

Practice

A 1 (a)   2 (a)

B ① Yes, we just came back to our room. It's 4 p.m. and housekeeping hasn't visited yet.

② Yes, that's right. I'd like for the linens to be changed and we will need fresh towels.

③ Thank you. Please send them right away.

Unit 04 Concierge Service

Listening 향상 팁
p. 62

A 1 (a) 2 (c) 3 (d) 4 (b)

1 Are there any good shows to see in town?
시내에 볼 만한 좋은 쇼 있나요?

2 I need to have my suit dry cleaned. Can you help me?
양복을 드라이 크리닝 해야 해서요. 좀 도와 주실래요?

3 I need to take my client out to dinner tonight. Where do you suggest?
오늘 저녁에 고객을 모시고 저녁을 해야 합니다. 추천해 주실 곳이 어디인가요?

4 What's the best way to get to the airport?
공항까지 가는 가장 좋은 방법이 뭔가요?

B 1 F 2 T

Situation I
pp. 63-64

Here are your room keys, and should you need help with anything special during your stay, please visit the concierge desk. The concierge will be happy to help you with many different things such as planning a sightseeing day, car rentals, train or bus tickets, or even reservations for a tour or to the theater. The concierge desk is to the left of the elevator bank, so please stop in any time.

여기 방 열쇠입니다. 머무르시다가 어떤 일이든 도움이 필요하시면 컨시어지(안내) 데스크를 방문해주세요. 콘시어지(안내) 직원은 관광 일정 짜기, 자동차 렌트, 기차나 버스표, 또는 투어나 영화 예매까지 여러 가지 다양한 일들을 기꺼이 도와드릴 것입니다. 안내데스크는 엘리베이터 통로 왼쪽에 있으니 언제든 들르시기 바랍니다.

Warm-up
room keys, your stay, concierge desk, sightseeing day, bus tickets, theater

Practice
A 1 (c) 2 (a) 3 (b)   B (b)   C 1 T 2 T

Dictation
① should ② concierge desk ③ sightseeing

④ car rentals ⑤ reservations ⑥ elevator bank
⑦ any time

Situation II
p. 65

A: Room Service, may I take your order please?
B: Yes, I had a question about the menu.
   Are all of the items available 24 hours a day?
A: The first four pages of the menu are, but the rest of the menu has the available times listed at the top of the page.
B: Ah, I see. Well it's rather late now, so can you recommend some vegetarian dishes for me?
A: Yes, we have lots of vegetarian dishes available such as the veggie burger, vegetable fried rice, sesame noodles and tofu, or the fruit platter.
B: Oh, the sesame noodles sound great. Could I have an order of that and then a fruit platter, please?

A: 룸 서비스입니다. 주문하시겠습니까?
B: 네. 메뉴에 대해 궁금한 점이 있습니다. 모든 음식이 24시간 이용 가능한가요?
A: 첫 네 페이지의 메뉴들은 그렇지만, 나머지 메뉴들은 페이지 상단에 이용 가능한 시간들이 표시되어 있습니다.
B: 아, 그렇군요. 그럼 지금은 꽤 늦었으니 저에게 채식 요리를 추천해 주시겠습니까?
A: 채식 요리가 많이 있는데요, 베지 버거, 채소 볶음밥, 참깨 국수와 두부, 또는 모듬 과일 같은 것들이 이용 가능합니다.
B: 아. 참깨 국수가 좋겠네요. 그것과 모듬 과일을 주문해 주시겠어요?

Warm-up (b), (c)

Practice
A 1 room service   2 at any time
  3 vegetarian dishes 4 noodles and fruit
B ① Yes, I had a question about the menu.
     Are all of the items available 24 hours a day?
  ② Ah, I see. Well it's rather late now, so can you recommend some vegetarian dishes for me?
  ③ Oh, the sesame noodles sound great.
     Could I have an order of that and then a fruit platter, please?

Week 04 Transportation
Unit 01 Getting Directions to the Tour Site

Listening 향상 팁 p. 70

A 1 (b) 2 (d) 3 (a) 4 (c)
B 1 Boulevard 2 Street 3 Avenue 4 Keep
C 1 T 2 F

Situation I pp. 71-72

The walking tour of the National Mall is a great way to see the major sites of DC. Start early at Smithsonian Station. If you come out Exit 4 and walk straight, you'll find the Smithsonian Castle and the information center. It's best to ask for staff advice when planning your day. Continue walking in the same direction until you reach 3rd St. SW, and then turn left. After you reach Madison Dr. NW, you will turn left again and you can continue your tour down the National Mall until you reach the Washington Monument.

내셔널 몰 도보 투어는 워싱턴 DC의 주요 장소를 볼 수 있는 가장 좋은 방법입니다. 스미스소니언 역에서 이른 시간에 시작하세요. 4번 출구로 나와서 쭉 걸으시면 스미스소니언 캐슬과 안내소를 찾으실 수 있을 것입니다. 일정을 짤 때 직원에게 조언을 구하는 것이 가장 좋은 방법입니다. 3번가 남서쪽에 이를 때까지 같은 방향으로 계속 걸으시고, 그 다음 좌회전하세요. 매디슨 드라이브 북서쪽에 다다른 후에 한 번 더 좌회전하시면 내셔널 몰을 따라 워싱턴 기념비에 도착할 때까지 투어를 계속하실 수 있습니다.

Warm-up

walking tour, National Mall, information center, in the same direction, turn left, until you reach

Practice

A 1 (a) 2 (b) 3 (b)   **B** (b)   **C** 1 F 2 F

Dictation

① walking tour ② walk straight ③ Continue walking
④ same direction ⑤ turn left ⑥ reach
⑦ Washington Monument

Situation II p. 73

A: Excuse me. Do you know where Madison Dr. NW is?
B: It's just one block south, back the way you came. What are you looking for?
A: We are on a walking tour, and we are just trying to get back to the Washington Monument.
B: I would suggest you keep going straight here. If you walk about 15 minutes on this road, you'll come to the White House.
A: Oh, that's cool. Is that far from the Washington Monument?
B: No, not at all. When you come to the White House, just take a left and go south down 15th St. NW. You can't miss it.

A: 실례합니다. 매디슨 드라이브 북서쪽이 어디인지 아세요?
B: 왔던 길로 되돌아가셔서 남쪽으로 한 블록만 가시면 돼요. 무엇을 찾고 계신데요?
A: 우리는 지금 도보 투어를 하고 있는데, 워싱턴 기념비 쪽으로 다시 돌아가려고 하는 중이에요.
B: 여기로 쭉 걸어가시는 게 좋을 것 같아요. 이 길로 15분 정도 걸어가시면 백악관에 닿으실 겁니다.
A: 오, 잘됐네요. 거기는 워싱턴 기념비에서 먼가요?
B: 아니요, 전혀요. 백악관이 보이면 왼쪽으로 돌아서 15번가 북서쪽에서 남쪽으로 내려가시면 됩니다. 바로 찾으실 겁니다.

Warm-up (a)

Practice

A (b), (c)

B ① It's just one block south, back the way you came. What are you looking for?

② I would suggest you keep going straight here. If you walk about 15 minutes on this road, you'll come to the White House.

③ No, not at all. When you come to the White House, just take a left and go south down 15th St. NW. You can't miss it.

Unit 02 Buying Tickets

Listening 향상 팁
p. 74

A 1 a lot of 2 out of 3 kind of, to the
4 sick of 5 for an 6 for a, of

B 1 T 2 T

Situation I
pp. 75-76

Are you looking for a quick escape from the city? Come and visit us at the Lucky Farm for a day of fresh air, country life, and good home cooking! We are located a quick 35 minute train or 50 minute bus ride from the city center, and offer all kinds of activities for kids, adults, and groups. Visit our website or call us today for more information. We look forward to welcoming you soon. Discounts of 15% off entrance are offered to the first 50 visitors every day!

도시로부터 재빠르게 탈출하고 싶으신가요? 럭키 농장을 방문하셔서 상쾌한 공기와 전원생활, 그리고 맛있는 가정요리를 위한 하루를 만들어 보세요! 우리 농장은 도심에서 빠르게 기차로 35분 혹은 버스로 50분이 걸리는 곳에 있으며, 아이, 어른, 그리고 단체를 위한 모든 종류의 활동을 제공합니다. 더 많은 정보를 위해서는 오늘 홈페이지에 방문하시거나 전화 주시기 바랍니다. 여러분을 곧 만나 뵙기를 기대합니다. 매일 첫 50명의 방문객께는 입장료 15% 할인 쿠폰이 제공됩니다!

Warm-up

a quick escape, country life, city center, all kinds of activities, for more information, 15% off

Practice

A 1 (b) 2 (c) 3 (c)   **B** (b)   **C** 1 T 2 T

Dictation

① from the ② and ③ or ④ of ⑤ to ⑥ off
⑦ are

Situation II
p. 77

A: Hello? Is this Mr. Clarkson?
B: Yes, it is.

A: Hello sir. This is the front desk, and I am calling about your train tickets for tomorrow. You had asked us to book tickets for you and your family on the 9 a.m. train tomorrow, but I'm afraid it is all sold out.
B: Oh no. Is there any other train available?
A: Yes, sir. There is a train at 6 a.m. and one at 11 a.m. that both go to the same destination.
B: I think the 11 a.m. one will be fine. Will you please book tickets for two adults and two children on that train?

A: 안녕하세요? 클락슨 씨 되시나요?
B: 네, 그런데요.
A: 안녕하세요. 프런트 데스크입니다. 내일 기차표 때문에 전화 드렸습니다. 내일 오전 9시 기차로 고객님과 가족분들의 표를 예매해 달라고 부탁하셨는데요, 안타깝게도 모두 매진입니다.
B: 어, 이런. 이용 가능한 다른 기차가 있을까요?
A: 네, 있습니다. 오전 6시와 오전 11시에 있는데, 둘다 같은 목적지로 가는 것입니다.
B: 오전 11시 것이 좋을 것 같네요. 그 기차로 어른 두 명과 아이들 두 명 표를 예매해 주시겠어요?

Warm-up

front desk, your train tickets, to book, the 9 a.m. train, other train, on that train

Practice

A (c)

B ① Yes, it is.
② Oh no. Is there any other train available?
③ I think the 11 a.m. one will be fine. Will you please book tickets for two adults and two children on that train?

Unit 03 Finding the Right Stop

Listening 향상 팁
p. 78

A 1 Take, at 2 Get off, transfer to
3 Go, off 4 Go out

B 1 Take 2 Transfer to 3 Get off 4 miss

C 1 T 2 T

Situation I
pp. 79-80

A: Sorry, could I ask for your help?
B: Yeah, what's up?
A: We are looking for Gravely Street Station. Do you know if we're close?
B: Yeah, it's in 3 more stops. Almost there.
A: Oh, excellent. We were worried we had missed it.
B: Don't worry. It's coming up soon, and the doors will be on the left.

A: 죄송합니다만 도움을 요청해도 될까요?
B: 네, 무슨 일이세요?
A: 그래이블리 스트리트 역을 찾고 있는데요, 저희가 그곳과 가까이 있는지 아시나요?
B: 네, 역 세 개를 더 가야 해요. 거의 다 왔어요.
A: 아, 잘됐네요. 놓쳤을까 봐 걱정했어요.
B: 걱정하지 마세요. 얼마 안 남았어요. 그리고 문은 왼쪽에 있을 거예요.

Warm-up
ask for, looking for, close, almost there, worried, on the left

Practice
A 1 (c) 2 (b) 3 (b)　　B (c)　　C 1 F 2 F

Dictation
① Sorry　② what's up　③ looking for　④ know if
⑤ more stops　⑥ there　⑦ left

Situation II
p. 81

A: Excuse me, could you help us?
B: I will sure try. What's wrong?
A: We are looking for Splash Park Extreme, and we thought it was supposed to be right here at Exit 4.
B: Well, this is Exit 4, but you're at West Park Station. I think that water park is at Grand Park West Station.
A: Oh no! Is it far from here?
B: You'll need to take the train two stops north and then transfer to the central line. It will take you about 20 minutes.

A: 실례합니다. 저희 좀 도와주시겠어요?
B: 그럼요. 무슨 일이세요?
A: 스플래쉬 파크 익스트림을 찾고 있는데 여기 4번 출구에 있을 거로 생각했어요.
B: 글쎄요. 여기는 4번 출구이긴 한데 웨스트 파크 역이에요. 그 수상 공원은 그랜드 파크 웨스트 역에 있는 것 같아요.
A: 아, 안돼! 여기서 먼가요?
B: 기차로 북쪽으로 역 두 개를 더 가야 하고 그 다음에 중앙선으로 갈아타셔야 해요. 약 20분 정도 걸릴 거예요.

Warm-up (a)

Practice
A (a)
B ① I will sure try. What's wrong?
　② Well this is Exit 4, but you're at West Park Station. I think that water park is at Grand Park West Station.
　③ You'll need to take the train two stops north and then transfer to the central line. It will take you about 20 minutes.

Unit 04 Missing a Train

Listening 향상 팁
p. 82

A 1 Harry is my best friend. I love (him).
　2 I'm (going to) take the next train.
　3 I (want to) rebook the next available train.
　4 I have a sweet tooth. I love (chocolate).
B 1 (You've) just missed the 3 o'clock train.
　2 You can take the next one. (It'll) arrive 30 minutes later.
　3 (That'll) cost a small rebooking fee.
　4 I thought I (could've) made it.
C 1 T 2 F

Situation I
pp. 83-84

A: Hi! I am so flustered. I think I just missed my train. Here is my ticket.
B: Oh, yes, the train just departed. I can offer you a seat on the next train that leaves in 35 minutes. It is a slower train though, so it's going to arrive two hours later than you

would've originally. The next high speed train leaves in an hour, so it only arrives one hour later than your original arrival time. There is a rebooking fee of $35 either way.

A: 안녕하세요! 정말 당황스럽네요. 저 방금 기차를 놓친 것 같아요. 여기 제 티켓이요.
B: 아, 네. 그 기차는 막 출발했어요. 35분 후에 떠나는 다음 기차에 대한 좌석을 제공해드리겠습니다. 그런데 이건 좀 더 느린 기차여서 원래 도착 시간보다 2시간 늦게 도착합니다. 다음 빠른 기차는 한 시간 뒤에 출발하기 때문에 고객님의 원래 도착 시간보다 한 시간 만 늦게 도착합니다. 두 방법 모두 35 달러의 재예약비가 있습니다.

Warm-up
flustered, missed, a slower train, one hour later, original arrival time, a rebooking fee

Practice
A **1** (c) **2** (b) **3** (b)   B (a)   C **1** F **2** F

Dictation
① missed ② departed ③ 35 minutes ④ going to ⑤ would've ⑥ later than ⑦ rebooking fee

Situation II
p. 85

A: Excuse me, but where can we find Platform 13?
B: You want to take the escalators on the right over there. Were you on the 346 for Boston?
A: Yes, we were. We're running so late!
B: I'm very sorry, but that train just departed. You've missed it.
A: Oh no! That's terrible. What can we do?
B: If you visit the ticket counter, they will try and arrange a transfer for you to the next available train.

A: 실례합니다만 어디로 가면 13번 승강장을 찾을 수 있나요?
B: 저기 오른쪽에 있는 에스컬레이터를 타시면 됩니다. 보스턴행 346번을 타셨었나요?
A: 네, 그랬어요. 너무 늦을 것 같아요!
B: 정말 유감스럽지만, 그 기차는 방금 막 출발했습니다. 놓치셨어요.
A: 아, 안돼! 큰일 났어요. 어떻게 해야 하죠?
B: 매표창구에 가시면 그쪽에서 고객님께서 이용 가능한 다음 기차에 갈아탈 수 있게 조치해 드릴 것입니다.

Warm-up
(a)

Practice
A **1** Platform 13 **2** Boston **3** missed **4** the ticket counter
B ① You want to take the escalators on the right over there. Were you on the 346 for Boston?
② I'm very sorry, but that train just departed. You've missed it.
③ If you visit the ticket counter, they will try and arrange a transfer for you to the next available train.

Week 05 At the Restaurant
Unit 01 Making a Reservation

Listening 향상 팁
p. 90

A **1** (c) **2** (a) **3** (b) **4** (d)

1 May I have a phone number where we can reach you, sir?
저희가 연락드릴 수 있는 전화 번호 알려주시겠습니까?
2 What name should I make a reservation under?
어떤 이름으로 예약해 드릴까요?
3 How large is your party, ma'am?
일행이 몇 분이시죠?
4 For which date? 날짜는요?

B **1** make a reservation **2** booked solid
C **1** T **2** F

Situation I
pp. 91-92

Thank you for calling Palace Garden Restaurant. The service staff is currently occupied, but your call will be answered shortly. If you are calling to make a reservation, please be ready with the date, time, and the number in your party. Please note that reservations are not accepted for lunch, Valentine's Day, or Christmas. The restaurant is closed the third Sunday of every month, and last orders are taken nightly at 10:30 p.m. Please continue to hold and someone will be with you shortly.

팰리스 가든 레스토랑에 전화 주셔서 감사합니다. 서비스 직원이 다른 업무로 바쁘지만 곧 연결될 겁니다. 예약을 위해 전화하셨다면 예약하실 날짜와 시간, 인원 수를 미리 생각해 두세요. 점심 시간, 밸런타인데이, 크리스마스에는 예약이 불가능함을 유의하시길 바랍니다. 저희 레스토랑은 매월 셋째 주 일요일 휴무이며 마지막 주문 가능 시간은 밤 10시 반입니다. 전화를 끊지 말고 기다리시면 곧 연결될 겁니다.

Warm-up

service staff, occupied, shortly, make a reservation, Valentine's Day, last orders

Practice

A 1 (b) 2 (c) 3 (a) **B** (c) **C** 1 F 2 T

Dictation

① service staff ② occupied ③ make a reservation
④ date, time ⑤ not accepted ⑥ third
⑦ last orders

Situation II   p. 93

A: Thank you for waiting. Palace Garden Restaurant. How may I help you?
B: Yes, I was calling to make a reservation for next Tuesday.
A: Okay. That would be the 17th, correct? How many in your party and what time, ma'am?
B: Yes, the 17th. There will be 8 of us for 1 p.m.
A: Oh. I am terribly sorry, but we don't take reservations for lunch. First come, first served.
B: Oh, I see. Well I will think about it then.

A: 기다려주셔서 감사합니다. 팰리스 가든 레스토랑입니다. 어떻게 도와 드릴까요?
B: 다음 주 화요일에 예약을 하려고 전화 드렸습니다.
A: 네, 17일 말씀이시죠? 몇 시에 몇 분이 오시나요?
B: 네, 17일 맞아요. 오후 1시에 8명이요.
A: 오, 정말 죄송합니다만 저희는 점심 시간에 예약을 받지 않습니다. 선착순이거든요.
B: 아, 그렇군요. 그럼 생각 좀 해볼게요.

Warm-up

make a reservation, 17th, how many, what time, terribly sorry, first served

Practice

A a Tuesday **b** 17th **c** 1 p.m.
B ① Yes, I was calling to make a reservation for next Tuesday.
   ② Yes, the 17th. There will be 8 of us for 1 p.m.
   ③ Oh, I see. Well I will think about it then.

Unit 02 Introducing a Restaurant

Listening 향상 팁   p. 94

A 1 so 2 on the other hand
B 내용 전환 by the way 추가 also 결과 as a result
   강조 in particular 조건 in that case 순서 first
C 1 T 2 F

Situation I   pp. 95-96

Are you hungry? Do you love bacon? In that case, come on down to Jimmy's Fast Food Joint and try our new Ultimate Bacon Double Cheeseburger! It's two patties topped with three strips of bacon and also covered in cheese. Each burger is made fresh and based on your order, so I know you won't be disappointed! For a limited time only, each order will come with fries and a drink at no extra charge! Be sure to come in to try it. Again, it's for a limited time only!

배가 고프신가요? 베이컨을 좋아하시나요? 그렇다면 지미의 패스트푸드점에 오셔서 신 메뉴인 얼티미트 베이컨 더블 치즈버거를 한번 드셔보세요! 이 버거에는 치즈로 코팅된 두 장의 패티가 들어 있고 세 장의 베이컨이 토핑되어 있습니다. 주문에 따라 만들어 진 신선한 버거는 여러분을 실망시키지 않을 것입니다. 한정된 기간 동안 감자 튀김과 음료수를 무료로 받으실 수 있습니다. 꼭 오셔서 한번 드셔 보세요. 다시 한번 말씀 드립니다. 행사기간은 한정되어 있답니다!

Warm-up

hungry, in that case, come on down, three strips of bacon, based on your order, for a limited time

Practice

A 1 (b) 2 (b) 3 (a) **B** (c) **C** 1 T 2 F

Dictation
① In that case ② two patties ③ cheese
④ fresh ⑤ so ⑥ at no extra ⑦ Again

Situation II
p. 97

A: Welcome to Jimmy's Fast Food Joint. May I take your order, please?
B: Yes, I want a cheeseburger combo with a cola.
A: Okay, but there is a special for the new Ultimate Bacon Double Cheeseburger right now, and I can offer you a drink and fries for free.
B: Oh, that's great. So it's cheaper than a regular cheeseburger combo?
A: Yes, sir. It's $5.78. Shall I ring one up with a cola for you?
B: Yes, for here, please. And then, could I have a sundae, too?

A: 지미의 패스트푸드점에 어서 오세요. 주문 하시겠어요?
B: 네, 치즈버거 콤보 하나 주세요. 음료는 콜라로요.
A: 네. 그런데 지금 신 메뉴인 얼티미트 베이컨 더블 치즈버거 이벤트가 있어요. 그래서 음료랑 감자 튀김은 무료입니다.
B: 오, 그거 좋네요. 그렇게 하면 일반 치즈버거 콤보 보다 저렴한가요?
A: 네. 5달러 78센트예요. 음료는 콜라로 해서 주문해 드릴까요?
B: 네, 먹고 갈게요. 그리고 선데도 하나 주시겠어요?

Warm-up
take, a cheeseburger combo, offer, cheaper, regular, $5.78

Practice
A (a)
B ① Yes, I want a cheeseburger combo with a cola.
  ② Oh, that's great. So it's cheaper than a regular cheeseburger combo?
  ③ Yes, for here, please. And then, could I have a sundae, too?

Unit 03 Advertising a New Product

Listening 향상 팁
p. 98
A 1 (c) 2 (b)

1 (a) Over easy, please. 노른자를 살짝 익혀 주세요.
  (b) I want it scrambled. 스크램블 해 주세요.
  (c) With cone, please. 옥수수랑 같이 주세요.
2 (a) I'd like oil and vinegar. 오일앤비니거로 할게요.
  (b) Whole wheat will be good. 통밀 빵이 좋겠어요.
  (c) With Italian, please. 이탈리안 드레싱과 같이 주세요.

B 1 rare, steamed 2 rye, over hard
C 1 T 2 F

Situation I
pp. 99-100

Have you visited Shirley's Sub Shop yet? We just opened three new locations around town including one right outside of Downtown Park! Our delicious subs make the perfect picnic food, so stop by on your way into the park! All of our subs are made right in front of you, and you can choose from six different kinds of bread, five different meats, ten different vegetables, and five kinds of sauces! We also have all kinds of drinks, chips, and cookies. Looking forward to serving you soon.

셜리네 샌드위치 가게에 방문해 보셨나요? 다운타운 공원 바로 바깥에 있는 가게를 포함해 마을에 총 세 가게를 새로 오픈 했습니다. 저희의 맛있는 샌드위치는 피크닉 음식으로 안성맞춤입니다. 공원으로 오시는 길에 한번 들러 보세요. 모든 샌드위치는 바로 눈앞에서 만들어 지고 여섯 가지 종류의 빵, 다섯 가지 종류의 고기, 열 가지 종류의 야채, 그리고 다섯 가지 종류의 소스를 고르실 수 있습니다. 저희는 모든 종류의 음료, 감자 튀김과 쿠키도 판매하고 있습니다. 방문을 기다리고 있겠습니다.

Warm-up
Sub Shop, three new locations, including, five different meats, five kinds of sauces, cookies

Practice
A 1 (b) 2 (a) 3 (c)   B (c)   C 1 T 2 T

Dictation
① right outside ② picnic food ③ six ④ five
⑤ vegetables ⑥ five kinds of ⑦ drinks, chips

Situation II
p. 101

A: Welcome back, sir. How can I help you?

B: There is something wrong with my order. We got into the park, and I think all the breads and fillings got mixed up.
A: Oh, I'm sorry, sir. I'd be happy to remake them for you at no charge.
B: Thank you. I had a ham and cheese on wheat and a turkey avocado on flatbread. Both with only lettuce, onions, and mustard.
A: I'll make them right away, sir. If you'd like to have a seat, I'll bring them to you when they are ready.
B: Okay. Thanks.

A: 다시 찾아 주셔서 감사합니다. 어떻게 도와 드릴까요?
B: 아까 산 게 문제가 좀 있어요. 공원에 들어갔을 때 확인했는데 주문한 빵이랑 내용물이 제대로 안맞는 것 같아요.
A: 죄송합니다. 무료로 다시 만들어 드리겠습니다.
B: 감사합니다. 밀가루 빵에 햄과 치즈를 넣은 거랑 납작한 빵에 칠면조 아보카도를 넣은 빵을 주문했었어요. 둘 다 양배추, 양파랑 머스타드만 넣어주세요.
A: 바로 만들어 드리겠습니다. 앉아계시면 가져 드릴게요.
B: 네, 감사합니다.

Warm-up

something wrong, mixed up, at no charge, ham and cheese, turkey avocado, lettuce

Practice

A (a), (c)

B ① There is something wrong with my order. We got into the park, and I think all the breads and fillings got mixed up.
② Thank you. I had a ham and cheese on wheat and a turkey avocado on flatbread. Both with only lettuce, onions, and mustard.
③ Okay. Thanks.

Unit 04 Problems on Food

Listening 향상 팁   p. 102

A 1 /t/ 2 /t/ 3 /d/ 4 /id/ 5 /d/ 6 /id/

B 1 grilled 2 diced 3 blended

1 /d/ 2 /t/ 3 /id/

C 1 T 2 T

Situation I   pp. 103-104

Good evening, folks. My name is Patrick, and I'll be your server tonight. Before you look through the menus too much, I'd like to let you know about some specials that the chef is offering tonight. First, there is a New York strip steak grilled to order and served with roasted vegetables. Next, there is also a baked filet of trout. Purchased fresh this morning from the wharf, the trout is baked and served with mashed turnips and rosemary sauce.

반갑습니다, 여러분. 저는 오늘 밤 여러분의 주문을 도와 드릴 패트릭입니다. 메뉴판을 보시기 전에 저희 주방장의 오늘 밤 스페셜 메뉴를 먼저 소개해 드리겠습니다. 첫째로, 구운 채소와 함께 나오는 뉴욕 스트립 스테이크가 있는데, 구운 정도를 선택하실 수 있습니다. 뼈를 발라 낸 송어 구이도 있습니다. 오늘 아침에 부두에서 구매한 신선한 송어 구이는 으깬 순무와 로즈마리 소스가 같이 나옵니다.

Warm-up

look through, New York strip steak, roasted vegetables, baked filet, mashed turnips, rosemary sauce

Practice

A 1 (c) 2 (a) 3 (b)   **B** (b)   **C** 1 F 2 T

Dictation

① look through ② grilled ③ served ④ roasted
⑤ baked ⑥ Purchased ⑦ mashed

Situation II   p. 105

A: Here is your drink order. Are you ready to order?
B: I wanted to ask if the trout special could be served with anything other than turnips.
A: Certainly, you could have a green salad, roasted vegetables, mashed potatoes, or onion soup as an alternative.
B: I think I'd like the green salad.
A: Would you like vinaigrette, garlic cream dressing, or oriental sesame dressing?
B: I'll go with the garlic cream dressing, please.

A: 주문하신 음료 나왔습니다. 식사 주문하시겠어요?
B: 혹시 송어 스페셜에서 으깬 순무 말고 다른 걸로 주실 수 있나요?
A: 물론이죠. 야채 샐러드, 구운 채소, 으깬 감자 혹은 양파 수프로 바꾸실 수 있습니다.
B: 야채 샐러드가 괜찮을 것 같네요.
A: 드레싱은 비네그레트(식초) 소스, 갈릭 크림 소스, 혹은 오리엔탈 참깨 드레싱 중에 어떤 걸로 해 드릴까요?
B: 갈릭 크림 소스로 해주세요.

Warm-up

drink order, turnips, roasted vegetables, mashed potatoes, vinaigrette, garlic cream dressing

Practice

A 1 today's special 2 trout 3 green salad
  4 garlic cream dressing

B ① I wanted to ask if the trout special could be served with anything other than turnips.
  ② I think I'd like the green salad.
  ③ I'll go with the garlic cream dressing, please.

Week 06 At the Mall
Unit 01 Mall Opening

Listening 향상 팁   p. 110

A 1 Please remember / to visit the new bakery, / Bread Factory, / on the first floor.
  2 I heard an announcement / about a sale, / but I didn't catch the location.
  3 If you will take the escalators / behind you, / then the café will be / on your right.
  4 I'm having a party / at that restaurant / next Saturday.

B 1 As always, / there are maps / at the escalators on / each floor.
  2 We have / to submit the proposal / by tomorrow / at all cost.

C 1 T 2 T

Situation I   pp. 111-112

Good morning, shoppers and welcome to Ridge Shopping Center. We are so happy to have you with us today. The doors to the center are now open, but shops in the east wing will not open for another hour. The basement food court will be open at 11:30. Please remember to visit the new pet store, Paws In, on the fourth floor. As always, there are maps at the escalators on each floor, and there are information desks at the central escalators on all even floors.

안녕하세요, 고객 여러분, 리지 쇼핑 센터에 오신 것을 환영합니다. 오늘 방문해 주셔서 정말 기쁩니다. 중앙 건물은 입장 가능하지만 동쪽 별관에 있는 상점들은 한 시간 뒤에 입장 가능합니다. 지하에 있는 푸드코트는 11시 반에 영업을 개시합니다. 4층에 애완동물 가게 포즈 인(Paws In)이 새로 들어왔으니 꼭 들러 주십시오. 각 층 에스컬레이터마다 안내 지도가 있고 모든 짝수 층 중앙 에스컬레이터에 안내데스크가 있습니다.

Warm-up

the doors to the center, for another hour, basement food court, remember, the new pet store, on all even floors

Practice

A 1 (b) 2 (b) 3 (b)   B (c)   C 1 F 2 F

Dictation

① to the center ② for another hour
③ remember to visit ④ on the fourth floor
⑤ there are maps ⑥ on each floor
⑦ on all even floors

Situation II   p. 113

A: Excuse me. Can you help me?
B: Ofcourse, sir. What can I do for you?
A: I heard an announcement about a new pet shop, but I didn't catch the location.
B: Paws In is the new pet store, and it's on the fourth floor.
A: What's the most direct route?
B: If you will take the escalators behind you up two floors, then Paws In will be on your right.

A: 실례합니다. 저 좀 도와 주실 수 있나요?
B: 그럼요. 뭘 도와 드릴까요?
A: 새로 생긴 애완 동물 가게에 대한 안내 방송을 들었는데 장소가 어딘지는 못 들었어요.
B: 새로 생긴 애완 동물 가게 이름은 포즈 인(Paws In)이고 4층에 있어요.
A: 어떻게 가야 가장 빨리 갈 수 있나요?
B: 당신의 뒤에 있는 에스컬레이터를 타고 두 개 층을 올라가시면 오른쪽에 있어요.

Warm-up

an announcement, a new pet shop, on the fourth floor, direct route, behind you, up two floors

Practice

A **1** pets **2** 2nd **3** an employee

B ① Of course, sir. What can I do for you?
② Paws In is the new pet store, and it's on the fourth floor.
③ If you will take the escalators behind you up two floors, then Paws In will be on your right.

Unit 02 Sales Announcement

Listening 향상 팁
p. 114

A **1** (a) **2** (b) **3** (b) **4** (a)   **B** **1** F **2** T

Situation I
pp. 115-116

Welcome to Deluxe Shopping Mall. We are so pleased you decided to shop with us today. There is a special sale going on in the Event Hall on the third floor today. At the sale, you'll find special clearance prices on kitchenware and dishes from Trappings Department Store. There is also an additional discount offered at Trappings on certain fragrances and cosmetics. Enjoy your shopping today.

디럭스 쇼핑몰에 오신 것을 환영합니다. 오늘 저희 쇼핑몰에 와 주셔서 정말 기쁩니다. 오늘 3층에 있는 이벤트 홀에서 특별 할인 행사가 진행 중입니다. 거기에 가시면 트래핑스 백화점에서 판매 하는 주방 용품과 그릇들을 특별 재고 정리 할인가로 만나 보실

수 있습니다. 트래핑스 백화점에서 추가 할인을 해주고 있는 특정 향수와 화장품도 만나 보세요. 즐거운 쇼핑 되시길 바랍니다.

Warm-up

pleased, decided to shop, a special sale, the Event Hall, on the third floor, additional discount

Practice

A **1** (b) **2** (a) **3** (c)   **B** (c)   **C** **1** T **2** F

Dictation

① pleased ② shop with us ③ a special sale
④ Event Hall ⑤ clearance prices
⑥ an additional discount ⑦ fragrances

Situation II
p. 117

A: Good morning, ma'am. How may I help you?
B: Yes, I heard the announcement about perfumes being on sale.
A: Please follow me this way, and I'll show you the selection we have.
B: Is Autumn Crisp on sale by chance?
A: Oh, I'm afraid not, but we have several others from the same designer on sale.
B: I'd like to try some samples of them.

A: 안녕하세요, 손님. 어떻게 도와 드릴까요?
B: 향수가 할인 중이라는 방송을 들어서요.
A: 이쪽으로 저를 따라오세요. 어떤 게 있는지 보여 드릴게요.
B: 혹시 어텀 크리습(Autumn Crisp)이 할인 중인가요?
A: 유감스럽지만 아닙니다. 하지만 같은 디자이너분의 상품 몇 개가 할인 중이에요.
B: 샘플 몇 개 뿌려 보고 싶네요.

Warm-up

announcement, perfumes, the selection, by chance, afraid not, some samples

Practice

A (b)

B ① Yes, I heard the announcement about perfumes being on sale.
② Is Autumn Crisp on sale by chance?
③ I'd like to try some samples of them.

Unit 03 Announcement About Parking

Listening 향상 팁 p. 118

A 1 (b) 2 (a) 3 (d) 4 (c)

> 1 Would the driver of a brown station wagon please return to your car? Your lights are on.
> 갈색 스테이션왜건 차량 소유주님, 지금 차로 돌아가 주실 수 있나요? 차량 라이트에 불이 들어와 있습니다.
>
> 2 There is an illegally parked convertible blocking the emergency vehicle entrance.
> 불법 주차된 컨버터블 차량이 응급차량 입구를 가로 막고 있습니다.
>
> 3 Illegally parked cars will be towed at once.
> 불법 주차된 차량은 즉시 견인될 예정입니다.
>
> 4 Would the driver of the white sedan with the license plate LP4868 please come to the parking lot immediately?
> LP4868번 하얀색 세단 소유주님, 지금 즉시 주차장으로 와 주 실 수 있나요?

B 1 F 2 T

Situation I pp. 119-120

> Attention, shoppers. Would the patron driving a white convertible with the license plate DGC 765 please come to the parking garage immediately? Your car is parked in a handicapped space, and must be moved at once. A tow truck is standing by, and the car will be removed from the parking deck in 15 minutes. Please come to the deck quickly to move your car. Again, white convertible with the license plate DGC 765 please come to the parking garage.
>
> 고객 여러분께 안내 말씀 드립니다. DGC 765번 흰색 컨버터블 차량 소유주님, 지금 주차장으로 즉시 와 주실 수 있나요? 고객님의 차량이 장애인 전용 주차 구역에 주차되어 있어서 빨리 빼 주셔야 합니다. 견인 트럭이 대기 중이고 15분 후에 차량을 주차장에서 견인할 것입니다. 주차장으로 빨리 오셔서 차를 빼 주세요. 다시 한번 말씀 드립니다. DGC 765번 흰색 컨버터블 차량 소유주님 주차장으로 와 주세요.

Warm-up

the patron, a white convertible, a handicapped space, a tow truck, parking deck, again

Practice

A 1 (b) 2 (c) 3 (a)   **B** (b)   **C** 1 F 2 T

Dictation

① a white convertible ② 765 ③ handicapped space ④ tow truck ⑤ 15 minutes ⑥ deck ⑦ parking garage

Situation II p. 121

> A: Oh my! I just heard that announcement. That's my car!
> B: I think you'd better go to the parking deck right away, ma'am.
> A: I didn't realize it was a handicapped spot! Can you hold these items for me?
> B: Yes, ma'am. I can keep them behind the counter for an hour.
> A: Thank you so much, I'll be back as soon as possible to buy them.
> B: Okay. It's no problem, ma'am.
>
> A: 오, 이런! 저 안내 방송 방금 들었어요. 저거 제 차예요!
> B: 지금 당장 주차장으로 가보셔야 할 것 같아요.
> A: 장애인 전용 주차 구역인 줄 몰랐어요! 이 물건들 좀 맡아 주실 수 있나요?
> B: 네. 카운터 뒤에 한 시간 동안 맡아 드릴 수 있습니다.
> A: 정말 감사 드려요. 결제하러 최대한 빨리 올게요.
> B: 네. 걱정 말고 다녀 오세요, 손님.

Warm-up

my car, you'd better, parking deck, a handicapped spot, hold, as soon as possible

Practice

A (a), (d)

B ① I think you'd better go to the parking deck right away, ma'am.

② Yes, ma'am. I can keep them behind the counter for an hour.

③ Okay. It's no problem, ma'am.

Unit 04 Mall Closing

Listening 향상 팁
p. 122

A 1 The store around the corner / will open / at 10 a.m.
2 I am sorry, / but all the stores close / at 9 p.m.
3 Mr. Brown / checked / everything that he needed / for the trip.
4 Please make sure / that you have all your possessions with you / as you exit.

B 1 T   2 F

Situation I
pp. 123-124

Attention, shoppers. The shopping center will be closing in 15 minutes. Please conclude your shopping and make your way to the exits. All stores will be closed in 15 minutes, and the mall doors will be locked in 20 minutes. Please make sure that you have all your possessions and purchases with you as you exit. Thank you for shopping with us today. We will be open tomorrow morning at 9 a.m., and we hope to see you again soon!

고객 여러분께 안내 말씀 드립니다. 폐점 시간 15분 전입니다. 쇼핑을 마무리하시고 출구로 나가 주시기 바랍니다. 모든 가게는 15분 후에 문을 닫고 쇼핑몰 출입구는 20분 후에 닫습니다. 모든 소지품과 쇼핑한 물건들을 잊지 말고 챙겨서 나가시길 바랍니다. 오늘 저희 쇼핑 센터를 이용해 주셔서 감사합니다. 저희는 내일 오전 9시에 문을 엽니다. 곧 다시 뵙기를 바랍니다!

Warm-up

shopping center, closing, conclude, in 20 minutes, possessions, purchases

Practice

A 1 (a)   2 (b)   3 (b)   **B** (a)   **C** 1 T   2 T

Dictation

① and make   ② to the exits   ③ in 15 minutes
④ will be locked   ⑤ Please make sure
⑥ as you exit   ⑦ at 9 a.m.

Situation II
p. 125

A: Are you closed?
B: Yes, ma'am. I'm sorry, but all the stores close at 9 p.m.
A: Oh, no! I really needed to make a purchase tonight.
B: I'm very sorry, ma'am, but all of our registers are already closed.
A: What time do you open in the morning?
B: We'll be open at 9 a.m., and will gladly help you at that time.

A: 영업 끝났나요?
B: 네. 죄송하지만 모든 가게는 밤 9시에 문을 닫습니다.
A: 이런! 오늘 밤에 꼭 사야 할 게 있었어요.
B: 정말 죄송합니다, 고객님. 모든 계산대가 이미 종료되었습니다.
A: 아침 몇 시에 여나요?
B: 오전 9시에 엽니다. 그 때 오시면 성심껏 도와드리겠습니다.

Warm-up

closed, at 9 p.m., make a purchase, at 9 a.m., gladly, at that time

Practice

A 1 past   2 late   3 employee   4 tomorrow

B ① Yes, ma'am. I'm sorry, but all the stores close at 9 p.m.
② I'm very sorry, ma'am, but all of our registers are already closed.
③ We'll be open at 9 a.m., and will gladly help you at that time.

Week 07 On the Street
Unit 01 Getting Directions

Listening 향상 팁
p. 130

A 1 First, ①   2 Third, ③   3 Second, ②

B ① In the beginning   ② Next   ③ Then   ④ Finally

Okay, you'll go down this street and find the market. In the beginning, there are a lot of food stalls. Next, the shops are all selling souvenirs and trinkets. Then, there are mostly clothing stores. Finally, you'll find the jewelry shops you are looking for.

네, 이 길을 따라 쭉 내려가시면 시장을 찾을 수 있을 거예요. 맨 처음, 그곳에는 수 많은 음식 노점들이 있어요. 그 다음, 모든 가게에서 기념품이나 자질구레한 장신구를 팔아요. 그리고 그 후, 주로 옷 가게가 있습니다. 끝으로, 찾고 있던 귀금속점이 나올 거예요.

C 1 T 2 F

Situation I   pp. 131-132

A: Excuse me, but I'm a bit lost. I'm looking for Waterford Park. Do you know where it is?
B: Sure. Do you know the city well?
A: Sorry. I'm not from around here.
B: That's all right. Okay, here's what you do. First, drive straight down this street about one kilometer. Then, at the third stop light, turn to the right.
A: What should I do after that?
B: Just drive straight for about five minutes. The park will be right in front of you. There's no way you can miss it.

A: 실례합니다만, 제가 길을 잃어서요. 워터포드 공원을 찾고 있어요. 어디 있는지 아시나요?
B: 물론이죠. 여기 시내를 잘 아시나요?
A: 미안한데, 제가 이 주위를 잘 몰라요.
B: 괜찮아요. 자, 이렇게 하시면 됩니다. 먼저 이 거리를 따라 약 1킬로미터 정도 쭉 내려가세요. 그리고 세 번째 신호등에서 우회전해야 됩니다.
A: 그 다음에는 어떻게 해야 하죠?
B: 약 5분 동안 쭉 직진하세요. 공원이 바로 앞에 있을 겁니다. 절대 지나칠 수 없어요.

Warm-up

lost, the city, first, then, at the third stop light, after that

Practice

A 1 (a) 2 (a) 3 (c)   **B** (b)   **C** 1 F 2 F

Dictation

① lost ② from around here ③ First ④ Then
⑤ after that ⑥ about five minutes ⑦ no way

Situation II   p. 133

A: Hello. Do you know where the Museum of Natural History is? I can't find it.
B: Of course. It's located at the corner of Whitson Street and Baker Drive.
A: Um... I don't know the city, so could you please give me directions there?
B: No problem. You're on Whitson Street right now, so it will be easy to find.
A: Do you mean I just need to go straight?
B: Actually, you're going the wrong way. First, do a U-turn. Next, go straight three blocks. You'll see the museum on your right.

A: 안녕하세요. 자연사 박물관이 어디인지 아세요? 못 찾겠네요.
B: 물론이죠. 윗슨 스트리트와 베이커 드라이브의 코너 쪽에 위치해 있어요.
A: 제가 이 도시를 잘 몰라서 그런데 그쪽까지 가는 길을 좀 알려 주실 수 있을까요?
B: 물론이죠. 당신이 지금 윗슨 스트리트에 있으니까 찾기 쉬울 거예요.
A: 그 말은 그냥 직진하면 된다는 말인가요?
B: 실은 반대길로 가고 있으시네요. 먼저 유턴하세요. 그 다음에 세 블록을 직진하세요. 그럼 오른쪽에 박물관이 보일 겁니다.

Warm-up (c)

Practice

A 1 a stranger 2 the wrong 3 turn around

B ① Of course. It's located at the corner of Whitson Street and Baker Drive.
② No problem. You're on Whitson Street right now, so it will be easy to find.
③ Actually, you're going the wrong way. First, do a U-turn. Next, go straight three blocks. You'll see the museum on your right.

Unit 02 Shopping for Souvenirs

Listening 향상 팁   p. 134

A 1 (a) kinds of   (b) to choose from
2 (a) Pick up   (b) Get
3 (a) today only   (b) one-day only
4 (a) $50 or more   (b) over $50

B 1 T 2 T

Situation I
pp. 135-136

Welcome, shoppers, to Gerald's Souvenir Shop. We've got all kinds of souvenirs for sale. You can get postcards, T-shirts, stuffed animals, and books. We also have key chains and pictures. Pick up some items for yourself in order to remember your trip. Or buy some items for your friends and family members back home. Now, I'd like to tell you about a special sale we're having today only. Spend $50 or more, and you'll get 20% off your entire purchase. That's a deal which simply can't be beat. Enjoy shopping here at Gerald's Souvenir Shop.

안녕하세요, 제럴드네 기념품점 쇼핑객 여러분. 우리는 모든 종류의 기념품을 갖추고 있습니다. 여러분께서는 우편 엽서, 티셔츠, 봉제 인형, 책을 사실 수 있습니다. 또한 열쇠 고리와 사진도 갖추고 있습니다. 여러분의 여행을 기억할 만한 물건을 몇 가지 고르시면 됩니다. 아니면 여러분의 친구나 집에 있는 가족을 위해 몇 가지 사 보세요. 이제, 오늘만 적용되는 특별 할인에 관해 말씀 드리겠습니다. 50달러 이상을 사시면 구입 물품 전체를 20% 할인 받으실 수 있습니다. 더할 나위 없는 좋은 조건입니다. 그러면 제럴드네 기념품 점에서 쇼핑을 즐기시길 바랍니다.

Warm-up (a), (b), (d)

Practice
A 1 (b) 2 (a) 3 (b)   B (b)   C 1 T 2 F

Dictation
① all kinds of   ② items for yourself
③ for your friends   ④ special sale   ⑤ $50 or more
⑥ 20% off   ⑦ can't be beat

Situation II
p. 137

A: Good morning. Are you looking for anything in particular?
B: Not really. I enjoyed my time at the museum, and I want some souvenirs. But I don't know what to buy.
A: Why don't you get a few postcards? We've got some really nice ones that you can mail to your friends from here.
B: Do they have pictures of the exhibits on them?
A: Yes, here. I can show you the postcards. And I'd like to show you some books about the museum's exhibits. You'll love them.
B: All right. Thank you very much.

A: 안녕하세요. 특별히 찾는 거 있으세요?
B: 아니요. 박물관을 좀 구경했는데 기념품 좀 사려고요. 그런데 뭘 사야 할 지 모르겠네요.
A: 엽서를 몇 장 사시는 게 어떠세요? 여기에 친구들에게 보낼 수 있는 좋은 게 몇 개 있어요.
B: 거기에 전시품 사진도 나와 있나요?
A: 네, 여기요. 엽서들을 보여 드릴 수 있어요. 그리고 박물관 전시품에 대한 몇몇 책자도 보여 드릴게요. 좋아하실 거예요.
B: 알겠습니다. 정말 고맙습니다.

Warm-up
in particular, souvenirs, postcards, pictures, some books, exhibits

Practice
A (c)
B ① Not really. I enjoyed my time at the museum, and I want some souvenirs. But I don't know what to buy.
② Do they have pictures of the exhibits on them?
③ All right. Thank you very much.

Unit 03 Bargaining

Listening 향상 팁
p. 138

A 1 a little high   2 halfway   3 have to pass
B 1 (c) 2 (b) 3 (a)
C 1 T 2 T

Situation I
pp. 139-140

A: Good afternoon, ma'am. Do you see anything that you like?
B: I think this blue wool sweater looks wonderful, but it's a bit out of my price range. I can't pay that much for it.
A: How much would you like to pay?

B: How about 60 dollars? I think that's a reasonable price.
A: I can't accept that offer. I won't make a profit at that price. What about paying 75 dollars for it? That's a discount of 20 dollars.
B: You've got a deal. Do you take cash?

A: 안녕하세요, 손님. 맘에 드시는 것이 있나요?
B: 이 파란색 모 스웨터가 멋진데, 제 예산 범위를 약간 넘기네요. 이만큼 낼 수가 없어요.
A: 얼마에 사고 싶으신데요?
B: 60달러 어떤가요? 괜찮은 가격인 듯 한데요.
A: 그건 받아들일 수 없네요. 그 가격에는 남는 게 없거든요. 75달러로 사는 건 어떠세요? 20달러나 깎아 드린 거예요.
B: 좋아요. 현금도 받으시죠?

Warm-up

my price range, how much, a reasonable price, make a profit, discount of, a deal

Practice

A 1 (c) 2 (b) 3 (a)   **B** (a)   **C** 1 F 2 F

Dictation

① looks wonderful ② my price range
③ How much ④ How about ⑤ reasonable
⑥ make a profit ⑦ a discount of

Situation II   p. 141

A: Can I interest you in this pair of gold earrings?
B: They look beautiful. How much are they?
A: They cost one hundred dollars, but I can give you a special price. I can sell them to you for 90 dollars today.
B: I'm afraid that's too much money. I'm looking for something which costs about half that amount.
A: Shall I show you a few other items then? I've got just the right thing in mind for you.
B: Great. I'd love to see what you have.

A: 이 금 귀걸이 보실 의향 있으세요?
B: 아름답네요. 그거 얼마예요?
A: 100달러인데요 손님께 특별 가격으로 드릴 수 있어요. 오늘 손님께는 90달러에 판매할게요.
B: 좀 비싼 것 같네요. 그것의 절반 정도 되는 가격의 물건을 찾고 있는 중이거든요.

A: 그럼 제가 다른 상품 몇 개 보여 드릴까요? 손님 마음에 딱 드실 만 한 게 마침 있는데요.
B: 좋아요. 갖고 계신걸 보고 싶네요.

Warm-up

cost, a special price, too much money, looking for, half that amount, the right thing

Practice

A (b), (c)
B ① They look beautiful. How much are they?
② I'm afraid that's too much money. I'm looking for something which costs about half that amount.
③ Great. I'd love to see what you have.

Unit 04 Enjoying Street Food

Listening 향상 팁   p. 142

A 1 I, (c) 2 he, (b) 3 asked, (a) 4 what, (d)
B 1 (b) 2 (c) 3 (a)
C 1 T 2 T

Situation I   pp. 143-144

Good evening, sir. Can I interest you in some of the food I'm selling? I'd like you to know that I have the best hot dogs in town. They're absolutely delicious. You'll love them if you try them. I've got ketchup, mustard, and relish for you to put on your hot dog. And if you don't just want a regular hot dog, why don't you try one of my chili dogs? The combination of the hot dog and chili will be something you'll never forget. Yum! You can get regular-sized hot dogs or foot-long hot dogs. So what do you say? Interested?

좋은 저녁입니다. 제가 파는 음식 좀 추천해도 될까요? 저는 시내에서 가장 맛있는 핫도그를 팔고 있습니다. 끝내주게 맛있습니다. 맛보시면 정말 좋아하실 겁니다. 핫도그에 뿌릴 케첩, 머스타드, 렐리시도 있습니다. 평범함 핫도그를 원하지 않으시면 칠리도그는 어떤가요? 핫도그와 칠리의 조합은 당신이 절대 잊지 못할 맛이 될것입니다. 꿀꺽! 일반 사이즈나 1 피트 길이의 핫도그도 있습니다. 어떠신가요? 땡기시나요?

Warm-up

interest you, some of the food, the best hot dogs, absolutely, love them, chili dogs

Practice

A 1 (b)   2 (c)   3 (c)   **B** (a)   **C** 1 T   2 F

Dictation

① best   ② absolutely   ③ on your hot dog
④ my chili dogs   ⑤ never forgot   ⑥ Yum
⑦ Interested

Situation II   p. 145

A: Excuse me, but what are you selling?
B: These are pretzels. Would you like one? I can put mustard on it if you like.
A: Mustard on a pretzel? Gross! How could anyone like that?
B: Actually, most people prefer to eat their pretzels that way. I tell you what…. Try a pretzel with mustard. If you don't like it, you don't have to pay me anything.
A: It's a deal…. Hey! This is pretty good. Thanks. How much do I owe you?
B: That will be two dollars and fifty cents, please.

A: 실례하지만 뭘 팔고 계신가요?
B: 이건 프레즐입니다. 한번 드셔 보시겠어요? 원하시면 머스타드를 뿌려 드릴 수도 있어요.
A: 프레즐에 머스타드를 뿌린다고요? 맛이 이상할 것 같은데요? 어떻게 사람들이 이걸 좋아할 수 있죠?
B: 사실 대부분의 사람들은 그렇게 프레즐을 먹는 것을 좋아해요. 있잖아요…. 머스타드랑 같이 프레즐을 한번 드셔 보세요. 만약에 맛이 없으면 돈을 안 내셔도 돼요.
A: 좋아요…. 저기요! 이거 꽤 맛있는데요. 감사해요. 얼마 드려야 하죠?
B: 2달러 50센트입니다.

Warm-up

pretzels, mustard, actually, prefer to eat, a deal, pretty good

Practice

A 1 street vendor   2 mustard   3 more   4 pretzel

B ① These are pretzels. Would you like one? I can put mustard on it if you like.
② Actually, most people prefer to eat their pretzels that way. I tell you what…. Try a pretzel with

mustard. If you don't like it, you don't have to pay me anything.
③ That will be two dollars and fifty cents, please.

Week 08 At the Tourist Site
Unit 01 Purchasing Tickets

Listening 향상 팁   p. 150

A 1 (b)   2 (a)   3 (b)

1 How much are the different seats?
  다른 좌석들은 얼마인가요?
2 Can I cancel my reservation?
  제 예약을 취소할 수 있을까요?
3 Where do you want to sit?
  어디에 앉고 싶으신가요?

B 1 T   2 T

Situation I   pp. 151-152

A: Hi. I'd like to buy tickets for today's show.
B: There are three different performances today. Which show would you like to see, the 4:00, 6:30, or 8:00 one?
A: Hmm…. I'd prefer to see the one at 6:30.
B: No problem. Where in the theater do you want to sit? Here is a seating chart.
A: Let me see…. I'd like seats in the front. I need two tickets. How much do they cost?
B: Each ticket costs $25, so you owe a total of $50.

A: 안녕하세요. 저는 오늘 쇼의 공연 표를 사고 싶어요.
B: 오늘 공연이 3개 있습니다. 4시, 6시 30분, 8시 공연에서 어느 것을 보고 싶으신가요?
A: 음 … 네. 6시 30분 것으로 주세요.
B: 네. 극장의 어느 자리에 앉고 싶으신가요? 여기 좌석표가 있습니다.
A: 잠깐만요 …. 앞자리에 앉고 싶네요. 표 두 장이 필요해요. 얼마죠?
B: 한 장당 25달러이므로 50달러입니다.

Warm-up

tickets, performances, in the theater, in the front, you owe, a total of

Practice
A 1 (b) 2 (b) 3 (c)   B (a)   C 1 F 2 F

Dictation
① today's show ② three different performances
③ the one at 6:30 ④ seating chart ⑤ in the front
⑥ Each ticket ⑦ a total of $50

Situation II
p. 153

A: Excuse me. I want to purchase three tickets for the dolphin show starting in ten minutes.
B: I'm very sorry, but it's all sold out.
A: That's too bad. When is the next time the show will be performed?
B: You're in luck. Since today is the weekend, there are two more shows today. One is at 3:30, and the other is at 6:00. Which one do you prefer?
A: I'll take tickets for the 3:30 show, please. What do they cost?
B: They are just $5 apiece. You can pay with cash or a credit card.

A: 실례합니다. 10분 후에 시작하는 돌고래 쇼 표를 세 장 사고 싶습니다.
B: 죄송하지만 그 공연은 매진입니다.
A: 너무 아쉽네요. 다음 공연은 언제 하나요?
B: 운이 좋으시네요. 오늘이 주말이라 오늘 공연이 두 개 더 있습니다. 하나는 3시 30분에 있고요, 다른 하나는 6시에 있습니다. 어느 것이 더 좋으세요?
A: 3시30분 공연 티켓을 살게요. 얼마죠?
B: 한 장에 5달러입니다. 현금이나 카드로 결제하실 수 있습니다.

Warm-up
(b)

Practice
A 1 cannot 2 on the weekdays 3 $15
B ① I'm very sorry, but it's all sold out.
  ② You're in luck. Since today is the weekend, there are two more shows today. One is at 3:30, and the other is at 6:00. Which one do you prefer?
  ③ They are just $5 apiece. You can pay with cash or a credit card.

Unit 02 Booking a Tour

Listening 향상 팁
p. 154

A 1 Rising 2 Falling 3 Fall-Rise
B 1 (b) 2 (a)
C 1 F 2 T

Situation I
pp. 155-156

A: Good morning, I can book tours of the city here, can't I?
B: That's correct. Are you interested in the full-day tour or the half-day one?
A: I'm not sure. I'll get to see more sights on the full-day tour, right?
B: Uh-huh. The full-day tour takes you to the museum and the harbor area. The half-day tour doesn't do that.
A: Hmm.... I think I'd rather go on the full-day tour then. I definitely want to visit the museum.
B: Excellent. How many tickets would you like to purchase?

A: 안녕하세요, 시내 관광을 여기서 예약할 수 있죠, 그렇죠?
B: 맞습니다. 종일 코스를 원하시나요, 아니면 반나절 코스를 원하시나요?
A: 잘 모르겠네요. 종일 코스이면 더 많이 볼 수 있겠네요. 맞죠?
B: 네. 종일 코스를 하시면 박물관과 부두 지역을 가시게 되는데, 반나절 코스는 그게 없습니다.
A: 음… 그러면 종일 코스로 갈게요. 박물관을 꼭 가고 싶거든요.
B: 잘 하셨어요. 표 몇 장을 사실 건가요?

Warm-up
book, tours of the city, full-day tour, more sights, harbor area, how many tickets

Practice
A 1 (b) 2 (c) 3 (b)   B (c)   C 1 F 2 T

Dictation
① can't I ② full-day tour ③ right ④ Uh-huh
⑤ museum ⑥ definitely ⑦ purchase

Situation II
p. 157

A: Hello. I need to book one of your tours, please.
B: Of course. Which tour would you like to make a reservation for?
A: The walking tour of the historic district. You run that tour every day, don't you?
B: I'm afraid not. Our tour guide is only available on Mondays, Wednesdays, and Saturdays this summer.
A: Okay. Well.... Tomorrow is Wednesday, so... it's possible to take that tour, isn't it?
B: It sure is. We still have space. Why don't you sign your name right here on this list?

A: 안녕하세요. 여기 투어 상품 중 하나를 예약하고 싶어요.
B: 물론이죠. 어떤 상품을 예약하고 싶으세요?
A: 역사지구 도보 투어요. 그 투어는 매일 있잖아요, 그렇죠?
B: 죄송합니다. 저희 투어 가이드가 올 여름은 월요일, 수요일 토요일에만 시간이 되네요.
A: 알겠습니다. 그러면.... 내일이 수요일이니까... 그 여행 상품을 예약할 수 있네요, 그렇죠?
B: 그렇습니다. 아직 남은 자리도 있고요. 여기 이 명단에 서명해 주시겠어요?

Warm-up (a), (b)

Practice

A (b)

B ① Of course. Which tour would you like to make a reservation for?
② I'm afraid not. Our tour guide is only available on Mondays, Wednesdays, and Saturdays this summer.
③ It sure is. We still have space. Why don't you sign your name right here on this list?

Unit 03 Rules at Tourist Sites

Listening 향상 팁
p. 158

A **1** to, for **2** a, for **3** to, or
B **1** can **2** can't
C **1** T **2** F

Situation I
pp. 159-160

Before we enter the gallery, I need to tell you a few things. First of all, photography is strictly prohibited. Camera flashes can harm the paintings. Fortunately, you can purchase postcards or pictures of the artwork at the souvenir shop. Next, please keep your voices down at all times. Many of our patrons like to observe the art in silence. Therefore, you should try not to disturb them. Furthermore, we request that you turn off your mobile phones. If you need to speak on your phone, you may leave the gallery and go to the main lobby.

미술관에 들어가기 전에 몇 가지 말씀 드리겠습니다. 먼저 사진 촬영이 엄격히 금지됩니다. 사진기 조명이 미술품에 손상을 입히기 때문입니다. 다행히 기념품 점에서 미술품 그림이 담긴 엽서나 사진을 사실 수 있습니다. 그리고 항상 목소리를 낮추세요. 많은 미술관 관람객은 조용히 작품을 감상하기를 좋아합니다. 그러므로 방해가 되지 않도록 조심하세요. 또한 휴대폰을 꺼 주셔야 합니다. 휴대폰으로 통화하시려면 관람실을 나가 1층 로비로 가십시오.

Warm-up
first of all, photography, prohibited, at all times, patrons, furthermore

Practice

A **1** (c) **2** (b) **3** (c) B (a) C **1** l **2** l

Dictation
① to ② can ③ can ④ or ⑤ at ⑥ your ⑦ at

Situation II
p. 161

A: Hold on a minute. I want to get something to eat from my bag.
B: What? You can't do that. You're not supposed to eat anything here.
A: Why not?
B: It's against the rules. There's no eating or drinking allowed inside because this is an historic building. However, if you're really hungry, we can drop by the snack bar out front.
A: Hmm.... I guess I can wait a few minutes. We've almost finished touring the building, haven't we?

B: Yes, we only have two more rooms to look at. Then, we'll have seen everything of interest here.
A: 잠깐만요. 제 가방에서 먹을 것 좀 가져 올게요.
B: 뭐라고요? 그렇게 못해요. 여기에서는 아무것도 먹을 수 없는걸요.
A: 왜 안 되는데요?
B: 규칙에 어긋나는 거예요. 안에서는 먹거나 마실 수 없게 되어 있거든요. 왜냐하면 이곳은 역사적인 기념 건축물이잖아요. 하지만 정말 배가 고프시다면 입구 쪽에 있는 스낵 바에 잠시 들를 수 있어요.
A: 음... 몇 분 정도는 참을 수 있을 것 같아요. 우리 건축물 투어하는거 거의 끝나 가잖아요, 그렇죠?
B: 네, 두 군데만 더 보면 돼요. 그러면 이곳에서 흥미로운 것은 모두 다 본 거예요.

Warm-up
something to eat, from my bag, not supposed, against, historic building, of interest

Practice
A (c), (d)

B ① What? You can't do that. You're not supposed to eat anything here.
② It's against the rules. There's no eating or drinking allowed inside because this is an historic building. However, if you're really hungry, we can drop by the snack bar out front.
③ Yes, we only have two more rooms to look at. Then, we'll have seen everything of interest here.

Unit 04 Touring a Site

Listening 향상 팁   p. 162

A 1 (a) 2 (a) 3 (b)

1 We are open every day from 9 to 7.
저희는 매일 9시부터 7시까지 문을 엽니다.
2 We have tours available in English, French, Chinese, and Spanish.
저희는 영어, 프랑스어, 중국어, 스페인어로 투어를 진행할 수 있습니다.
3 The museum is closed weekly on Mondays.
박물관은 매주 월요일에 문을 닫습니다.

B 1 T 2 T

Situation I   pp. 163-164

Welcome to the Peabody Museum. We hope you enjoy viewing our collection. There are three floors here. The third floor contains our art collection. You can view art from European, Asian, and American masters. I'm sure you'll love the paintings and sculptures. On the second floor, you can see our collection of ancient Greek and Roman relics. We have some special items on loan from the Athens Museum. Be sure to check them out. Finally, on the first floor, as you can see, we have dinosaur fossils. Now, please have a great time for the next two hours.

피바디(Peabody) 박물관에 오신 걸 환영합니다. 전시품 감상을 즐기시길 바랍니다. 이 박물관은 세 개 층이 있습니다. 3층에는 미술 작품들이 있습니다. 유럽, 아시아, 미국의 대가들이 그린 미술 작품을 보실 수 있습니다. 회화와 조각 작품들을 좋아하시게 될 겁니다. 2층에는 고대 그리스와 로마 시대 유물들을 보실 수 있습니다. 아테나 박물관에서 임대해 온 특별 전시물도 있습니다. 반드시 관람해 보세요. 마지막으로 1층에는 보시다시피 공룡 화석이 있습니다. 자, 다음 두 시간 동안 좋은 시간 보내시길 바랍니다.

Warm-up
museum, our collection, sculptures, on loan, dinosaur fossils, next two

Practice
A 1 (c) 2 (c) 3 (b)   B (c)   C 1 T 2 T

Dictation
① three floors ② our art collection
③ European, Asian, American
④ ancient Greek, Roman ⑤ on loan
⑥ dinosaur fossils ⑦ the next two hours

Situation II   p. 165

A: Which room in the palace is this?
B: This is the throne room. The king and queen used to sit here on various occasions.
A: I like the artwork on the walls. When were these paintings made?

B: Most of them are more than 400 years old. The kingdom was wealthy during that time, so its rulers spent lots of money on artwork.
A: What are we going to see next?
B: We're going to visit the royal quarters. A lot of antique furniture is on display in those rooms. The crown jewels are located there as well.

A: 궁전에서 이 곳은 어떤 방인가요?
B: 이곳은 접견실이에요. 왕과 왕비가 여러 경우에 이곳에 앉곤 했답니다.
A: 벽에 있는 그림이 마음에 드는데요. 이 그림들은 언제 만들어진 건가요?
B: 대부분의 것들은 400여년 전에 만들어 진 거예요. 왕국이 그 당시 동안에는 풍요로웠거든요. 그래서 그 때의 통치자들은 그림에 많은 돈을 썼죠.
A: 다음에는 무엇을 볼 건가요?
B: 왕과 왕비의 침소에 가볼 겁니다. 침실에는 많은 고가구들이 전시되어 있지요. 왕관 보석들도 그곳에 놓여 있습니다.

1 Thank you for your cooperation. See you then.
협조해 주셔서 감사합니다. 그때 뵙겠습니다.

2 Something came up. I have to take care of it.
일이 생겼어요. 제가 해결해야 합니다.

3 Unfortunately, I can't make it at 3:00.
죄송하지만 3시에 갈 수 없겠네요.

4 No problem. I'll be available then.
괜찮습니다. 그때 시간 됩니다.

B 1 T 2 T

Warm-up

palace, the throne room, various occasions, wealthy, the royal quarters, antique furniture

Practice

A 1 a palace 2 paintings 3 old furniture 4 royal quarters

B ① This is the throne room. The king and queen used to sit here on various occasions.

② Most of them are more than 400 years old. The kingdom was wealthy during that time, so its rulers spent lots of money on artwork.

③ We're going to visit the royal quarters. A lot of antique furniture is on display in those rooms. The crown jewels are located there as well.

Situation I
pp. 171-172

Good morning, Ms. Eastwood. This is Cedric Thompson calling from Dynamic Systems. I received your e-mail and would love to have a meeting with you. Unfortunately, I cannot meet today because I am too busy. But I am free on Wednesday in the morning. How about meeting at 10 AM? I can visit your office in Springfield because I have another meeting there in the afternoon. I need directions to your office though. How about calling me back at 457-3934? Talk to you soon. Goodbye.

안녕하세요, 이스트우드씨. 저는 다이나믹 시스템즈의 세드릭 톰슨입니다. 귀하의 이메일을 받았고, 귀사와 미팅을 갖고 싶습니다. 안타깝게도 오늘은 너무 바빠서 만날 수 없네요. 하지만 수요일 오전은 시간이 있습니다. 오전 10시에 미팅하는 건 어떠세요? 제가 스프링필드에 있는 사무실로 가겠습니다. 왜냐하면 그쪽에서 오후에 또 다른 미팅이 있거든요. 그래도 사무실 위치 좀 알려주세요. 457-3934로 제게 연락을 주시는 건 어떨까요? 조만간 또 통화하죠. 안녕히 계세요.

Warm-up

received your e-mail, unfortunately, visit your office, another meeting, directions, calling me back

Practice

A 1 (a) 2 (b) 3 (c)   **B** (a)   **C** 1 F 2 T

Dictation

① your e-mail ② Unfortunately ③ too busy
④ How about meeting ⑤ visit your office
⑥ need directions ⑦ calling me back

Week 09 On the Phone
Unit 01 Arranging a Meeting

Listening 향상 팁
p. 170

A 1 (c) 2 (b) 3 (a) 4 (d)

Situation II

p. 173

A: We need to have a staff meeting to talk about the merger with the Dolson Corporation.
B: How about tomorrow? Does everyone have time?
A: No, the training session for the computer software is being held all day. And Thursday is no good because the CEO is coming here.
B: Then we'd better have the meeting today. We can have it during lunch.
A: All right. I'll call Sal's Deli right now and have a bunch of sandwiches and chips delivered. You send an e-mail to everyone.
B: Right. I'll do that immediately.

A: 돌슨 주식회사와의 합병에 대해 얘기하기 위해 직원 회의를 해야 합니다.
B: 내일은 어떤가요? 모두 시간 괜찮나요?
A: 아니요, 컴퓨터 소프트웨어 교육 일정이 하루 종일 잡혀 있습니다. 그리고 목요일은 CEO가 여기 오시기 때문에 별로 좋지 않고요.
B: 그러면 오늘 회의를 하는 게 좋겠군요. 점심 시간 동안 할 수 있잖아요.
A: 알겠습니다. 제가 바로 살스델리에 전화를 걸어서 샌드위치와 감자칩을 좀 배달시킬게요. 직원들에게 이메일 좀 보내주세요.
B: 알겠습니다. 지금 바로 하죠.

Warm-up

a staff meeting, merger, training session, the CEO, during lunch, an e-mail

Practice

A 1 CEO   2 a training session   3 during

B ① How about tomorrow?
     Does everyone have time?
   ② Then we'd better have the meeting today. We can have it during lunch.
   ③ Right, I'll do that immediately.

Unit 02 Getting a Complaint Call

Listening 향상 팁

p. 174

A 1 complain, damaged   2 everything, ordered
   3 received, missing

B 1 (b)   2 (b)

1 A: Hi, I'm calling about a problem with a shipment.
  B: Yes, ma'am. What's the problem?
  A: Every item in my box was broken when I got it!
  A: 안녕하세요, 배달 온 것 때문에 전화드렸습니다.
  B: 네, 고객님. 무엇이 문제이신가요?
  A: 내가 받아 보니, 상자에 든 것이 모두 깨져 있었어요.

2 A: ABC Credit Card Company. How can I help you?
  B: Yes, I just got my new card and my name is spelled wrong!
  A: Oh, no. I will issue a new one to you right away.
  A: ABC 신용카드사입니다. 무엇을 도와 드릴까요?
  B: 네, 새 카드를 방금 받았는데, 제 이름 철자가 잘못되어 있네요.
  A: 아, 이런. 바로 새 카드를 발급해 드리겠습니다.

C 1 F   2 T

Situation I

pp. 175-176

A: Hello. This is customer service. Janet speaking. How may I be of assistance?
B: Hello. My name is Brian Washington. I purchased some clothes on your website, and they were just delivered to me. But there are a couple of problems.
A: What's the matter with them, sir?
B: One of the shirts is the wrong size, and the pants I ordered don't fit, either.
A: I'm terribly sorry about that. Can I have your order number, please? Then, I can arrange to send you the right items.
B: Sure. My order number is CR5403M1.

A: 안녕하세요. 고객센터의 자넷입니다. 어떻게 도와 드릴까요?
B: 안녕하세요. 제 이름은 브라이언 워싱턴입니다. 귀사의 웹사이트에서 옷을 몇 개 샀고 옷들이 방금 저에게 배달되었습니다. 그런데 몇 가지 문제들이 좀 있어서요.
A: 어떤 문제들이 있으신가요?

B: 셔츠 중에 하나는 사이즈가 잘못 됐고요 제가 주문한 바지도 맞지 않아요.
A: 정말 죄송스럽게 생각합니다. 주문 번호를 말씀해 주시겠어요? 그러면 제가 제대로 된 상품을 준비해 놓도록 하겠습니다.
B: 물론이죠. 제 주문번호는 CR5403M1입니다.

Warm-up

speaking, of assistance, the shirts, the pants, order number, arrange to send

Practice

A 1 (a) 2 (a) 3 (b)   B (b)   C 1 F 2 T

Dictation

① purchased ② delivered to
③ a couple of problems ④ the wrong size
⑤ don't fit ⑥ arrange to send ⑦ order number

Situation II   p. 177

A: Hi. I bought a vacuum cleaner at your store a couple of hours ago, but it won't work.
B: What exactly is the problem with the item you purchased, ma'am?
A: When I plugged it in, it wouldn't turn on.
B: I see. Why don't you bring the item back to the store and exchange it for another one?
A: I don't have time to return the vacuum cleaner today. I guess I can do that tomorrow morning.
B: Great. Be sure to bring the receipt with you. And I'm very sorry about this.

A: 안녕하세요. 몇 시간 전에 매장에서 청소기를 샀는데요. 작동을 안 하네요.
B: 손님께서 구매하신 상품에 정확히 어떤 문제가 있는 건가요?
A: 청소기의 전원을 연결하면 켜지질 않아요.
B: 알겠습니다. 상품을 매장으로 가져오셔서 다른 것으로 교환하시는 게 어떨까요?
A: 오늘은 청소기를 반납할 시간이 없네요. 내일 오전에 할 수 있을 것 같아요.
B: 좋습니다. 영수증도 함께 가져오시는 것 잊지 마세요. 정말 죄송합니다.

Warm-up (c)

Practice

A (c)
B ① What exactly is the problem with the item you purchased, ma'am?
② I see. Why don't you bring the item back to the store and exchange it for another one?
③ Great. Be sure to bring the receipt with you. And I'm very sorry about this.

Unit 03 Transferring a Call

Listening 향상 팁   p. 178

A 1 set up, have in mind
  2 How, sound, wide open
  3 works for, at, at

B 1 T 2 T

Situation I   pp. 179-180

A: Hello. May I speak with Jason Cartwright, please?
B: I'm sorry, but he no longer works here. What do you need to speak with him about?
A: He was the person who processed my loan. I need to speak to him about repaying it. I'd like to change the terms a bit.
B: Ah, okay. All of Mr. Cartwright's accounts are being handled by Janet Morgan. Would you like me to transfer you to her?
A: Yes, please. That would be great.
B: All right. Hold on just one moment, please.

A: 여보세요. 제이슨 카트라이트 씨와 통화할 수 있을까요?
B: 죄송합니다만 그분은 더 이상 이곳에서 근무하지 않습니다. 그분과 무엇에 대해 얘기하시려고 했나요?
A: 그분이 제 대출을 담당했던 분인데요. 대출금 상환에 대해서 얘기해야 해서요. 조건들을 조금 바꾸고 싶어요.
B: 아, 알겠습니다. 카트라이트 씨가 관리하던 계좌들은 모두 자넷 모건 씨가 관리하고 있습니다. 그분께 전화를 돌려 드릴까요?
A: 네, 부탁합니다. 그러면 좋겠네요.
B: 알겠습니다. 잠시만 기다려 주세요.

Warm-up

no longer, my loan, the terms, accounts, transfer, hold on

Practice
A 1 (b) 2 (b) 3 (c)   B (b)   C 1 T 2 T

Dictation
① speak with ② no longer works
③ processed my loan ④ about repaying
⑤ change the terms ⑥ being handled ⑦ transfer

Situation II   p. 181

A: Hello. Thank you for calling Swanson's. This is Marcia. How may I help you?
B: Hi. I'm calling about the special offer for sweaters that I saw advertised on television. How can I purchase a couple of them?
A: You need to speak with someone in the Sales Department.
B: I'm afraid that I don't know the extension. Could you let me know it, please?
A: Of course. It's 54. But if you wait a minute, I can transfer your call. I'll put you on the line with Steve.
B: Thanks a lot.

A: 안녕하세요. 스완슨에 전화 주셔서 감사합니다. 저는 마르시아입니다. 어떻게 도와 드릴까요?
B: 안녕하세요. 텔레비전 광고에 나온 스웨터 특별 할인에 대해서 전화 드렸습니다. 그 물건들 몇 개를 어떻게 구매할 수 있을까요?
A: 영업부 직원과 말씀을 나눠 보셔야 할 것 같네요.
B: 죄송하지만 제가 내선 번호를 모르는데요. 저에게 알려 주시겠어요?
A: 물론입니다. 54번입니다. 그런데 조금 기다려 주신다면 제가 전화를 돌려 드릴 수 있어요. 스티브와 연결시켜 드리겠습니다.
B: 정말 감사합니다.

Warm-up   (c)

Practice
A (a), (d)

B ① Hi. I'm calling about the special offer for sweaters that I saw advertised on television. How can I purchase a couple of them?
② I'm afraid that I don't know the extension. Could you let me know it, please?
③ Thanks a lot.

Unit 04 Changing a Project Schedule

Listening 향상 팁   p. 182
A 1 however 2 on the other hand 3 otherwise
  4 as a result 5 consequently 6 therefore
B 1 T 2 T

Situation I   pp. 183-184

All right, everyone, I have some news. Apparently, Johnson Construction needs to start building as soon as possible. So we have to finish the blueprints faster than we had planned. As a result, the final due date is no longer December 1st. It's been moved up to November 15th. I realize this only gives us two more weeks to complete everything. But please remember that we're already in the final stages. However, we're going to have to work plenty of overtime, so expect to stay late every night and to come in on the next two weekends.

자, 여러분, 소식이 좀 있습니다. 아시다시피, 존슨 건축에서 가능한 한 빨리 건설을 시작하기를 바랍니다. 그래서 우리는 우리가 계획했던 것 보다 더 빨리 도면 설계를 끝내야 해요. 따라서, 최종 마감일은 더 이상 12월 1일이 아닙니다. 최종 마감일은 11월 15일로 변경되었습니다. 이 말은 우리가 모든 것을 끝내는데 2주 정도의 시간 밖에 없다는 것을 의미합니다. 하지만 우리는 이미 마지막 단계에 있다는 것을 잊지 말아 주세요. 그러나 우리는 야근을 많이 해야 할 것입니다. 매일 밤 늦게까지 일하고 다음 2주 동안 주말에도 출근할 것을 알고 계세요.

Warm-up
apparently, the blueprints, as a result, final due date, in the final stages, however

Practice
A 1 (b) 2 (a) 3 (c)   B (b)   C 1 F 2 T

Dictation
① Apparently ② So ③ As a result
④ November 15th ⑤ But ⑥ However ⑦ so

Situation II
p. 185

A: Susan, we've got to delay our delivery of items to Sherman Motors.
B: Why? I thought we could send them the parts they wanted by this Friday.
A: That was the original plan, but we had to shut down one of the assembly lines. It needs to be repaired.
B: Okay. Then when do you think we can deliver everything?
A: I'm positive we can do that by next Tuesday. However, we'll have to operate the assembly lines over the weekend.
B: That will require paying the workers overtime, but we don't want to lose this contract. Let's do it.

A: 수잔, 쉐르만 모터스에 보낼 상품 배송을 좀 지연시켜야 할 것 같아요.
B: 왜요? 그들이 원했던 부품들을 이번 주 금요일까지 보낼 수 있을 줄 알았는데요.
A: 그게 원래 계획이지만, 조립 라인 중 하나를 멈춰야만 했잖아요. 수리를 해야겠더라고요.
B: 알겠습니다. 그러면 모든 것을 언제쯤 배송할 수 있을 거라고 생각하세요?
A: 다음 주 화요일에는 우리가 할 수 있을 거라고 확신해요. 하지만 주말 동안에 조립 라인을 작동해야 할 거예요.
B: 그렇게 하면 작업자들에게 초과 근무 비용을 지불해야 할겁니다. 하지만 이 계약을 놓칠 순 없죠. 그렇게 하죠.

Warm-up
delay, delivery, the original plan, assembly lines, positive, this contract

Practice
A **1** this Friday **2** assembly lines
   3 work **4** more

B ① Why? I thought we could send them the parts they wanted by this Friday.
  ② Okay. Then when do you think we can deliver everything?
  ③ That will require paying the workers overtime, but we don't want to lose this contract. Let's do it.

Week 10 At the Office
Unit 01 Introducing the New Manager

Listening 향상 팁
p. 190

A **1** out, (c) **2** made, (a) **3** count on, (b)
   4 get acquainted with, (d)
B **1** T **2** T

Situation I
pp. 191-192

May I have your attention, please? We made a decision on the new director of the Accounting Department. We couldn't be happier with the choice we made. Best of all, we didn't have to go outside the company. We found her right here. So it's my great pleasure to tell you that Sabrina Wilson is your new boss. Sabrina is one of the hardest working employees at the company. She's got more experience than almost anyone here, and I'm sure she'll get the most out of all of you. How about a big round of applause for Sabrina?

저에게 주목해 주시겠습니까? 우리는 회계 부서의 새로운 관리자를 결정했습니다. 저희가 내린 결정에 정말 만족합니다. 무엇보다도 회사 밖에서 찾지 않아도 됐었죠. 우리는 그녀를 바로 이곳에서 찾았습니다. 그래서 여러분께 사브리나 윌슨이 여러분의 새로운 상사라는 것을 발표할 수 있게 되어 정말 기쁘게 생각합니다. 사브리나는 회사에서 가장 열심히 일하는 직원들 중에 한 명입니다. 그녀는 이곳의 대부분의 사람들이 갖고 있는 것보다 더 많은 경험을 갖고 있고 그녀가 여러분의 능력을 최대한 발휘할 수 있도록 해 줄 것이라고 믿습니다. 사브리나에게 큰 박수를 보내 주면 어떨까요?

Warm-up
attention, made a decision, the new director, the Accounting Department, best of all, one of the hardest working

Practice
A **1** (b) **2** (b) **3** (c)   B (c)   C **1** F **2** T

Dictation
① the new director ② the choice we made
③ Best of all ④ the hardest working employees
⑤ more experience than ⑥ get the most out of
⑦ a big round of applause

Situation II

p. 193

A: Karen, you should know that we have a new supervisor in the office.
B: Is that so? Who is it?
A: It's Jason Carter. I believe that you met him when he came here to interview. He made quite an impression on upper management.
B: I know exactly what they saw in him. He is definitely the best candidate for the job.
A: Well, he's going to be starting here next Monday. I'd like for you to help him get acquainted with everyone here.
B: You can count on me.

A: 카렌, 사무실에 새로운 상사가 올 거래요.
B: 그래요? 누군데요?
A: 제이슨 카터예요. 그 분이 여기에 인터뷰하러 왔을 때 만났을 거예요. 고위 경영진에게 꽤 깊은 인상을 줬어요.
B: 그들이 그의 어떤 점을 좋아하는지 분명히 알겠네요. 그는 분명 그 일에 최고의 적임자예요.
A: 자, 그는 다음 주 월요일부터 여기로 출근하실 거예요. 당신이 그가 여기 모든 사람들과 잘 지낼 수 있도록 도와주세요.
B: 저만 믿으세요.

Warm-up

a new supervisor, interview, quite an impression, upper management, definitely, candidate, get acquainted with

Practice

A 1 Jason 2 met 3 woman

B ① Is that so? Who is it?
   ② I know exactly what they saw in him. He is definitely the best candidate for the job.
   ③ You can count on me.

Unit 02 Announcing a Training Session

Listening 향상 팁

p. 194

A 1 People watch movies.
  2 The people are watching movies.
  3 Men read books.
  4 The men read books.

B 1 T 2 T

Situation I

pp. 195-196

I've got some great news, everyone. I know you've all been complaining about the new software we started using. Well, the company that sold it to us has agreed to send someone here to lead a training session. Isn't that welcome news? He's going to be here all day long tomorrow. He's going to lead three sessions, each of which will be two hours long. Up to twenty of you can be in one session. I've got the sign-up sheets here, so why don't all of you come up here and choose which time you'd like to get your training?

여러분, 좋은 소식이 있습니다. 여러분 모두 우리가 사용하기 시작한 새로운 프로그램에 불만이 있다는 것을 알고 있습니다. 그래서 그것을 판 회사에서 우리 회사로 교육을 진행할 사람을 보내 주기로 했습니다. 반가운 소식 아닌가요? 그 사람이 내일 하루 종일 이곳에 있을 거예요. 그 분이 세 개의 수업 시간을 진행할 건데 하나가 두 시간 정도 됩니다. 최대 20명이 한 수업에 들어갈 수 있어요. 여기 신청서가 있으니 여러분 모두 앞으로 나와서 어떤 시간의 수업을 들을 것인지 골라 보시는 건 어떨까요?

Warm-up

some great news, complaining about, the new software, a training session, all day long, the sign-up sheets

Practice

A 1 (c) 2 (b) 3 (c)   B (c)   C 1 F 2 F

Dictation

① some great news ② the new software
③ to lead a training session ④ all day long
⑤ Up to twenty of you ⑥ why don't all of you
⑦ which time

Situation II

p. 197

A: Mr. Wright called to tell me that the training session for new employees is this Friday.
B: Excellent! That's when I was hoping it would be.
A: And he said that he wants you to assist with it.
B: Sure. What exactly does he want me to do?

A: You're going to give the introductory speech and also train the workers on their basic duties.
B: No problem at all. I've done both of those two or three times before, so I know precisely how to teach them.

A: 라이트씨가 전화해서 이번 주 금요일에 신입 직원들 교육이 있다고 하네요.
B: 잘됐네요! 딱 그때쯤 하면 좋겠다고 생각했는데요.
A: 그리고 그가 당신이 그것을 좀 도와주면 좋겠다고 했어요.
B: 물론이죠. 그가 정확히 저에게 무엇을 해주길 바라는 거죠?
A: 당신은 소개 발표를 할 거예요 그리고 또 직원들에게 기본 업무에 대해서도 교육하고요.
B: 전혀 문제가 안되죠. 두 개 다 전에 두 세 번은 해 본 거라서 그들을 어떻게 가르쳐야 할지 잘 알아요.

Warm-up

training session, new employees, assist, exactly, introductory speech, their basic duties

Practice

A (b), (d)

B ① Excellent! That's when I was hoping it would be.
② Sure. What exactly does he want me to do?
③ No problem at all. I've done both of those two or three times before, so I know precisely how to teach them.

Unit 03 Announcing a Conference

Listening 향상 팁   p. 198

A 1 (a) 2 (b) 3 (a) 4 (a) 5 (b)

1 Are you into Jazz?
재즈를 좋아하시나요?
2 This offer is valid until the end of the week.
이 제안은 주말까지 유효합니다.
3 We should make quarterly reports.
분기 보고서를 작성해야 합니다.
4 Take the express bus to get there.
거기 가시려면 고속 버스를 타세요.
5 She paid the taxi fare for the group.
그녀가 그 일행의 택시비를 냈습니다.

B 1 F 2 T

Situation I   pp. 199-200

There is one more thing to mention before we finish this meeting. Next month, the annual conference for mechanical engineers will be held in San Diego. It's going to last from July 19th to 22nd. There are several great speakers, workshops, and other special events scheduled. If you're interested, talk to Sylvia. She has some brochures for the conference. You can attend the event, and we'll pay your registration fee. However, the company won't be able to cover your travel expenses or accommodations while you're there. Still, it might be a worthwhile venture to go.

회의를 끝내기 전에 한 가지 더 말씀 드릴게요. 다음 달에 기계 공학자들을 위한 연례 컨퍼런스가 샌디에이고에서 열립니다. 7월 19일부터 22일까지 지속될 것입니다. 몇몇 저명한 연설자들, 워크샵들, 그리고 다른 특별 행사들이 계획되어 있습니다. 관심 있으시면 실비아에게 말씀해 주세요. 그녀가 그 컨퍼런스 브로슈어를 좀 갖고 있습니다. 여러분은 행사에 참가하실 수 있고, 회사가 여러분의 등록비를 지불할 것입니다. 그러나 거기 있는 동안의 여행 비용이나 숙박료는 지불해 드리기가 어렵습니다. 그래도 가볼 만한 가치가 있는 곳일 겁니다.

Warm-up

mechanical engineers, last, workshops, brochures, registration fee, worthwhile

Practice

A 1 (b) 2 (c) 3 (b)   B (a)   C 1 T 2 F

Dictation

① the annual conference
② special events scheduled
③ some brochures ④ your registration fee
⑤ cover ⑥ travel expenses or accommodations
⑦ a worthwhile venture

Situation II   p. 201

A: I saw on Marino Enterprises' website that the firm is sponsoring a conference next week.
B: Seriously? I had no idea. What do you know about it?

A: Well, the keynote speaker is Tina Struthers. She's one of the top names in the industry.
B: You can say that again. When is the conference going to be held?
A: On August 4th and 5th. That's Tuesday and Wednesday. We'll need to receive authorization from Mr. Jenkins to attend.
B: Let's find out more about the conference first. Then, we can inquire with him.

A: 마리노 회사 홈페이지에 들어가 봤는데 그 회사가 다음 주에 있는 컨퍼런스를 후원하더라고요.
B: 정말요? 그건 몰랐네요. 그것에 대해서 뭘 알고 있어요?
A: 음, 기조 연설자가 티나 스트러더스예요. 그녀는 이 업계에서 가장 명성 있는 사람 중에 한 명이죠.
B: 두말하면 잔소리죠. 컨퍼런스는 언제 열려요?
A: 8월 4일과 5일이에요. 화요일과 수요일이에요. 참가하려면 젠킨스 씨의 허락을 받아야 할 거예요.
B: 우선 그 컨퍼런스에 대해서 조금 더 알아봅시다. 그리고나서 우리가 그에게 허락을 구할 수 있을 거예요.

Warm-up

website, sponsoring, a conference, seriously, keynote speaker, Tuesday

Practice

A (a), (b)

B ① Seriously? I had no idea. What do you know about it?
② You can say that again. When is the conference going to be held?
③ Let's find out more about the conference first. Then, we can inquire with him.

Unit 04 Overcoming Problems

Listening 향상 팁   p. 202

A 1 (c)   2 (a)   3 (b)
B 1 (c)   2 (b)   3 (a)

1 We need to talk about a serious issue. We have been losing clients, and need to figure out why.
중요한 문제에 관해 논의해야 합니다. 고객들이 빠져 나가고 있는데, 왜 그런지 파악해야 합니다.

2 Something in the factory seems to be wrong. A lot of products are failing the quality control check.
공장에 뭔가 문제가 있습니다. 많은 제품이 품질 검사를 통과하지 못하고 있습니다.

3 I need your help. I think I sent the samples to the wrong address.
좀 도와 주세요. 틀린 주소로 샘플을 보낸 것 같아요.

C 1 F   2 T

Situation I   pp. 203-204

I've got an important announcement to make. We're in a bit of a crisis because we don't have enough contracts to be profitable. Fortunately, there are several projects we're bidding on. Each bid is due by the middle of next week. If we win at least two, we'll become financially stable again. But it's going to require hard work by everyone to make sure that happens. I've assigned each of you to a team to work on separate bids. I e-mailed the list to you now. So check it out and meet your teammates, and then let's get to work.

중요하게 발표할 사항이 있습니다. 우리는 수익을 낼 만한 계약들이 충분하게 없어서 지금 약간의 위기에 처해 있습니다. 다행히도, 우리가 입찰할 수 있는 몇 개의 프로젝트들이 있네요. 각각의 입찰 마감이 다음 주 중반입니다. 만약에 우리가 입찰에서 최소 두 건을 따낸다면 우리는 재정적으로 다시 안정을 찾을 것입니다. 그러나 그렇게 되기 위해서는 여러분 모두가 열심히 일해 주셔야 합니다. 각 입찰 별로 팀을 나눠 여러분을 각 팀에 배정했습니다. 제가 지금 여러분께 그 리스트를 이메일로 보냈어요. 그러니 확인해 보시고 여러분의 팀원들과 만나 일을 시작합시다.

Warm-up

announcement, a crisis, enough contracts, bidding on, due, financially stable

Practice

A 1 (b)   2 (b)   3 (a)   **B** (c)   **C** 1 T   2 T

Dictation

① announcement ② a crisis ③ is due by
④ financially stable ⑤ require hard work
⑥ on separate bids ⑦ check it out

Week 11 Business Trips
Unit 01 Renting a Car

Listening 향상 팁
p. 210

A **1** c **2** b **3** a **4** b **5** c

1 I'm flying to San Francisco on September 8th.
나는 9월 8일에 비행기 타고 샌프란시스코로 갑니다.

2 He'll arrive in Chicago on June 18th.
그는 6월 18일에 시카고에 도착할 것입니다.

3 My boss, Mr. Ross will call you tomorrow.
제 상사인 로스 씨가 내일 전화 드릴 것입니다.

4 I'm calling to make a reservation for a car.
차를 예약하려고 전화했습니다.

5 We have a teleconference twice a week.
일주일에 두 번씩 화상 회의를 합니다.

6 We had a meeting at my office for two hours.
내 사무실에서 두 시간 동안 회의를 했습니다.

B **1** F **2** T

Situation II
p. 205

A: Jeremy, I got the sales report you wrote from Ms. Powell. She's pretty unhappy about it.
B: Unhappy? How come?
A: Apparently, you inserted the wrong sales figures. The ones you used were for March, but you were supposed to put the May figures in the file.
B: Oh... That's not good. Do you think you can help me fix it?
A: Yes, that's why Ms. Powell wanted me to speak with you. Let's go to my office and rewrite the report.
We need to finish before noon.
B: Thanks a lot, Stephanie.
I'll treat you to lunch once we're done.

A: 제레미, 당신이 쓴 영업 보고서를 포웰 씨에게서 받았어요. 그녀는 그것에 만족스러워 하지 않아요.
B: 마음에 들어 하지 않는다고요? 아니, 왜요?
A: 보다시피 당신이 판매 수치를 잘못 입력했어요. 당신이 사용한 수치는 3월 기예요, 하지만 파일에 5월 숫자를 입력했어야 했는데 말이죠.
B: 오… 저런.
당신이 제가 그것을 바로 잡을 수 있도록 도와 줄 수 있나요?
A: 네, 포웰 씨가 그래서 저한테 딩신과 얘기해 보라고 한 거예요. 제 사무실로 가서 보고서를 다시 써 봅시다. 우리는 정오 전에는 끝내야 해요.
B: 고마워요, 스테파니. 일 끝나고 내가 점심을 한번 대접할게요.

Situation I
pp. 211-212

Hello. My name is Claudia Bryant. I'm calling to make a reservation for a car. I'm flying to New York City on January 12th. I'll need a car from then until January 19th. I'm going to be driving a lot, so I'd like a vehicle that gets good gas mileage and is easy to drive. In addition, there will be three people accompanying me. Therefore, we need a midsized car with plenty of legroom. Could you please call me back at 954-9404 to let me know if you have any vehicles available then? Thank you. Goodbye.

안녕하세요. 제 이름은 클로디아 브라이언트입니다. 차를 예약하려고 전화했습니다. 1월 12일에 비행기를 타고 뉴욕에 갑니다. 그때부터 1월 19일까지 차가 필요합니다. 운전을 많이 할 거니까 연비가 좋고 운전하기 쉬운 차가 좋겠습니다. 그리고 세 명이 저와 동행합니다. 그래서 자리가 넓은 중형차가 필요합니다. 그때 이용 가능한 차가 있으면 954-9404로 전화해서 알려 주실래요? 고맙습니다. 안녕히 계세요.

Warm-up

the sales report, apparently, the wrong sales figures, fix, rewrite, treat

Practice

A **1** the man's **2** March **3** woman **4** pay for

B ① Unhappy? How come?
② Oh… That's not good. Do you think you can help me fix it?
③ Thanks a lot, Stephanie. I'll treat you to lunch once we're done.

Warm-up

make a reservation, January 12th, good gas mileage, accompanying, a midsized car, plenty of legroom

Practice
A **1** (c)　**2** (b)　**3** (c)　　B (b)　　C **1** F　**2** T

Dictation
① make a reservation　② New York City
③ until January 19th　④ good gas mileage
⑤ easy to drive　⑥ plenty of legroom
⑦ any vehicles available

Situation II
p. 213

A: Good afternoon. Do you happen to have any cars available to rent right now?
B: Yes, we do. What kind of car do you need?
A: I've got five people with me, so I think an SUV would be perfect.
B: We've got one of those available. It will seat that many people in addition to your luggage.
A: Great. How much will it cost to rent it per day? I need it for the next five days.
B: We charge $75 a day to rent our SUV. If you need insurance, that will cost extra.

A: 안녕하세요. 지금 바로 렌트가 가능한 자동차가 있을까요?
B: 네, 있습니다. 어떤 종류의 차를 원하시죠?
A: 제가 다섯 명의 사람들과 함께 해요. 그래서 SUV가 좋을 것 같은데요.
B: 그 중에 가능한 것이 있네요. 그 정도 많은 사람들과 짐까지 실을 수 있을 겁니다.
A: 좋습니다. 렌트하는데 하루에 얼마죠? 앞으로 5일 동안 필요하거든요.
B: 저희 SUV는 렌트하는데 하루에 75달러입니다. 보험이 필요하시면 그건 추가로 비용이 들 거고요.

Warm-up　(c)

Practice
A **1** an SUV　**2** five　**3** more than

B ① Good afternoon. Do you happen to have any cars available to rent right now?
② I've got five people with me, so I think an SUV would be perfect.
③ Great. How much will it cost to rent it per day? I need it for the next five days.

Unit 02 At a Meeting Place

Listening 향상 팁
p. 214

A **1** so that　**2** In order to
B **1** (c)　**2** (a)　**3** (b)

1 Strong showers will be in the area from this afternoon. Due to heavy rains, be careful of flash floods.
오늘 오후부터 지역에 강한 비가 내리겠습니다. 폭우로 인해 물이 넘치는 것을 조심하십시오.

2 Scattered thunderstorms will be in the area tonight. Some severe weather is expected through tomorrow.
오늘 밤 산발적인 뇌우가 있겠습니다. 내일부터 날씨가 험한 날씨가 예상됩니다.

3 We are predicting 3 to 4 inches of snow accumulation overnight. Driving conditions are very poor throughout the greater city region this morning.
밤 사이에 3~4인치 정도의 눈이 쌓일 것으로 예상됩니다. 내일 아침 시내 많은 지역에서 운전하는데 아주 불편할 것입니다.

C **1** T　**2** T

Situation I
pp. 215-216

Everyone, please listen carefully. We're about to arrive at Symington Manufacturing to conduct the negotiations regarding the merger. We'll be met at the front desk by a couple of executives. Be sure to introduce yourselves and to pass out business cards. Now, when the meeting starts, Carter is going to take the lead because he's the most knowledgeable on the topic. As for the rest of you, don't speak up unless I ask you a question. In that case, I'd like you to provide the information I request and nothing else. Just give facts, not opinions.

여러분, 주목해 주십시오. 우리는 합병에 관한 협상을 진행하러 시밍턴 매뉴팩처링에 곧 도착할 것입니다. 몇 명의 회사 중역들을 프런트 데스크에서 만날 것입니다. 반드시 여러분을 소개하고 명함을 건네도록 하세요. 그리고 회의가 시작하면 카터가 이 문제에 관해 가장 잘 알기 때문에 회의를 이끌어 갈 겁니다. 나머지 분들은 제가 질문하지 않으면 말하지 마세요. 제가 질문한다면 여러분은 제가 요청한 정보만 주시고 그 이외에는 나서지 마세요. 의견이 아니라 사실만 말하세요.

Warm-up
negotiations, the merger, executives, business cards, the most knowledgeable, nothing else

Practice
A **1** (b) **2** (a) **3** (b)   B (b)   C **1** T **2** F

Dictation
① conduct the negotiations ② the merger
③ business cards ④ take the lead
⑤ don't speak up ⑥ information I request
⑦ not opinions

Situation II
p. 217

A: Welcome to FTR Productions, Ms. Venne. Why don't you have a seat here in the conference room?
B: Thank you very much.
A: Would you like to have some refreshments before we start the meeting? Would you like some coffee or tea?
   We also have some snacks here on the table.
B: Coffee would be great.
A: If you need to use your laptop, you can plug it in right next to your seat. This room also has Wi-Fi if you require it. Would you like to know the password?
B: Yes, please. I would.

A: FTR 프로덕션에 오신 것을 환영합니다, 벤 씨. 컨퍼런스룸에서 이 자리에 앉으시겠어요?
B: 대단히 감사합니다.
A: 회의를 시작하기 전에 다과를 좀 드시겠어요? 커피나 차 어떠세요? 탁자 위에 간식도 조금 마련했습니다.
B: 커피가 좋겠습니다.
A: 노트북을 사용하셔야 하면 좌석 바로 옆에 전원을 꽂으세요. 이 방은 필요하시면 와이파이도 쓸 수 있습니다. 비밀번호를 알려 드릴까요?
B: 네, 알려 주세요.

Warm-up (a)

Practice
A (a), (b)
B ① Welcome to FTR Productions, Ms. Venne. Why don't you have a seat here in the conference room?

② Would you like to have some refreshments before we start the meeting? Would you like some coffee or tea? We also have some snacks here on the table.
③ If you need to use your laptop, you can plug it in right next to your seat. This room also has Wi-Fi if you require it. Would you like to know the password?

Unit 03 Business Lunch

Listening 향상 팁
p. 218

A **1** Exactly, (c) **2** How about, (d)
  3 What I mean is, (b) **4** So, (a)
B **1** F **2** T

Situation I
pp. 219-220

A: Thank you for agreeing to meet me for lunch today. We can do some business while we eat.
B: It's no problem at all. Shall we look at the menu? I've never been here before.
A: In that case, why don't you let me order? I've been here several times in the past.
B: Sounds good. What do you recommend?
A: Let's have the seafood pasta.
   I'll call a waiter over so that I can order.
B: Great. After you order, let's get down to business then. We have a lot to discuss today.

A: 오늘 점심 때 만나기로 동의해 주셔서 감사합니다.
   우리는 식사를 하면서 사업 이야기를 좀 하죠.
B: 별말씀요. 메뉴판을 볼까요? 저는 예전에 여기 와 본 적이 없어요.
A: 그러시다면 제가 주문해도 될까요? 저는 예전에 여기 몇 번 와 보았습니다.
B: 좋네요. 추천 좀 해주실래요?
A: 해물 파스타를 먹죠. 웨이터를 불러 주문할게요.
B: 좋습니다. 먼저 주문하고 나서 사업 이야기로 들어갑시다. 오늘 의논할 것이 아주 많네요.

Warm-up
agreeing to meet, for lunch, do some business, in that case, why don't you, recommend

Practice

A **1** (b) **2** (c) **3** (a)   B (c)   C **1** T **2** T

Dictation

① do some business ② Shall we
③ why don't you ④ Let's have
⑤ call a waiter over ⑥ let's get down
⑦ a lot to discuss

Situation II
p. 221

A: I think we've got a bit more time until the entrée arrives. So what do you think of our offer?
B: It looks good overall. But the price is a bit more than we were hoping to pay. How about lowering it?
A: We can probably do that, but we'd need a guarantee that you'd buy a specific number of products every month.
B: That sounds reasonable. I can agree to do that.
A: Excellent. Well, why don't we discuss the numbers that will satisfy both of us after we eat?
B: I'm all for that.

A: 제 생각에 주 요리가 나올 때까지 시간이 좀 있는 것 같아요. 그러니까 저희가 드린 제안에 대해서 어떻게 생각하시는지요?
B: 전반적으로 좋아 보입니다. 하지만 가격이 우리가 생각했던 것 보다 약간 더 높네요. 가격을 낮추는 것은 어떠세요?
A: 그렇게 할 수도 있지만 매달 특정 수량의 상품을 구매하겠다는 보장을 해주셔야 합니다.
B: 합리적으로 들리네요. 거기에는 동의할 수 있습니다.
A: 좋습니다. 그럼 식사 후에 우리 둘다 만족할 수 있는 가격에 대해 논의하는 것이 어떨까요?
B: 좋습니다.

Warm-up

a bit more time, entrée, overall, lowering, a guarantee, a specific number

Practice

A (b), (c)

B ① It looks good overall. But the price is a bit more than we were hoping to pay.
How about lowering it?
② That sounds reasonable. I can agree to do that.

③ I'm all for that.

Unit 04 Accepting Invitations

Listening 향상 팁
p. 222

A **1** (c) **2** (a) **3** (b) **4** (e) **5** (d)
B **1** T **2** T

Situation I
pp. 223-224

Hello, Ms. Carpenter. This is Jerry Stratford responding to the e-mail you sent me this morning. Thank you for inviting me to visit your office for a meeting. I'd be more than happy to give you a demonstration of my firm's newest products. It just so happens that I'm in Springfield right now, so I can drop by your office tomorrow morning. How does ten in the morning sound? I'll need about two hours to show you everything. So I imagine I'll finish around noon. Perhaps we can have lunch together afterward. I'll see you tomorrow. Goodbye.

안녕하세요, 카펜터 씨. 저는 제리 스트랫퍼드이며 오늘 아침에 보내신 이메일에 답을 하겠습니다. 회의를 위해 당신 사무실에 방문해 달라 요청해 주셔서 감사합니다. 저희 회사의 최신 제품을 시연할 수 있게 되어 매우 기쁩니다. 그런데 저는 지금 스프링필드에 있으므로 내일 오전에 당신 사무실에 들를 수 있습니다. 아침 10시 괜찮으신가요? 다 보여 드리려면 약 두 시간 정도 걸립니다. 그럼 정오쯤 끝낼 수 있을 것 같습니다. 그 후 점심을 같이 할 수도 있을 듯 합니다. 내일 뵙겠습니다. 안녕히 계세요.

Warm-up

responding, the e-mail, inviting me, newest products, drop by, afterward

Practice

A **1** (c) **2** (a) **3** (a)   B (a)   C **1** T **2** T

Dictation

① to visit your office ② a demonstration of
③ newest products ④ tomorrow morning
⑤ about two hours ⑥ around noon
⑦ have lunch together

Situation II
p. 225

A: Mr. Porter, would you be interested in seeing our factory? I can show you how we manufacture our products.
B: I would like that very much. When can you do that?
A: If you're not busy, we can go there right now.
B: Sure. Does this factory use the new manufacturing technique created by Jason Schmidt?
A: It sure does. You can see it in action in about five minutes. Shall we go?
B: Definitely. If it's possible, I'd like to meet Mr. Schmidt as well.

A: 포터 씨, 저희 공장을 둘러보시겠어요? 제가 저희 상품이 어떻게 생산되는지 보여 드릴 수 있습니다.
B: 정말 그러고 싶습니다. 언제 보여 주실 수 있나요?
A: 바쁘지만 않으시면, 지금 당장 거기에 가볼 수 있어요.
B: 좋습니다. 이 공장에서는 제이슨 슈미츠가 개발한 신제조 기술을 사용하나요?
A: 네, 그렇습니다. 그것이 작동하는 것을 약 5분 정도 후에 볼 수 있습니다. 가실까요?
B: 네. 그리고 만약 가능하다면 슈미츠 씨도 뵙고 싶습니다.

Warm-up
interested, our factory, products, technique, in action, as well

Practice
A **1** the factory **2** the woman's **3** technique

B ① I would like that very much. When can you do that?
② Sure. Does this factory use the new manufacturing technique created by Jason Schmidt?
③ Definitely. If it's possible, I'd like to meet Mr. Schmidt as well.

Week 12 Speech / Presentation
Unit 01 Opening and Closing a Presentation

Listening 향상 팁
p. 230

A **1** (a) **2** (b) **3** (a) **4** (b)

1 Ladies and gentlemen, it's an honor to be here.
신사숙녀 여러분, 이 자리에 서게 되어 영광입니다.
2 My name is Hana Kim, a director of Englishunt.
제 이름은 김하나이며, 잉글리시헌트의 국장입니다.
3 Today I'm here to say how to increase the productivity.
오늘 생산성을 늘리는 방법을 말하려 여기 섰습니다.
4 That covers all I wanted to say today.
이게 제가 오늘 말하려 했던 내용의 전부입니다.

B **1** F **2** T

Situation I
pp. 231-232

Thank you for coming this morning. My name is Malorie Smith, and I represent Johnson Labs. Today, I'm going to speak about a brand-new pharmaceutical which my company will begin selling next month. It took us ten years to develop and get it approved, but I believe that time was well spent. This medicine, which we call Proximal, will be used by people suffering from various heart ailments. The effects of Proximal are dramatic. I'll tell you all about them in a moment. If you would hold your questions until the end, I'd appreciate it. Now, let me begin.

오늘 아침에 방문해 주셔서 감사합니다. 제 이름은 말로리 스미스이고, 저는 존슨 연구소를 대표합니다. 오늘 저는 다음 달부터 저희 회사가 판매할 신약에 대해 말씀 드리려고 합니다. 저희는 그것을 개발하고 승인 받는데 10년이 걸렸지만, 저는 그 시간이 의미 있었다고 믿습니다. 저희가 프록시멀이라고 부르는 이 약은 다양한 심장 질환을 앓고 있는 사람들이 사용하게 될 것입니다. 프록시멀의 효과는 정말 뛰어납니다. 잠시 후에 그 효과들에 대해 말씀 드리겠습니다. 질문은 끝날 때까지 참아 주시면 감사하겠습니다. 이제 시작하겠습니다.

Warm-up
brand-new, pharmaceutical, suffering from, effects, dramatic, until the end

Practice
A **1** (a) **2** (b) **3** (b)   B (c)   C **1** T **2** F

Dictation
① pharmaceutical ② get it approved
③ people suffering from ④ heart ailments
⑤ The effects ⑥ in a moment

⑦ hold your questions

Situation II   p. 233

And that brings me to the end of my presentation. You should now have a clear understanding of what projects the R&D Department here is working on. While we have several products that should be able to be marketed this year, we also have many others in the pipeline. Several are quite promising and could prove to be extremely lucrative to our company. Now, since I have concluded my remarks, I'd like to allow everyone here to speak up. I am positive some of you must have questions for me to answer. Anyone?

그리고 그것이 제 프리젠테이션의 마지막입니다. 이제 이곳에 있는 연구 개발 부서가 어떤 프로젝트를 진행하고 있는지 명확하게 이해하셨을 겁니다. 저희는 올해 판매할 수 있는 제품이 몇 가지 있지만, 개발중인 다른 제품들도 많습니다. 몇몇은 꽤 유망하고 우리 회사에 매우 이익이 된다는 것을 증명할 수 있습니다. 자, 이제 제 말은 모두 끝났으니, 여기 계신 분들이 말씀하실 수 있도록 허락해 드리겠습니다. 여러분들 중 몇몇은 분명 제가 대답했으면 하는 질문이 있다고 생각합니다. 누구 계신가요?

Warm-up (a)

Practice

A **1** finish **2** introducing **3** profitable

B ① You should now have a clear understanding of what projects the R&D Department here is working on.
② Several are quite promising and could prove to be extremely lucrative to our company.
③ I am positive some of you must have questions for me to answer. Anyone?

Unit 02 Linking Ideas

Listening 향상 팁   p. 234

A **1** (a) goal   (b) goal
  2 (a) ongoing   (b) ongoing
  3 (a) extensive (b) extensive
  4 (a) raise   (b) raise

B **1** T **2** F

Situation I   pp. 235-236

Now that I've concluded my opening remarks, I'd like to get to the heart of the matter. We need to come up with enough private investment so that we can expand our facilities this year. Thanks to the popularity of our products, we're getting more and more purchase requests than ever. But we're not able to meet the high demand for our items right now. I've come up with a few ideas on how we can raise the money we need. It won't be easy to raise half a billion dollars, but I believe it's an attainable goal.

이제 개회사를 마쳤으니, 저는 그 문제의 핵심을 말씀 드리고 싶습니다. 저희는 올해 시설을 확장할 수 있도록 충분한 민간 투자를 확보해야 합니다. 저희 제품의 인기 덕분에, 우리는 그 어느 때보다도 더 많은 구매 요청을 받고 있습니다. 하지만 우리는 지금 우리의 품목에 대한 수요를 충족시킬 수 없습니다. 우리가 필요로 하는 돈을 어떻게 모금할 수 있는지에 대해 저는 몇 가지 아이디어를 생각해 봤습니다. 5억달러를 모으는 것은 쉽지 않겠지만, 저는 그것이 달성할 수 있는 목표라는 것을 믿습니다.

Warm-up

opening remarks, the heart of the matter, private investment, popularity, purchase requests, raise

Practice

A **1** (a) **2** (c) **3** (a)   B (b)   C **1** T **2** F

Dictation

① concluded   ② enough private investment
③ expand our facilities   ④ Thanks to
⑤ meet the high demand   ⑥ raise the money
⑦ an attainable goal

Situation II   p. 237

We've spent a considerable amount of time on the Washington Project. Unfortunately, our client is not pleased with the solutions that we've given him. He claims they're both expensive and unfeasible. We therefore need to come up with some new ideas. We've decided to create a task force that will focus only on this ongoing project.

It's going to be led by April Devine, who has done extensive research on this type of situation. I'm going to turn this presentation over to April right now and let her discuss what she is planning to do. April?

저희는 상당한 양의 시간을 워싱턴 프로젝트에 투자했습니다. 유감스럽게도, 우리의 고객은 우리가 그에게 준 해결책에 만족하지 않았습니다. 그는 그것들이 모두 비싸고 불가능하다고 주장합니다. 따라서 우리는 새로운 아이디어를 생각해 내야 합니다. 우리는 이 진행 중인 프로젝트에만 집중할 수 있는 TF팀을 만들기로 결정했습니다. 이 팀은 이런 유형의 상황에 대해 광범위한 연구를 해 온 에이프릴 드바인이 주도하게 될 것입니다. 저는 이제 프리젠테이션을 에이프릴에게 넘기고 그녀가 무엇을 할 계획인지에 대해 논의하게 하려고 합니다. 에이프릴?

Warm-up

considerable, the solutions, come up with, this ongoing project, extensive research, let her discuss

Practice

A (b), (d)

B ① Unfortunately, our client is not pleased with the solutions that we've given him.
② We've decided to create a task force that will focus only on this ongoing project.
③ I'm going to turn this presentation over to April right now and let her discuss what she is planning to do. April?

Unit 03 Emphasizing Important Points

Listening 향상 팁
p. 238

A 1 (a)   2 (c)   3 (b)

B 1 Do you like to watch a movie?
2 Did she give her presentation yesterday?

C 1 T   2 T

Situation I
pp. 239-240

According to our projections, we're set to make a profit of $500,000 this year. Let me reiterate. That's half a million dollars in profits. We're going to make the first profit in our five-year history. And we're going to make an enormous one. So what's the reason for this sudden turnabout? It's simple. One of our ads went viral on the Internet, so that attracted attention to us. The ad was for our newest toothpaste, so sales went up. How far up? They went up 347%. Naturally, sales of other products increased, so everything started selling well.

저희의 예상에 따르면 저희는 올해 50만 달러의 이익을 내도록 되어 있습니다. 거듭 말씀 드립니다. 그것은 백만 달러의 절반의 수익입니다. 5년 역사상 첫 번째 수익을 창출하게 되는 것입니다. 그리고 그 수익은 정말 막대할 것입니다. 그래서 이런 갑작스러운 반전의 이유가 무엇이냐고요? 간단합니다. 저희 광고들 중 하나가 인터넷에서 입소문이 나서 저희에게 관심이 쏠린 거죠. 그 광고는 저희 새로 나온 치약이었는데요, 그래서 판매량이 올라갔죠. 얼마나 많이 올랐을까요? 347%까지 올랐어요. 자연스럽게 다른 상품 판매량도 증가했고요 그래서 모든 것이 잘 팔리기 시작했습니다.

Warm-up

projections, make a profit, reiterate, the first profit, an enormous one, naturally

Practice

A 1 (c)   2 (a)   3 (c)   **B** (a)   **C** 1 T   2 F

Dictation

① half a million   ② in profits   ③ the first profit
④ an enormous one   ⑤ went viral
⑥ attracted attention to   ⑦ 347%

Situation II
p. 241

A: Now that I've concluded my remarks, does anyone in the audience have a question?
B: I have one. You said that your firm has developed a fast computer chip. Just how fast is it?
A: It's more than 50% faster than anything available on the market.
B: 50% faster? Are you serious?

A: Absolutely. Not only is it that much quicker than anything else, but we can manufacture it for a cheaper price than most of the chips on the market today.
B: If that's correct, it sounds like you've got a revolutionary new product on your hands.

A: 제 발표가 끝났으니, 여러분 중에 질문 있으신 분은 질문하세요.
B: 제가 질문 있습니다. 귀사가 빠른 컴퓨터 칩을 개발했다고 말씀하셨는데요. 그것이 얼마나 빠른 건가요?
A: 시장의 어떤 경쟁 상품보다 50% 이상 더 빠릅니다.
B: 50%나 더 빠르다고요? 정말인가요?
A: 물론입니다. 그 어느 것보다 그만큼 더 빠를 뿐아니라, 오늘날 시장에 나와 있는 대부분의 칩보다 더 싼 가격으로 생산할 수 있습니다.
B: 만약 그게 사실이라면, 혁명적인 신상품을 손에 쥐고 계시는 것 같네요.

Warm-up

the audience, developed, a fast computer chip, on the market, serious, absolutely

Practice

A (a), (c)

B ① I have one. You said that your firm has developed a fast computer chip. Just how fast is it?
② 50% faster? Are you serious?
③ If that's correct, it sounds like you've got a revolutionary new product on your hands.

Unit 04 Describing Graphs/Charts

Listening 향상 팁   p. 242

A **1** (b)   **2** (d)   **3** (a)   **4** (c)

1 Profits have fallen significantly these days.
최근에 이익이 상당히 떨어졌습니다.

2 Sales have flatten out.
매출이 차츰 평평해 지고 있습니다.

3 Our sales will rise gradually next quarter.
우리 매출이 다음 분기에 서서히 증가할 것입니다.

4 Profit margins stay constant.
이윤 폭이 일정합니다.

B **1** F   **2** F

Situation I   pp. 243-244

Please take a look at the pie chart up on the screen. This shows the market share for businesses in the local construction industry. As you can see, Anderson Construction has the top position at 32%. However, we're right behind in second place at 25%, and we've been increasing our market share lately. In third place, at 14%, is Kelly Construction, and the JT Company is in fourth place at 10%. Several smaller companies are getting the remainder of the business. Now, here's a graph that shows how each company's market share has been changing this year.

화면에 있는 원형 도표를 봐주시기 바랍니다. 이것은 지역 건축 산업의 회사별 시장 점유율을 보여 주고 있습니다. 보시는 것처럼 앤더슨 건축이 32%로 최고 자리를 차지하고 있습니다. 하지만 저희가 25%로 바로 뒤 2위 자리에 있고요, 최근에 저희 시장 점유율이 증가하고 있습니다. 3위에는 14%로 켈리 건축이 그리고 4위는 10%로 JT 컴퍼니입니다. 몇몇 작은 회사들이 이 사업의 나머지를 차지하고 있습니다. 이제 올해 각 회사의 시장 점유율이 어떻게 바뀌었는지 보여 주는 그래프를 보여드리겠습니다.

Warm-up

pie chart, top position, in third place, at 10%, remainder, has been changing

Practice

A **1** (b)   **2** (b)   **3** (a)   **B** (c)   **C** **1** F   **2** T

Dictation

① pie chart   ② market share
③ local construction   ④ at 32%
⑤ in second place   ⑥ increasing our market share
⑦ has been changing

Situation II   p. 245

A: This is a line graph showing spending in the past six months.
B: If I'm reading it correctly, our spending has increased each of the past six months.
A: That's correct. Since January, our spending has increased 77% on a monthly basis. That's simply unsustainable.

B: How does it compare to our revenue?
A: I've got another graph here. Revenue has been holding steady at around $2 million per month.
B: It looks as though we're going to start losing money unless we get our spending under control.

A: 이것은 지난 6개월 동안의 지출을 보여 주는 선 그래프입니다.
B: 제가 그래프를 제대로 읽은 거라면, 지난 6개월간 우리의 지출이 매달 증가해 왔네요.
A: 맞습니다. 1월 이후로, 우리의 지출은 매달 77%씩 증가했습니다. 그것은 좀 지속 불가능한 수준이에요.
B: 우리의 수익과 비교해서는 어떤가요?
A: 제가 여기 또 다른 그래프를 가져왔습니다. 수익은 매달 약 2백만 달러로 꾸준히 유지되고 있습니다.
B: 우리가 지출을 통제하지 않는다면 우리가 적자를 내기 시작할 것으로 보이네요.

Warm-up (c)

Practice

A **1** increased **2** remaining steady **3** out of

B ① If I'm reading it correctly, our spending has increased each of the past six months.
② How does it compare to our revenue?
③ It looks as though we're going to start losing money unless we get our spending under control.

초판1쇄 발행 | 2017년 11월 6일

| 총 괄 | 정문환 EBS 온라인사업부장
| | 한정림 ㈜잉글리시헌트 대표이사
| 기 획 | 잉글리시헌트연구소, EBS 차공근
| 집 필 | 잉글리시헌트연구소, Grace Kim
| 콘텐츠개발 | 양윤선, 김하나, 윤미숙, 옥경숙, 박건일
| | 이철희, 이순구, 심소연, 이아론
| 원어민감수 | Paul Edwards, Becky Elliot
| 편집디자인 | 구진희
| 사 진 | Shutterstock

발행처 | 지성공간
경기도 파주시 문발동 광인사길 71

전 화 | (031) 955-6952
팩 스 | (031) 955-6037
출판등록 제406-2008-000067호
온라인 / 모바일강의 www.ebslang.co.kr
ISBN | 979-11-86317-23-5

저작권자 ⓒ EBS, ㈜잉글리시헌트
All rights reserved including the rights of reproduction in whole or part in any form. Printed in Korea.